VMware vCloud Director Cookbook

Over 80 recipes to help you master VMware
vCloud Director

Daniel Langenhan

professional expertise distilled

BIRMINGHAM - MUMBAI

VMware vCloud Director Cookbook

First published: October 2013

Production Reference: 1171013

Published by Packt Publishing Ltd.
Livery Place
35 Livery Street
Birmingham B3 2PB, UK.

ISBN 978-1-78217-766-1

www.packtpub.com

Cover Image by Daniel Langenhan (daniel_langenhan@yahoo.com.au)

Credits

Author

Daniel Langenhan

Reviewers

Cody Bunch

Thomas Hepper

Mitesh Soni

Acquisition Editor

James Jones

Lead Technical Editor

Amey Varangaonkar

Technical Editors

Veena Pagare

Anand Singh

Copy Editors

Brandt D'mello

Kirti Pai

Alfida Paiva

Sayanee Mukherjee

Project Coordinator

Angel Jathanna

Proofreaders

Lindsey Thomas

Jonathan Todd

Indexer

Rekha Nair

Graphics

Ronak Dhruv

Abhinash Sahu

Production Coordinator

Prachali Bhiwandkar

Cover Work

Prachali Bhiwandkar

About the Author

Daniel Langenhan is a client-focused Virtualization Expert with more than 18 years of international industry experience.

His skills span the breadth of virtualization, ranging from architecture, design, and implementation for large multitier enterprise client systems to delivering captivating education and training sessions in security technologies and practices to diverse audiences.

In addition to this, he possesses an extensive knowledge and experience in process management, enterprise-level storage, Linux, and Solaris operating systems.

Utilizing his extensive knowledge, experience, and skills, he has a proven track record of successful integration of virtualization into different business areas, while minimizing cost and maximizing reliability and effectiveness of the solutions for his clients.

He has gained his experience with major Australian and international vendors and clients. Daniel's consulting company is well established with strong industry ties in many verticals, for example, finance, telecommunications, and print. His consulting business also provided services to VMware International.

Daniel is the author of *Instant VMware vCloud Starter, Packt Publishing* and *VMware View Security Essentials, Packt Publishing*.

I would like to thank my wife, Renata, for her tireless support and patience in all things. This book would not have been possible without her.

About the Reviewers

Cody Bunch is a Private Cloud/Virtualization Architect, VMware vExpert, and VMware VCP from San Antonio, TX. Cody has authored and co-authored several OpenStack and VMware books. Additionally, he has been a Technical Editor on a number of projects. Cody also regularly speaks at industry events and local user groups.

Cody has also worked on the *OpenStack Cloud Computing Cookbook Second Edition*, *OpenStack Security Guide*, *Automating VMware vSphere with vCenter Orchestrator*, *Managing VMware Infrastructure with PowerShell*, and *VMware VI and VMware vSphere SDK* books by *Packt Publishing*.

Thomas Hepper has worked for more than 20 years in the area of Computer Hardware and Software. With Silicon Graphics workstations, his long journey started through the Unix world (IRIX/HP-UX/AIX/Solaris/Linux). His first contact with the virtual world and Windows came later. Currently, he is responsible for an environment of approximately 1,300 VMs on approximately 150 physical systems, all running on VMware ESXi.

Mitesh Soni is a Technical Lead with iGATE's Cloud Services, Research & Innovation group. He is a Sun Certified Java Programmer, Sun Certified Web Component Developer, and VMware Cloud Professional. He has been involved in thought leadership and technology evangelization via papers, seminars, wikis, and creating solutions related to cloud computing. Mitesh has worked on cloud platforms such as Amazon Web Services, VMware vCloud, CloudStack, and CloudBees. He has published papers in national and international conferences. He is a regular author for cloud computing-related articles in the *Open Source For You* magazine.

Mitesh is interested in reviewing cloud computing-related books.

www.PacktPub.com

Support files, eBooks, discount offers and more

You might want to visit www.PacktPub.com for support files and downloads related to your book.

Did you know that Packt offers eBook versions of every book published, with PDF and ePub files available? You can upgrade to the eBook version at www.PacktPub.com and as a print book customer, you are entitled to a discount on the eBook copy. Get in touch with us at service@packtpub.com for more details.

At www.PacktPub.com, you can also read a collection of free technical articles, sign up for a range of free newsletters and receive exclusive discounts and offers on Packt books and eBooks.

http://PacktLib.PacktPub.com

Do you need instant solutions to your IT questions? PacktLib is Packt's online digital book library. Here, you can access, read and search across Packt's entire library of books.

Why Subscribe?

- ▶ Fully searchable across every book published by Packt
- ▶ Copy and paste, print and bookmark content
- ▶ On demand and accessible via web browser

Free Access for Packt account holders

If you have an account with Packt at www.PacktPub.com, you can use this to access PacktLib today and view nine entirely free books. Simply use your login credentials for immediate access.

Instant Updates on New Packt Books

Get notified! Find out when new books are published by following @PacktEnterprise on Twitter, or the *Packt Enterprise* Facebook page.

Table of Contents

Preface

VMware vCloud has evolved to be one of the most exciting technologies in the last few years. It is not only the follow-up product to VMware Lab Manager but it also opens up your vSphere infrastructure for customer-based management. VMware vCloud allows you to manage your vSphere infrastructure and lets you push work from the administrators back onto the customers. This enables customers to self provide and self administer their resources without impacting their security or resource management.

This book contains the most up-to-date and enterprise-proven concepts to enhance your vCloud productivity. Not only do we discuss vCloud 5.1, but we also talk about the newest release, vCloud 5.5. You will see how to integrate these new features and increase your productivity even more.

We will present recipes that not only deal with the daily tasks but also present you with new ideas and concepts that you may not have thought of before, as well as give you some great tips and shortcuts.

What this book covers

Chapter 1, *Setting Up Networks*, walks you through the creation of the different networks that exist in vCloud. We will go from External Networks, through VXLANs, and the Cisco 1000v to Edge networks.

Chapter 2, *vCloud Networks*, plays with all the vCloud networking, routing, and isolation possibilities. Accessing isolated network, working with vCloud routers, as well as Edge and fencing will be investigated.

Chapter 3, *Better vApps*, delves into all that you can do with vApps. We will discuss the import and export of vApps as well as Guest Customization.

Chapter 4, *Datastores and Storage Profiles*, focuses on Datastores, storage profiles, and linked clones.

Chapter 5, Working with the vCloud API, introduces you to working with the vCloud API. We will be using PowerShell, PHP, vCenter Orchestrator as well as the REST API to build VMs.

Chapter 6, Improving the vCloud Design, will give you a new understanding of how to design a productive and effective vCloud environment.

Chapter 7, Operational Challenges, introduces you to solutions to combat common and uncommon operational problems. This chapter is a collection of all kinds of useful recipes that will provide you with tips and tricks on how to be more efficient with vCloud Director.

Chapter 8, Troubleshooting vCloud, focuses on logfiles, error finding, and recovery.

Appendix, contains a list of all the abbreviations used used in this book.

What you need for this book

The book was written using vCloud 5.1 and vCloud 5.5; therefore you need at least:

- VMware vSphere 5.1 environment (or better)
- VMware vCloud Director 5.1 (or better)
- VMware vCloud Network and Security (vCNS) 5.1 (or better)

You can obtain trial licensing for vCloud from `http://www.vmware.com/try-vmware`.

In this book we will also discuss recipes that require the following software:

Generally used tools:

- Flash 11 (or better)
- Java 7 (or better)
- Firefox or Internet Explorer
- SSH
- SCP/SFTP

Tools for networks (*Chapter 1, Setting Up Networks* and *Chapter 2, vCloud Networks*):

- Cisco 1000v and Cisco NSM
- m0n0Wall

Tools for API usage (*Chapter 5, Working with the vCloud API*):

- VMware vCenter Orchestrator 5.1 (vCO) (or better; the appliance is OK too)
- VMware PowerCLI

- ▶ PowerGUI
- ▶ Firefox with the REST client
- ▶ PHP

Who this book is for

VMware vCloud Director Cookbook is aimed at system administrators and technical architects moving from a virtualized environment to cloud environments.

This book assumes some previous knowledge of vCloud that can be obtained by referring to *Instant VMware vCloud Starter* by *Daniel Langenhan*. You need basic knowledge of the vCloud GUI as well as some experience with vSphere. An understanding of basic network terminology is beneficial.

The book was written using vCloud 5.1 and vCloud 5.5, but most of the concepts and recipes will also work with vCloud 1.5.

Conventions

In this book, you will find a number of styles of text that distinguish between different kinds of information. Here are some examples of these styles, and an explanation of their meaning.

Code words in text, database table names, folder names, filenames, file extensions, pathnames, dummy URLs, user input, and Twitter handles are shown as follows: "Choose if you would like to create pre-copies into the transfer storage of the vCD cell (the /data/ transfer directory)."

A block of code is set as follows:

```
if ((exists user-class) and (option user-class = "gPXE")){
# STAGE 2 GPXE BOOTFILE
        filename = "https:// [TFTP Server]:6501/vmw/rbd/tramp";
}
```

When you are required to enter any additions to the code it will appear between [ ]:

```
get-Org -name [Name of Org]
```

Any command-line input or output is written as follows:

```
/opt/vmware/vcloud-director/jre/bin/keytool -keystore /opt/vmware/
certificates.ks -storetype JCEKS -genkey -keyalg RSA -alias [http |
consoleproxy]
```

New terms and **important words** are shown in bold. Words that you see on the screen, in menus or dialog boxes for example, appear in the text like this: "Clicking the **Next** button moves you to the next screen."

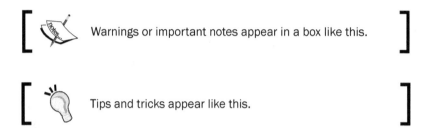

Warnings or important notes appear in a box like this.

Tips and tricks appear like this.

Reader feedback

Feedback from our readers is always welcome. Let us know what you think about this book—what you liked or may have disliked. Reader feedback is important for us to develop titles that you really get the most out of.

To send us general feedback, simply send an e-mail to feedback@packtpub.com, and mention the book title via the subject of your message.

If there is a topic that you have expertise in and you are interested in either writing or contributing to a book, see our author guide on www.packtpub.com/authors.

Customer support

Now that you are the proud owner of a Packt book, we have a number of things to help you to get the most from your purchase.

Downloading the example code

You can download the example code files for all Packt books you have purchased from your account at http://www.packtpub.com. If you purchased this book elsewhere, you can visit http://www.packtpub.com/support and register to have the files e-mailed directly to you.

Errata

Although we have taken every care to ensure the accuracy of our content, mistakes do happen. If you find a mistake in one of our books—maybe a mistake in the text or the code—we would be grateful if you would report this to us. By doing so, you can save other readers from frustration and help us improve subsequent versions of this book. If you find any errata, please report them by visiting http://www.packtpub.com/submit-errata, selecting your book, clicking on the **errata submission form** link, and entering the details of your errata. Once your errata are verified, your submission will be accepted and the errata will be uploaded on our website, or added to any list of existing errata, under the Errata section of that title. Any existing errata can be viewed by selecting your title from http://www.packtpub.com/support.

Piracy

Piracy of copyright material on the Internet is an ongoing problem across all media. At Packt, we take the protection of our copyright and licenses very seriously. If you come across any illegal copies of our works, in any form, on the Internet, please provide us with the location address or website name immediately so that we can pursue a remedy.

Please contact us at copyright@packtpub.com with a link to the suspected pirated material.

We appreciate your help in protecting our authors, and our ability to bring you valuable content.

Questions

You can contact us at questions@packtpub.com if you are having a problem with any aspect of the book, and we will do our best to address it.

1
Setting Up Networks

In this chapter, we will see how to set up the various network resources that we will use in the next chapter. We will cover the following recipes:

- ▶ Setting up an External Network
- ▶ Creating 1,000 isolated networks without VXLANs
- ▶ Making VXLANs work
- ▶ Integrating Cisco 1000v into vCD
- ▶ Giving your networks an Edge
- ▶ Doing it all(most) without a Distributed Switch

Introduction

Network virtualization is what makes vCloud Director such an awesome tool. However, before we go full out in the next chapter, we need to set up network virtualization, and it is what we will be focusing on here.

When we talk about isolated networks, we are talking about vCloud Director making use of different methods of the Network layer 3 encapsulation (OSI/ISO model). Basically, it's the same concept that was introduced with VLANs. VLANs split up the network communication in a network in different totally-isolated communication streams. vCloud makes use of these isolated networks to create networks in Organizations and vApps.

vCloud Director has three different network items listed as follows:

▸ **External Network**: This is a network that exists outside vCloud, for example, a production network. It is basically a port group in vSphere that is used in vCloud to connect to the outside world. An External Network can be connected to multiple Organization Networks. External Networks are not virtualized and are based on existing port groups on vSwitch or a Distributed Switch (also called a vNetwork Distributed Switch or vNDS).

▸ **Organization Network**: This is a network that exists only inside one organization. You can have multiple Organization Networks in an organization. Organizational networks come in three different types:

   ❑ **Isolated**: An isolated Organization Network exists only in this organization and is not connected to an External Network; however, it can be connected to vApp Networks or VMs. This network type uses network virtualization and its own network settings.

   ❑ **Routed Network** (**Edge Gateway**): An Organization Network connects to an existing Edge Device. An Edge Gateway allows defining firewall, NAT rules, DHCP services, Static Routes, as well as VPN connections and the load balance functionality. Routed Gateways connect External Networks to vApp Networks and/or VMs. This network uses virtualized networks and its own network settings.

   ❑ **Directly connected**: This Organization Network is an extension of an External Network into the organization. They directly connect External Networks to vApp Networks or VMs. These networks do NOT use network virtualization and they make use of the network settings of an External Network.

▸ **vApp Network**: This is a virtualized network that only exists inside a vApp. You can have multiple vApp Networks inside one vApp. A vApp Network can connect to VMs and to Organization Networks. It has its own network settings. When connecting a vApp Network to an Organization Network, you can create a router between the vApp and the Organization Network, which lets you define DHCP, firewall, NAT rules, and Static Routing.

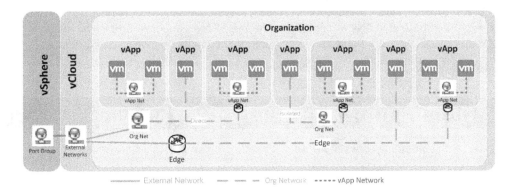

To create isolated networks, vCloud Director uses **Network Pools**. Network Pools are a collection of VLANs, port groups, and VLANs that can use layer 2 in the layer 3 encapsulation. The content of these pools can be used by Organizations and vApp Networks for network virtualization.

Network Pools

There are four kinds of Network Pools that can be created:

- **Virtual eXtensible LANs** (**VXLAN**): VXLAN networks are layer 2 networks that are encapsulated in layer 3 packets. VMware calls this **Software Defined Networking** (**SDN**). VXLANs are automatically created by **vCloud Director** (**vCD**); however, they don't work out of the box and require some extra configuration in vCloud Network and Security (refer to the *Making VXLANs work* recipe).

- **Network isolation-backed**: These have basically the same concept as VXLANs; however, they work out of the box and use MAC-in-MAC encapsulation. The difference is that VXLANs can transcend routers whereas Network isolation-backed networks can't (refer to the *Creating isolated networks without 1,000 VXLANs* recipe).

- **vSphere port groups-backed**: vCD uses pre-created port groups to build the vApp or Organization Networks. You need to pre-provision one port group for every vApp/Organization Network you would like to use.

- **VLAN-backed**: vCD uses a pool of VLAN numbers to automatically provision port groups on demand; however, you still need to configure the VLAN trunking. You will need to reserve one VLAN for every vApp/Organization Network you would like to use.

VXLANs and Network isolation-backed networks solve the problems of pre-provisioning and reserving a multitude of VLANs, which makes them extremely important. However, using a port group or VLAN Network Pools can have additional benefits that we will explore later.

So let's get started!

Setting up an External Network

Let's start with something very simple, such as setting up an External Network.

Getting ready

Creating an External Network requires an existing port group in vSphere. This port group can be on a vSwitch, a Distributed vSwitch, or a Cisco 1000v Distributed Switch. The port group can be supported by a VLAN or a physical network.

How to do it...

1. Log in to vCloud Director with a system administrator (SysAdmin) role.
2. Click on **Manage & Monitor**.
3. Click on **External Networks**.
4. Click on the green plus icon (**+**). Now, the **New External Network** wizard starts.
5. Select the vCenter that contains the port group and then select the port group you want the External Network connected to. If you have many networks, there is a filter just on the right above the list of the networks, as seen in the following screenshot:

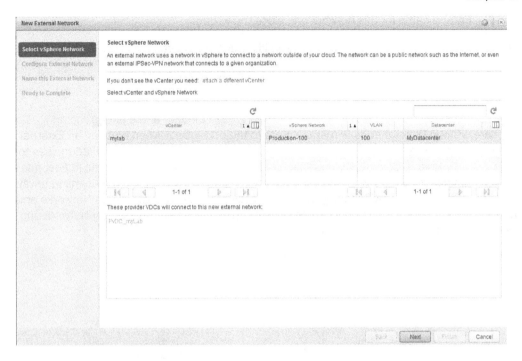

6. Add a subnet definition that contains at least the **Gateway address**, **Network mask**, and a **Static IP pool** by clicking on **Add**, as shown in the following screenshot:

7. Enter a name for this network and close the wizard.

The External Network will now be created and is ready to be used.

How it works...

An External Network is just a connection between vCloud Director and a port group on vSphere. vCloud Director adds IP management to the port group. When creating an External Network, you have to define a pool. This pool is used to automatically assign IP addresses to VMs, Edge Gateways, or vApp routers attached to this External Network. A Static IP Pool has to contain a minimum of one IP, but can contain the maximum available IPs minus the gateway address. vCloud Director will manage all the IPs assigned though Organization Networks and Edge devices. The IP assignments can be seen by right-clicking on the External Network and selecting **IP Allocations** as shown in the following screenshot:

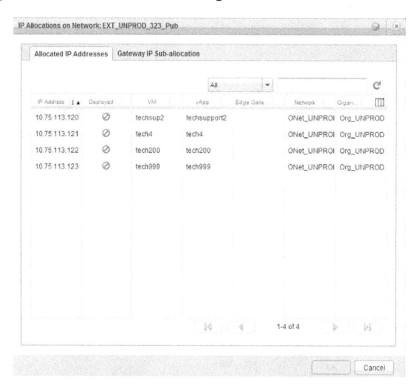

Using only one IP in an External Network Static IP Pool is interesting only if all IPs for VMs are assigned manually and no Edge or vApp router is used. If this is not the case, one should assign at least 5 to 10 IPs to the Network Pool. We will make excessive use of the External Network and we will use its IP pool for load balancing, VPNs, and much more.

There's more...

You can assign more than one IP range to an External Network, making it possible to create more than one IP range that can be used. However, IP allocation happens automatically and you are not able to control which IP from what range will be allocated to which specific VM. Creating multiple IP network ranges in External Networks is preferable when used together with IP suballocation in Edge devices.

When a VM is destroyed or undeployed, the IP will be released back to the pool. The setting of the default time for the IP release is set by navigating to **Administration | General | IPaddress release timeout**. The default value is 0 seconds. This setting specifies how long discarded IP addresses should be held before they can be reused. Think about your ARP tables and how long you have set your router's refresh time. If IP addresses are reallocated to new MAC addresses, a router might not be able to route it properly.

Creating 1,000 isolated networks without VXLANs

Network Pools are essential for network virtualization. If you are not sure about VXLAN networks, here is how you create 1,000 networks using only one VLAN.

Getting ready

As I have already mentioned, we need one VLAN that is trunked to a Distributed Switch. The VLAN doesn't need to be routed. The only other requirement is that the network gear can accommodate a higher MTU.

How to do it...

1. In the system organization, we click on **Manage & Monitor** and then on **Network pools**.

2. Now click on the green plus (**+**) icon to add a Network Pool.

3. Now click on **Network Isolation-backed** as shown in the following screenshot:

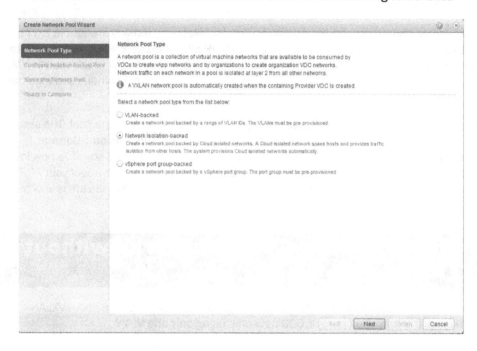

4. Define how many networks you would like to create. The maximum is 1,000:

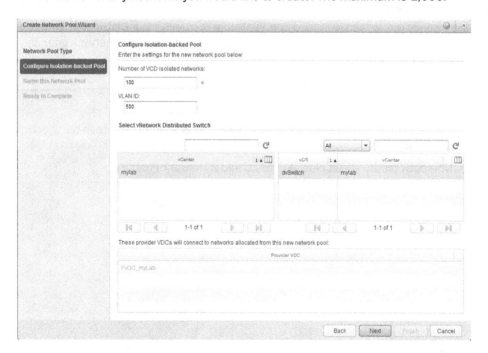

5. Type in the VLAN number you would like to use for the Network Pool.

6. Now select the vCenter and the Distributed Switch you want to use.

7. Give the Network Pool a name.

8. After clicking on **Next**, you will see all the values you have entered.

9. Click on **Finish** in order to create the Network Pool.

10. Now we need to set the MTU for this VLAN to a minimum of `1524`.

    A safer choice is `1600`, as this makes sure you have enough room for additional encapsulations down the track. Make sure that your physical switching infrastructure can use a higher MTU than the default `1500`.

11. Click on the created Network Pool and select **Properties**.

12. Click on **Network pool MTU** and set the MTU to `1600` as shown in the following screenshot:

13. Click on **OK**.

How it works...

Network isolation-backed networks actually don't use layer 2 and layer 3 encapsulations, but they use the MAC-in-MAC encapsulation. When a new vApp or Organization Network is created, vCD will create a new port group and will then use this port group to encapsulate the traffic on a MAC basis. The same technique was used in VMware Lab Manager, which was then called Host Spanning Networks. This doesn't come without cost. Because of the additional encapsulation, another 24 bits are required for each package, meaning that the MTU should be increased to a minimum of `1524`. If you don't change the MTU, you will have a network frame fragmentation.

The good thing is that Network isolation-backed Network Pools are quite fast and easy to configure and set up. They provide you with 1,000 isolated networks for each VLAN. You can define more than one Network isolation-backed network. However, you can only assign one Network Pool to an **Organizational virtual Datacenter** (**OvDC**), as there is a one-to-one relationship between them. You cannot create isolated networks before you assign a Network Pool to an OvDC.

To assign a Network Pool to an OvDC:

1. Navigate to **Manage & Monitor | Organizational VDC**.

2. Right-click on the OvDC you want the pool assigned to and select **Properties**.

3. Click on **Network pool & Services**.

4. Select the network pool you like to assign as shown in the following screenshot:

5. Select the number of networks you would like to assign to the OvDC as shown in the following screenshot.

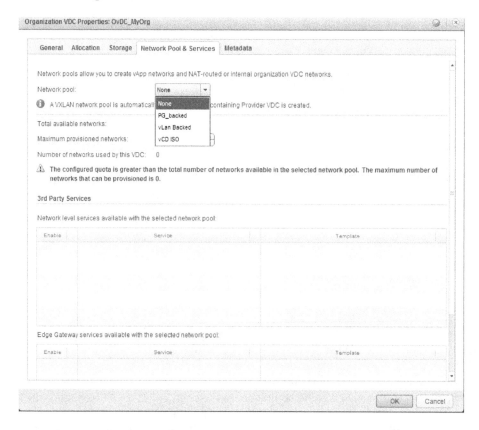

One of the disadvantages is that the networks are isolated, meaning we can't use them for anything other than vCloud Director.

See also

▶ We will work extensively with vApp and Organization Networks in *Chapter 2, vCloud Networks*

Making VXLANs work

VXLANs are great, but they don't work out of the box. In the following sections, we discuss how to set them up.

Getting ready

As you already have vCloud set up, you must have a **vCloud Network and Security appliance** (**vCNS**) deployed (formally known as **vShield**), and it should be configured to use your vCenter. For this recipe, you will need to be able to log in to the vCNS appliance with an administrator account.

Additionally, we need a VLAN on which the VXLANs will exist, and having a DHCP in that VLAN makes things easier. If no DHCP is accessible on this VLAN, you will need to provide one IP address per ESXi server in this VLAN.

The Segment ID you have to enter in step 14 in the *How to do it...* section is rather important, especially when you have multiple vCNS or vCloud installations (not multiple cells). Each of these installations should have a different range. If this is your first VXLAN installation, just use the range that is supplied in the steps.

Last but not least, you should have a multicast address range (see http://en.wikipedia. org/wiki/Multicast_address); this is best arranged with the network administrator. If you can't figure out what to use, the range given in the steps will work fine for a VXLAN that exists only in one location.

 If you are using the Cisco 1000v, please check out the *Integrating the Cisco 1000v into vCD* recipe before continuing here.

How to do it...

1. Open a browser and browse to the vCNS appliance `https://[ip of vCNS]`.
2. Log in to the appliance (the default username is `admin` and the password is `default`).
3. Make sure that you have switched to the **Host & Clusters** view.
4. Expand the `Datacenters` folder.
5. Click on your data center.
6. On the right side of the screen, you should now find multiple menus; one of them says **Network virtualization**, so click on it.

7. Now select **Preparation** and then **Connectivity** as shown in the following screenshot:

8. Click on **Edit**.

9. Select your **Cluster**.

10. Select the Distributed Switch as well as the VLAN ID for the VXLAN that you want to use and click on **Next** as shown in the following screenshot:

11. Now select a **Teaming policy** (for example, **Fail Over**) and its **MTU** (for example, **1600**) as shown in the following screenshot:

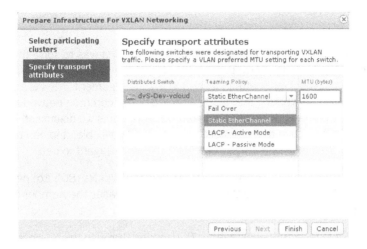

12. Click on **Finish**.

13. Wait until the agents are installed on all the ESXi servers. The status should then show **Normal** (you might need to refresh).

14. Click on **Segment ID** and then on **Edit** as shown in the following screenshot:

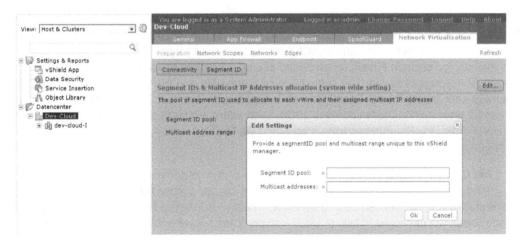

15. You have to now enter a range for the Segment IDs (for example, `5000-6000`).

16. Now enter the **Multicast address range** (for example, `225.1.1.1-225.1.2.254`).

17. Click on **Finish**.

18. We are now done with vCNS and can leave the rest to vCloud Director.

19. Log in to vCloud Director and click on **Network pools**.

20. The VXLAN pool, which is automatically created with your PvDC, should now show a green tick. If this is not the case, right-click on it and select **Repair**.

How it works...

VXLANs were created by VMware together with Cisco. The idea was to solve the problems of modern data centers. Typically, these problems relate to the inflexibility of VLAN and Switching boundaries due to too much subnetting, IP, and VLAN management. The idea behind VXLANs is to create virtualized networking that is used on top of the common networking layer. They are in use just like the Network isolation-backed Network Pools we discussed in the other recipe; however, VXLANs have the benefit of being routable, flexible, and can transcend to different locations. This makes them extremely flexible and elegant to use.

VXLANs are actually like VLANs; the main difference is that VLANs (802.1q) have a 12-bit namespace whereas VXLANs have a 24-bit one, which increases the number of VLANs from 4,096 to more than 16 million unique namespaces.

VXLANs use layer 2 in layer 3 encapsulation. This means they use the Internet Protocol (IP, layer 3) to propagate the networks (from layer 2 upward), making them routable and far more flexible across network borders. One could envision VXLANs as a tunnel between two endpoints where additional networks exist.

There's more...

VXLANs don't really exist in vCloud Director; VXLANs are defined in the vCNS appliance. vCNS creates the VXLAN tunnel endpoints and manages the VXLANs for the whole virtual infrastructure. For all this to happen, vCNS must install an agent on each ESXi server. This is done when you click on **Finish**, as explained in step 12 in the *How to do it...* section of this recipe. These agents provide the connection between VMs and the VXLANs. As the VXLAN packages are bigger than the common network packages, we have to adjust the MTU to avoid frame fragmentation. A safe setting is 1600. Each agent will be deployed and connected to a new vmknic. The IP for the vmknic is assigned via DHCP; however, this can be changed in vCNS for each ESXi server.

The **Fail Over** policy that you set on the Distributed Switches depends on what the physical switching architecture can do. If EtherChannels are set up, choose them. **Link Aggregation Control Protocol** (**LACP**) can be chosen either in active or passive mode. LACP in an active mode sends out packages to talk to LACP-activated devices, whereas in a passive mode it waits until a LACP-activated device talks to it. If in doubt about all of this, please involve your network team.

If you want to configure VXLANs with Static IPs for each vmknic, follow the ensuing procedure:

1. Log in to vCNS as an administrator.

2. Navigate to **Hosts & Clusters View** | **Datacenter** | **[your datacentre]** | **Network Virtualization** | **Connectivity** as shown in the following screenshot:

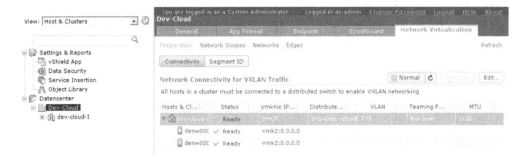

3. Write down which vmknic is used for VXLANs.

4. Log in to vCenter as an administrator.

5. Set a fixed IP for each of the vmknics on each ESXi server.

See also

The following are some links for further reading:

▶ VMware's easy to read explanation at http://www.vmware.com/solutions/datacenter/vxlan.html

▶ Cisco's *Digging deeper into VXLAN* at http://blogs.cisco.com/datacenter/digging-deeper-into-vxlan

▶ A good case study on VXLANs at http://it20.info/2012/05/typical-vxlan-use-case/

Integrating the Cisco 1000v into vCD

The Cisco 1000v Distributed Switch is an alternative to the VMware Distributed Switch; however, getting it working with vCloud is a challenge. In the following sections, we will see how to overcome it.

Getting ready

First and foremost, we need the Cisco 1000v installed (refer to the *How it works* section in this recipe). The next important thing is to hook the Cisco 1000v up to vCenter (refer to the *See also* section links in this recipe). After all this is done, you can use the Cisco 1000v in vSphere and we can now start linking it up to vCloud.

How to do it...

1. Log on to the Cisco 1000v **Virtual Supervisor Module** (**VSM**).

2. Run the following commands to activate the REST interface of the VSM:

```
1kv# conf t
1kv (Config)# feature network-segmentation-manager
1kv (Config)# feature segmentation
1kv (Config)# exit
1kv # copy running-config startup-config
[#####################################] 100%
1kv# exit
```

3. Log out of the Cisco 1000v.

4. Log in to the vCNS (vShield) as an administrator.

5. Click on **Settings & Reports**.

6. Click on **Networking** and then on **Add Switch Provider** as shown in the following screenshot:

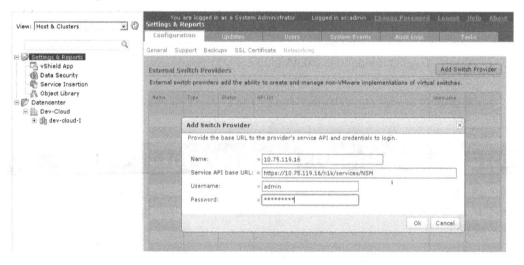

7. Now enter the Cisco VSM IP or hostname and the service API URL `https://[VSM IP] /n1k/services/NSM`.

8. Enter the admin credentials for the VSM and click on **OK**.

And that's it. Now you can use the *Making VXLANs work* recipe to create VXLANs using the Cisco 1000v.

How it works...

The Cisco 1000v replaced the VMware Distributed Switch. The benefit of this is that you can use the Cisco tools and Cisco language to configure it. For all intents and purposes, it acts and behaves like a Cisco physical switch. One of the drawbacks is that there can be maximal 63 hosts (63 hosts and one Cisco v1000) connected to one Cisco 1000v and the integration between Cisco and VMware isn't as smooth as it may appear to be.

Cisco 1000v consists of two different items. The VSM is the management console and is basically a VM where the Cisco OS runs. The **Virtual Ethernet module** (**VEM**) is a plugin into the ESXi server that replaces the functionality of the VMware Distributed Switch.

There are basically two different designs for the Cisco 1000v installation. The first and easiest is to install the Cisco 1000v VSMs (Manager) as a VM on vSphere. This has considerable drawbacks as the Cisco 1000v VSMs can't be used with the Cisco 1000v itself, meaning you need to install it using normal vSwitches, which in return calls for a separate management cluster. The other better but more costly alternative is to use Cisco 1010. The Cisco 1010 is nothing else but a physical server that can contain up to six VSMs.

Flow for a Cisco 1000v installation is shown in the following diagram:

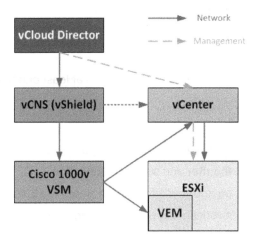

vCloud Director talks to vCenter for management (create VMs and so on), and talks to vCNS to create and manage complex networks (for example, Edge). The vCNS communicates with vCenter to create port groups and push out configurations to Distributed Switches. vCenter communicates with ESXi servers to facilitate management and to push network configurations out to the ESXi servers.

When the Cisco 1000v enters the picture, things change. Instead of vCNS talking to vCenter (the dotted line in the preceding figure), it now talks to the Cisco 1000v VSM. The VSM will then talk to vCenter and the VEM installed in the ESXi server to facilitate networking.

See also

The following are some useful links for the Cisco 1000v:

- ▶ Technical documentation at `http://www.cisco.com/en/US/products/ps9902/tsd_products_supPort_series_home.html`

- ▶ *Deployment Guide* for the 1000v at `http://www.cisco.com/en/US/prod/collateral/switches/ps9441/ps9902/guide_c07-556626.html`

- ▶ Implementing VXLAN with vCloud Director (more details) at `http://www.cisco.com/en/US/prod/collateral/switches/ps9441/ps9902/deployment_guide_c07-703595.html`

Giving your networks an Edge

For the recipes in the next chapter, we need an Edge. So, let's see how it works.

Getting ready

To create an Edge device in an organization, we need:

- ▶ One External Network, with some free IP addresses
- ▶ One organization
- ▶ One OvDC connected to one Network Pool with at least one free isolated network

How to do it...

1. Log in to vCloud (not the organization) as a `SysAdmin`.
2. Click on **Manage & Monitor** and select **Organization**.
3. Double-click on the organization you want to create the Edge in.
4. The Organization Network should now have opened as a separate tab.
5. Click on **Administration**.
6. Double-click on the OvDC your Network Pool is associated with.
7. Click on **Edge Gateways** as shown in the following screenshot:

8. To create a new Edge device, click on the green plus (**+**) sign.

The Edge wizard opens up and the first page lets you choose some very basic and important settings. I marked the settings that I will use for this installation so that it matches the need of the Edge device in the next chapter. All of them can be configured later too.

Perform the following steps for configuring the Edge Gateway:

1. Of the two Edge gateway configuration options, **Compact** and **Full**, select **Compact**. This option basically decides the resources that should be allocated to the gateway. **Compact** can be later upgraded to **Full**.

2. Uncheck the **Enable High Availability** option; if chosen, the gateway is protected against faults in ESXi hosts.

3. Check the **Configure IP Settings** option; it is used to manually configure the IP setting for the Edge.

4. Check the **Sub-Allocate IP Pools** option; it makes the IPs from the External Network available to the Edge.

5. Uncheck **Configure Rate Limits**; it is used to reduce the inbound and outbound bandwidth, as shown in the following screenshot:

Perform the following steps for configuring the External Networks:

1. Select the External Networks that the Edge should be connected to and click on **Add**.

2. If you select more than one External gateway, specify which one will be the default gateway.

3. Select the **Use default gateway for DNS Relay** option as it allows DNS forwarding for the Edge.

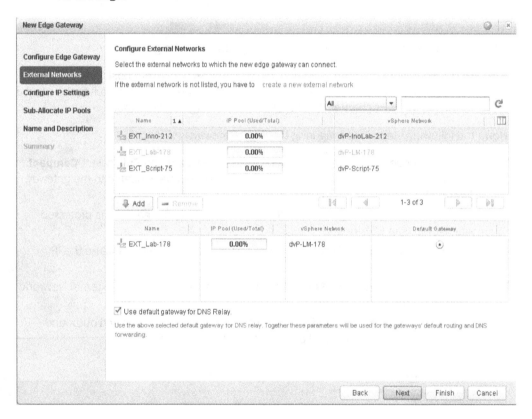

Perform the following for configuring the IP settings:

1. For each External Network, select if the gateway IP should be automatically taken from the pool or assigned manually.

2. Clicking on **Change IP Assignment** will open up a window where you can assign the IP manually.

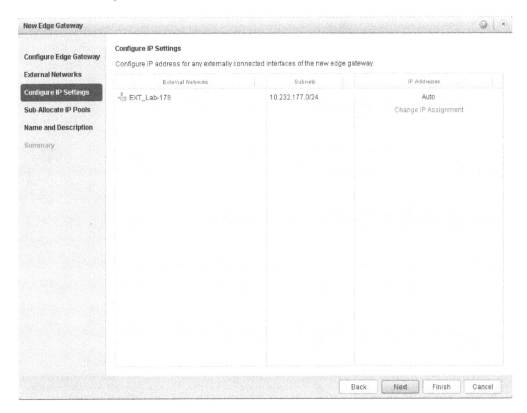

Perform the following steps to suballocate IP pools:

1. Select the External Network you would like to create a suballocation for.

2. Type the range you want to suballocate.

3. Click on **Add**.

4. Name the Edge device and click on **Next** to see the summary, or **Finish** to start the deploy of the Edge device.

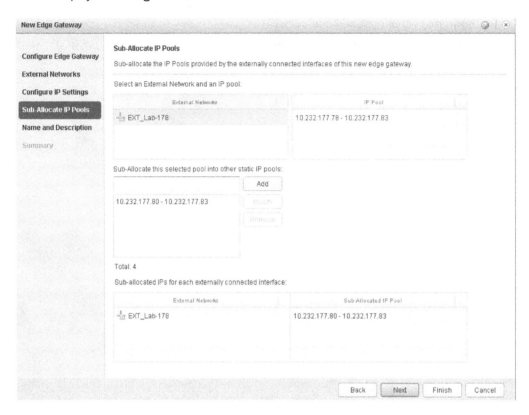

5. The Edge device is now deploying, which can take a moment. If you want, check out vCenter and see what's happening.

6. We now need an organization network connecting to the Edge. Click on **Org VDC Networks**.

7. Click on the green plus (**+**) sign to create a new Organization Network.

8. Select **Create a routed network...**, select the Edge device you have created, and click on **Next**.

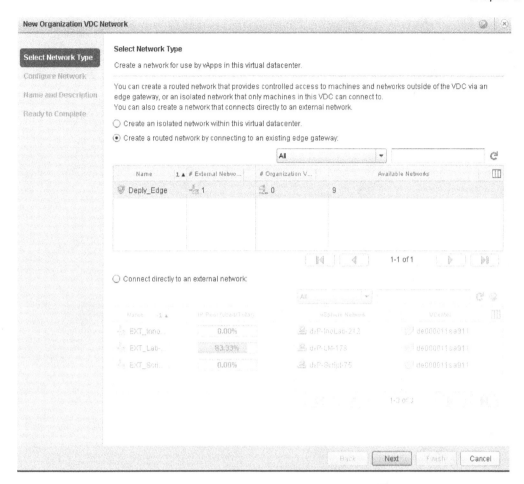

Perform the following steps for configuring the network:

1. Type in the addresses in the **Gateway address** and **Network mask** options.

2. The Edge can forward your DNS requests. If you don't want that and have your own DNS server in this Organization Network later configured, you can switch it off.

3. Specify a **Static IP pool** for this network.

4. Give the network a name and description.

5. Click on **Next** for a summary or **Finish** to create the Organization Network.as shown in the following screenshot:

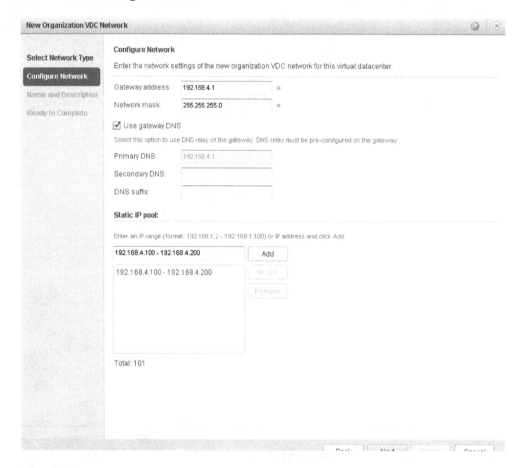

How it works...

The Edge is essentially a router with extras. It provides you with the ability to route between different networks, create firewall rules, create a DHCP service for Organization Networks, create load balancers, and also define a VPN network here.

The Edge devices are only accessible from the organization they were created in. The Edge has two sides: the northbound facing (External Networks) and the southbound facing (Organization Networks). For each Organization Network, the Edge provides a gateway address that can also act as a DNS forwarder. All communication through the Edge has to pass the firewall and can be controlled that way.

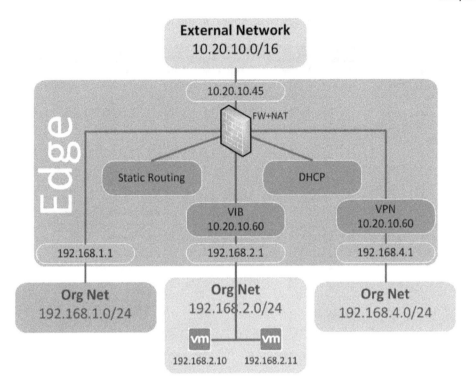

Each Organization Network can be configured with D-NAT and S-NAT, as well as DHCP and Static Routing. Load balancing can be configured and we will do that in the next chapter. As the Edge can be connected to multiple External Networks, it can serve as a hub for all kinds of connections, for example, direct Internet connections and local networks.

There's more...

I would strongly encourage you to take a trip into the vCNS and look at the Edge we created, and compare its vCNS options to the options vCloud Director presents you.

1. Log in to vCNS.
2. Expand **Datacenter** and click on your data center.
3. Select **Network Virtualization** and then **Edges**.

4. Double-click on your Edge device as shown in the following screenshot:

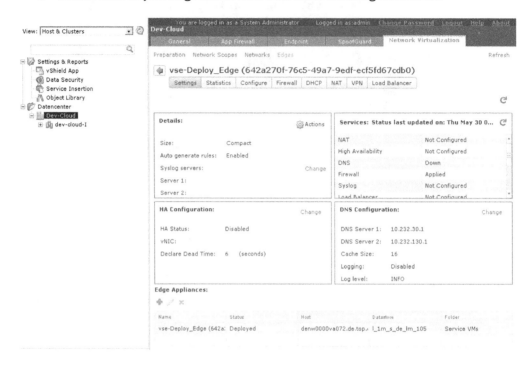

5. The settings for the vCloud Edge can be found when you right-click on **Edge** and then click on **Properties** as shown in the following screenshot:

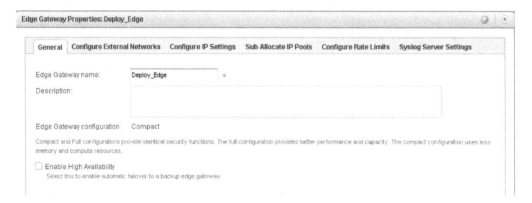

We will work with the Edge in the next chapter and find out what we can do with it

Doing it all(most) without a Distributed Switch

So you want vCloud, but you don't have a Distributed Switch; here is how you can enjoy vCloud using vSwitches.

Getting ready

Surprisingly, you don't need much, just a lot of port groups. Make sure that these port groups are created exactly the same on all ESXi hosts (case sensitive).

How to do it...

We discuss the changes required for each of the different networks:

- **External Networks**: Instead of using Distributed Switches, we will use normal vSwitches with port groups. No big drawbacks here.

- **Network Pools**: The only Network Pool type you can use is the port group-backed one. This also means that you will need to have one port group per isolated network. The drawback is that you can also only assign one Network Pool to each OvDC, making it a one-to-one relationship between the port group, OvDC, and isolated network.

How it works...

Using vSwitches instead of Distributed Switches with vCloud Director is a possibility, but normally this method is only used when VMware Enterprise Plus Licensing is not available. However, with the introduction of vCloud Suite (which comes with vSphere Enterprise Plus), it is not really needed anymore. Still, in some cases this might provide a solution.

2
vCloud Networks

In this chapter we will work with networks. Therefore, a look at the following recipes will give you a very good idea of what you can do with them:

- ▶ Deploying a vApp with vApp router
- ▶ Forwarding an RDP (or SSH) session into an isolated an isolated vApp
- ▶ Accessing a fully isolated vApp or Organization Network
- ▶ Using Organization Networks for interconnection between vApps
- ▶ Using templates with firewall and NAT settings
- ▶ Connecting a physical device to an isolated network
- ▶ Sharpening the Edge
- ▶ Using vApp Network fencing
- ▶ Creating multitiered vApp Networks
- ▶ Ensuring no change in IP after redeployment
- ▶ Automatic IP management for External Network Pools
- ▶ Creating load-balanced VMs in an organization
- ▶ Creating a secure connection between organizations (which can be in different vClouds)
- ▶ Monitoring which network resources have been used where

Introduction

In *Chapter 1, Setting Up Networks*, we looked into installing some rather special networks; now let's have a closer look at what one can do with networks in vCloud, but before we dive into the recipes, let's make sure we are all on the same page.

Usage of different Network types

vCloud Director has three different network items. An **External Network** is basically a port group in vSphere that is imported into vCloud. An **Organization Network** is an isolated network that exists only in an organization. The same is true for **vApp Networks**, which exists only in vApps. Have a quick look at the *Introduction* section of *Chapter 1, Setting Up Networks*, for some more information about them. We have already seen the following diagram in *Chapter 1, Setting Up Networks*, but now we will discuss the content one by one, from left to right in more detail. In each example you will also see a diagram of the specific network:

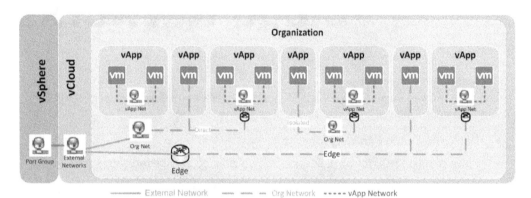

Isolated vApp Network

Isolated vApp Networks exist only inside vApps. They are useful if one needs to test how VMs behave in a network or to test using an IP range that is already in use (for example, production). The downside of them is that they are isolated, meaning that it is hard to get information or software in and out. Have a look at the *Forwarding an RDP (or SSH) session into an isolated vApp* and *Accessing a fully isolated vApp or Organization Network* recipes in this chapter to find some answers to this problem.

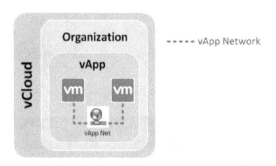

VMs directly connected to an External Network

VMs inside a vApp are connected to a Direct Organization Network that is again directly connected to an External Network, meaning that they will use the IPs from the External Network Pool.

Typically, these VMs are used for production, making it possible for customers to choose vCloud for fast provisioning of preconfigured templates. As vCloud manages the IPs for a given IP range (Static Pool), it can be quite easy to fast provision multiple VMs this way.

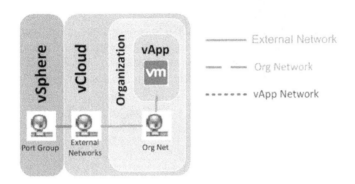

vApp Network connected via vApp router to an External Network

VMs are connected to a vApp Network that has a vApp router defined as its gateway. The gateway connects to a Direct Organization Network. The gateway will automatically be given an IP from the External Network Pool. The IPs of the VMs inside the vApp will be managed by the vApp Static Pool.

These configurations come in handy to reduce the amount of physical networking that has to be provisioned. The vApp router can act as a router with defined firewall rules, it can do S-NAT and D-NAT as well as define static routing and DHCP services. So instead of using a physical VLAN or subnet, one can hide away applications this way. As an added benefit, these applications can be used as templates for fast deployment.

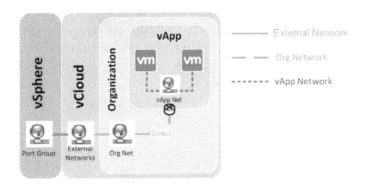

VMs directly connected to an isolated Organization Network

VMs are connected directly to an isolated Organization Network. Connecting VMs directly to an isolated Organization Network normally only makes sense if there's more than one vApp/VM connected to the same Organization Network.

These network constructs come in handy when we want to repeatedly test complex applications that require certain infrastructure services such as Active Directory, DHCP, DNS, database, and Exchange Servers. Instead of deploying the needed infrastructure inside the testing vApp, we create a new vApp that contains only the infrastructure. By connecting the test vApp to the infrastructure vApp via an isolated Organization Network, the test vApp can now use the infrastructure. This makes it possible to re-use these infrastructure services not only for one vApp but also for many vApps, reducing the amount of resources needed for testing. By using vApp sharing options, you can even hide away the infrastructure vApp from your users. Refer to the *Sharing a vApp* recipe in *Chapter 3, Better vApps*.

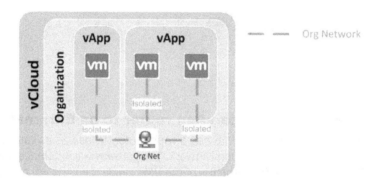

vApp connected via a vApp router to an isolated Organization Network

VMs are connected to a vApp Network that has a vApp router as its gateway. The vApp router gets its IP automatically from the Organization Network pool. The VMs will get their IPs from the vApp Network pool.

Basically, it is a combination of the network examples—VMs directly connected to an isolated Organization Network and a vApp Network connected via a vApp router to an External Network. A test vApp or an infrastructure vApp can be packaged this way and be made ready for fast deployment.

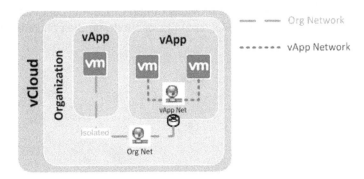

VMs connected directly to an Edge device

VMs are directly connected to the Edge Organization Network and get their IPs from the Organization Network pool. Their gateway is the Edge device that connects them to the External Networks through the Edge firewall.

A typical example for this is the usage of the Edge load balancing feature in order to load balance VMs inside the vApp. Another example is that organizations that are using the same External Network are secured against each other using the Edge firewall. This is mostly the case if the External Network is the Internet and each organization is an external customer.

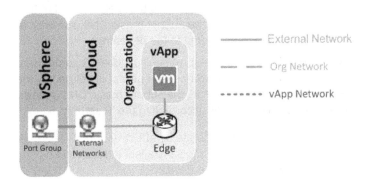

A vApp connected to an Edge via a vApp router

VMs are connected to a vApp Network that has the vApp router as its gateway. The vApp router will automatically get an IP from the Organization Network, which again has its gateway as the Edge. The VMs will get their IPs from the vApp Network pool.

This is a more complicated variant of the previous example, allowing customers to package their VMs, secure them against other vApps or VMs, or subdivide their allocated networks.

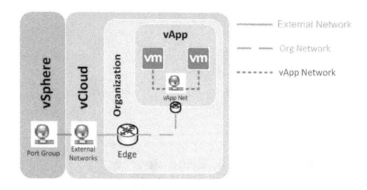

IP management

Let's have a look at IP management with vCloud. vCloud has the following three different settings for IP management of VMs:

▸ **DHCP**: You will need to provide a DHCP as vCloud doesn't automatically create one. However, a vApp router or an Edge can create one.

▸ **Static-IP Pool**: The IP for the VM comes from the Static IP Pool of the network it is connected to. In addition to the IP, the subnet mask, DNS, gateway, and domain suffix will be configured on the VM according to the IP settings.

▸ **Static-Manual**: The IP can be defined manually; it doesn't come from the pool. The IP you define must be part of the network segment that is defined by the gateway and the subnet mask. In addition to the IP, the subnet mask, DNS, gateway, and domain suffix will be configured on the VM according to the IP settings.

All these settings require Guest Customization to be effective. If no Guest Customization is selected, or if the VM doesn't have VMware tools installed, it doesn't work, and whatever the VM was configured with as a template will be used.

Some things you will need for all of the recipes for this chapter

Instead of wasting space and retyping what you need for each recipe every time, the following are some of the basic ingredients you will have to have ready for this chapter:

▸ An organization in which at least one OvDC is present

▸ The OvDC needs to be configured with at least three free isolated networks that have a network pool defined

▸ Some VM templates of an OS type you find easy to use (Linux or Windows)

▸ An External Network that connects you to the outside world (as in outside vCloud), for example, your desktop, and has at least five IPs in the Static IP Pool

Deploying a vApp with a vApp router

As usual, we will first do something light to warm up. Let's deploy a common vApp with a vApp router.

Getting ready

If you have everything I have described in the *Introduction* section, you're ready to go.

You can do this as `SysAdmin`, `OrgAdmin`, or `AppCreator`.

How to do it...

1. Log into your organization.
2. Click on **My Cloud**.
3. Click on 　to create a new vApp.
4. Give the vApp a name.
5. Choose at least one VM template to be added to this vApp.
6. Choose the OvDC and the storage profile.
7. When the time comes to choose the network, select **Add Network...** as shown in the following screenshot:

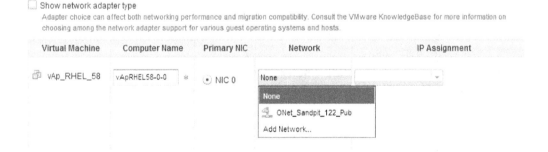

1. In the following wizard, define the network. vCloud will automatically present you with an 192.168.2.0/24 network that has a Static IP Pool. Either choose this or enter your own values.
2. Give the new vApp Network a name and finish the wizard.

8. Leave the IP assignment as **Static - IP Pool**.
9. Skip the **Configure Networking** section and close the vApp wizard.
10. After the vApp has been created, enter it and go straight to **Networking**.

11. Click on the green icon **+** to add another network to the vApp and perform the following:

    1. Choose **Organization VDC Network**.

    2. Choose the prepared Organization Network.

12. You will now see two networks. On the vApp Network you will notice a drop-down menu. Use this to connect the vApp Network to the Organization Network.

13. After you do this, the network will show the **NAT** and **Firewall** services activated as well as a yellow background color, as shown in the following screenshot:

14. Now click on **Apply** to save this configuration.

15. After the new setting is updated, right-click on the vApp Network and select **Configure Services**.

16. Now you can configure **DHCP**, **Firewall**, **NAT**, and **Static routing** for this vApp router (refer to the *Forwarding an RDP (or SSH) session into an isolated vApp* recipe in this chapter).

17. Click on **OK** when you're done.

18. Your VMs inside the vApp can now communicate with the outside VMs.

How it works...

The configuration we created is the same as in a home network that is attached to the Internet via a router. The devices at home can communicate out, but no one from the outside can connect inside.

In the background, vCloud talks to vCNS, and vCNS deploys a new appliance that handles the traffic through the firewall, NAT as well as any other traffic that passes through the vApp router. What really happens is that vCNS creates an Edge device and gives the user of vCloud only a limited amount of control of it. We will take a closer look into this in the *Sharpening the Edge* recipe in this chapter.

One rather important fact to know is what happens if things go wrong. A typical example is that the ESXi on which the vCNS (vShield) appliance lives has died, and with it the vApp router. To restore the network, follow the ensuing instructions:

1. Navigate to your vApp.

2. Click on **Networking**.

3. Right-click on the vApp Network and select **Reset Network**:

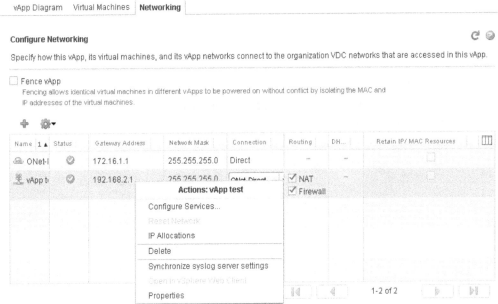

4. A warning will be displayed informing you that during reset, the networks are not accessible.

5. The vApp router is now redeployed in the background and everything should be back to normal.

Forwarding an RDP (or SSH) session into an isolated vApp

Isolated networks are good for testing; however, getting stuff in or out is hard. The following section shows how to make it easier. I call it "hole-in-the-Fence".

Getting ready

You need a fully deployed vApp with an internal vApp Network and at least one VM (preferably two) in it. You can use the *Deploying a vApp with vApp router* recipe in this chapter to get started. However, you will need to connect a Direct Organization Network to the vApp so that you can test this configuration using your desktop. To add a single VM to the vApp, have a look at the *Adding a VM to a vApp* recipe in *Chapter 3, Better vApps*.

How to do it...

1. Go into your deployed vApp by double-clicking on it.
2. Click on **Networking**.
3. Right-click on the vApp Network (not the Organization Network) and choose **Configure Services**.
4. Click on **Firewall**. You should see the following screen:

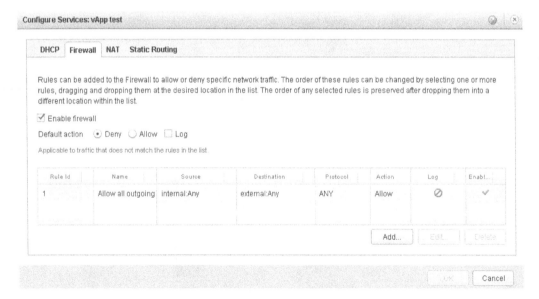

5. Select the first (and only) rule and then click on **Delete**.

6. Make sure that the **default action** option is set to **Deny**.

7. Click on **Add...** to add a new rule:

8. Enter the following settings:

	RDP	**SSH**
Name	RDP FW	SSH FW
Source	External	External
Source Port	Any	Any
Destination	Internal	Internal
Destination Port	3389	22
Protocol	TCP	TCP
Action	Allow	Allow
Login	Off	Off

9. Click on **OK** to add the new firewall rule.

10. Now click on **NAT**.

11. Select the NAT type as **Port Forwarding** and acknowledge the warning.

12. **Enable IP Masquerade** should be selected, and if the vApp is already deployed, you will see the IP of the external interface next to **Router external IP**.

13. Click on **Add...** to add a new rule and perform the following:

    1. Choose the **External Port** value as **3389** (or **22** for SSH).

    2. Set the **Forward Port** value to **3389** (or **22** for SSH).

    3. Choose a VM and click on **OK** to close the window:

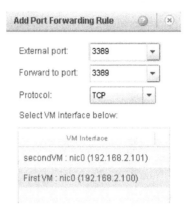

14. The setup is now finished. Click on **OK** to close the window. The following screenshot shows the correct NAT settings:

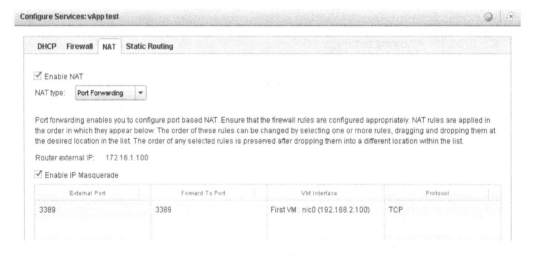

15. The vApp Network now appears in a yellow color, meaning that it has changed. Click on **Apply** to commit the changes.

16. After the changes have been deployed, we can now start configuring the VMs.

17. Log into the OS of your VMs using the vCloud Console.

18. Enable RDP in Windows or SSH in Linux.

19. Test the setting by using RDP or SSH from the secondary VM in the same vApp to log into the primary one.

20. Now that we are sure that RDP or SSH works, we can test from the outside. From your desktop, connect to the **Router external IP** that you found in step 11 (in my example, **172.16.1.100**). It might take longer than usual to get connected but this should now work.

How it works...

Basically, what we did is port forwarded one TCP port through the vApp router firewall. We also made sure that all other traffic won't pass the firewall. We have basically punched a hole in the wall. As the firewall keeps the state of the connections, it knows to let the return traffic through, but nothing else. The following diagram shows the setup we have created:

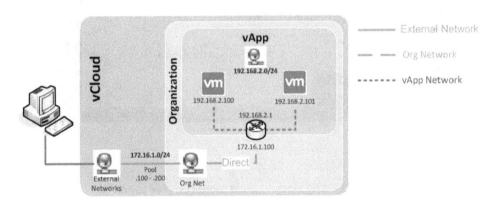

So we have now gotten a connection to a VM inside and we can use a remote screen. What's the big deal? We could do the same without that much trouble using the **vCloud Remote Console**. However, the vCloud Remote Console uses Flash and only runs as fast as your desktop. I have had users that have complained that their VMs were running slow; however, it was the Flash console that ran slow, not the VMs.

The other reason why RDP/SSH is better is that not only can we use the remote screen but also use the file transfer feature in RDP, or SCP/SFTP in Linux, as they all use the same port. You might need to switch on the file transfer in RDP, if this is the case, the following screenshot shows how to enable file transfer with RDP:

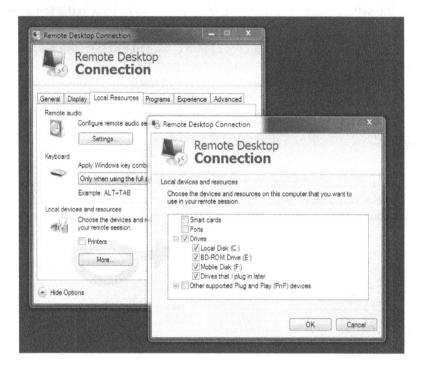

There's more...

We can expand on this basic building block to build more complex solutions.

Creating multiple forwards

So we have punched a hole in the wall and we can get *one* RDP/SSH session through to *one* VM, but how do we get RDP/SSH to the other VMs?

The answer is surprisingly easy. We don't use TCP 3389 and 22; we use different ports and forward them to each VM on the correct port. The only thing you need to know about the vApp router (Edge) is that the firewall will receive the communication first, then it will redirect it to the NAT to be forwarded to the VM (also called postrouting in network terminology). Therefore, we have to create one firewall rule and one port forwarding rule for each VM. Make sure you use ports that are not used by other protocols and that these ports are routed between your desktop and the vApp Router. For more information, refer to http://en.wikipedia.org/wiki/List_of_TCP_and_UDP_port_numbers.

You can also apply the same principle to an Edge and create port forwarding into isolated Organization Networks using the following values:

Firewall	VM 1	VM 2
Name	RDP VM1	RDP VM2
Source	External	External
Source Port	Any	Any
Destination	Internal	Internal
Destination Port	3389 (22)	33389 (22022)
Protocol	TCP	TCP
Action	Allow	Allow
Login	Off	Off

Port forward	VM 1	VM 2
External Port	3389 (22)	33389 (22022)
Internal Port	3389 (22)	3389 (22)
Protocol	TCP	TCP
VM	VM 1	VM 2

To connect to a VM using a nonstandard RDP or SSH port just type in the port as shown in the following screenshots:

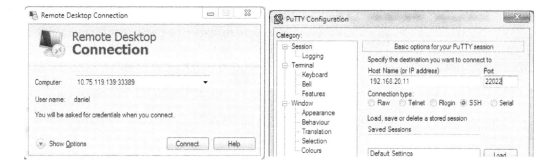

Logging network traffic

You can also log the network traffic of any of the vApp router firewall rules you implement by checking the checkbox **Log network traffic for firewall rule**. All traffic will be automatically forwarded to the Syslog server you have configured with vCloud. See the *See also* section.

Other ideas

You can use the same method for other purposes. Instead of forwarding an RDP/SSH connection to the vApp, you could allow a single connection from a specific VM on a specific port to a specific IP outside. This can, for example, be used to connect NFS or iSCSI from outside to the VM. However, you need to make sure you secure the firewall rules and don't let any other traffic out.

See also

For configuring a Syslog server, please refer to the *Troubleshooting vCloud Router traffic* and *Setting up and using vSphere Syslog Collector* recipes in *Chapter 8, Troubleshooting vCloud*.

Accessing a fully isolated vApp or Organization Network

It is basically the same idea as the previous recipe, but a very different solution; I call it "sitting-on-the-fence", but it is commonly known as a **Jumphost**.

Getting ready

This solution doesn't require a vApp router, and it works for isolated vApps and isolated Organization Networks. Depending on what you would like to build, you need different parts:

► **vApp Networks**: Create a vApp with multiple VMs and deploy an isolated vApp Network. Then add an additional VM of your preferred OS type (Windows or Linux).

► **Organization Networks**: Create an isolated Organization Network that is connected to some other vApps. Now create an additional vApp with only *one* VM of your preferred OS type (Windows or Linux).

To add a VM to a vApp, see the *Adding a VM to a vApp* recipe in *Chapter 3, Better vApps*.

This additional VM will be the Jumphost VM. Do not power on the Jumphost VM yet, as this is an important step in the recipe.

How to do it...

The recipe is the same for vApp and for Organization Networks. We will focus on the additional VM we have created. Perform the following steps:

1. Open your vApp and click on **Networking**.

2. Add the Direct Organization Network to the vApp (see the *Forwarding an RDP (or SSH) session into an isolated vApp* recipe).

3. Apply the new network configuration.

4. Click on **Virtual Machines**.

5. Right-click on the Jumphost VM and select **Properties**.

6. Click on **Hardware** and scroll down to **NICs**.

7. Add a new network card to the VM by clicking on **Add**.

8. Connect the Direct Organization Network to the new network card using a **Static - IP Pool** as shown in the following screenshot:

NICs

ℹ️ Guest customization is required to run for the NIC changes to take effect.

☐ Show network adapter type

Adapter choice can affect both networking performance and migration compatibility. Consult the VMware KnowledgeBase for more information on choosing among the network adapter support for various guest operating systems and hosts.

NIC#	Connected	Network	Primary NIC	IP Mode	IP Address	MAC Address	
1	☑	vApp Iso	○	Static - IP Pool	192.168.2.102	00:50:56:2a:00:39	Delete
2	☑	ONet-Direct	⦿	Static - IP Pool	172.16.1.101	00:50:56:2a:00:3a	Delete

➕ Add

 Choose the Direct Organization Network to be **Primary NIC**.

9. Click on **OK** to close the window.

10. Power on the Jumphost VM.

11. Check what IP has been assigned to the Jumphost VM from the Direct Organization Network.

12. Use RDP/SSH or any kind of file-sharing you may have configured on the gateway VM to connect to it.

13. Use the VMware console to access the Jumphost VM from the inside of the vApp.

How it works...

We have placed a dual-homed VM (Jumphost VM) on the border between the two networks (it is sitting on the fence). The Jumphost VM is assigned a public IP from the External Network Pool and a private IP from the isolated vApp or Organization Network. The important thing is that the public address is the primary gateway and has the gateway address assigned to it, making it possible to route back the connection to your desktop. This can also be achieved by adding static routing to the Jumphost VM's OS; however, for most people, this is rather confusing.

The following diagram shows a Jumphost configuration for a vApp and an organization configuration:

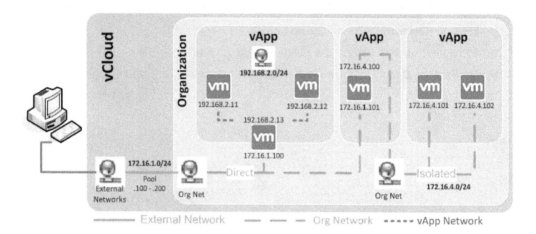

All vanilla Linux and Windows OSs have routing between interface cards disabled. It has to be explicitly activated (see the *See more* section of this recipe). This means that the Jumphost VM is sitting on both the networks without connecting them. This makes the Jumphost VM rather interesting. You can now access the Jumphost VM via RDP/SSH as well as any kind of file-sharing that has been set up. This makes it possible to connect to a fully isolated network and share files between the External Network and the isolated network.

There's more...

If you take this principle further, you could create your own router, load balancer, and other kinds of gateways.

If you are using this host as a bastion host, please be aware that you will need to harden it.

See also

▸ The *Activating Routing in Linux* blog by *Nikesh Jauhari* at `http://linuxpoison.blogspot.de/2008/01/how-to-enable-ip-forwarding.html`

▸ The *Activating Routing in Windows* section at `http://www.wikihow.com/Enable-IP-Routing`

Using Organization Networks for interconnection between vApps

Providing infrastructure for ever-changing test systems is a challenge; the following section gives one solution to the problem.

Getting ready

You need to create two vApps. You will fill one with the entire infrastructure VMs such as DHCP, DNS, Active Directory, database servers, and mail servers.

The other vApp contains your test set of VMs that will make use of the infrastructure VMs.

How to do it...

1. Create an isolated Organization Network with a Static IP Pool.
2. Create a new vApp that will contain the infrastructure VMs.
3. Add the isolated network to the infrastructure vApp.
4. Connect the entire infrastructure VMs to the isolated network with manual IPs that are outside the range of the pool (for example, `.10 - .50`).
5. Deploy the VMs so that they get the correct network settings.
6. Configure all the infrastructure VMs so that they work correctly.
7. Take a snapshot of the vApp, or add it to your catalog.
8. You are now ready to deploy your test set.
9. After the test set is deployed, configure your test VMs to work with the infrastructure VMs.
10. Test the vApp.
11. After you finish testing, undeploy and delete the test vApp.
12. Now use the **Revert to Snapshot** option for the infrastructure vApp or delete and redeploy from catalog.
13. You are ready for another test run.

How it works...

We haven't really done much. We have used the vApp concept to separate all VMs that are reusable, from the ones that are just there for testing. The following diagram shows the configuration for this recipe:

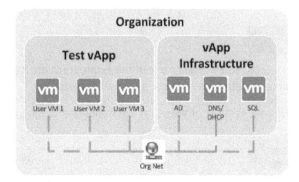

In addition, we use snapshotting or the catalog function to facilitate a new clean image of the reusable VMs.

There's more...

You could also add a Jumphost VM to the infrastructure vApp, making it accessible from the outside. See the *Accessing a fully isolated vApp or Organization Network* recipe in this chapter.

You can take this concept further to create a copy of your production infrastructure. This copy can be used to test out changes or to track faults.

To import your production VMs into vCloud without downtime, check out the *Importing a VM into vCloud* recipe in *Chapter 3, Better vApps*.

Using templates with firewall and NAT settings

One of the major problems is that vApp templates do not keep their vApp router settings when they are templated and redeployed. Using templates with firewall and NAT settings is a way around it.

Getting ready

We need a vApp that has been configured with a vApp router and contains some firewall and NAT rules. You can use the vApp you created in the *Forwarding an RDP (or SSH) session into an isolated vApp* recipe in this chapter.

How to do it...

1. Make sure the vApp that you want as a template is stopped.
2. Right-click on the vApp and choose **Copy to...**.
3. Choose a new **Name**, OvCD, and a **Storage Profile** for the vApp:

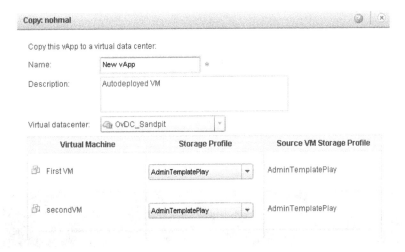

4. The vApp will now be copied.
5. After the vApp is copied, you can deploy it. It is now a full copy, including the vApp router rules of the original vApp.

How it works...

It is not the most ideal way to do this, but it works. There are several downsides of this solution. One is that you will need these templates in *each* organization; you cannot use them centrally. The other one is that users would be able to delete, alter, or otherwise use these templates' VMs. You can use sharing to resolve this problem, but then you lose the user's ability to self provision.

For sharing, see the *Sharing a vApp* recipe in *Chapter 3, Better vApps*.

There's more...

Another solution for this problem is to use vCenter Orchestrator to deploy vApp router rules on demand. There are a lot of scripts out there, and I would recommend googling for them. In the following screenshot you can see the existing scripts in the **vCenter Orchestrator** (**vCO**) library:

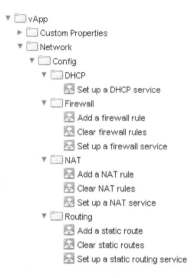

Connecting a physical device to an isolated network

A problem that turns up from time to time is that physical devices need to be connected to an isolated test environment. The following section gives an idea of how to do it.

Getting ready

We will need to have a physical device connected to a VLAN that is routed to the ESXi servers. This means that the VLAN should be trunked to the ESXi servers and added to a Distributed Switch (or vSwitch) as a new port group.

We have everything else to create on the spot.

How to do it...

1. Navigate to **System | Manage & Monitor | Network Pools**.

2. Click on the green icon (**+**) to create a new Network Pool.

3. Choose **vSphere port group-backed**.

4. Select the vCenter you connected the VLAN to.

5. Choose port group of the device to which the VLAN is attached and click on **Add** as shown in the following screenshot:

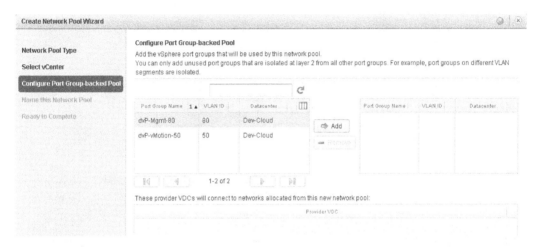

6. Give the Network Pool a name and finish the wizard.

7. You now have a Network Pool that is connected to the external VLAN.

8. We now need either a new OvDC or we need to assign the Network Pool to an existing OvDC.

9. Now we are ready to deploy a new vApp in the OvDC that we have assigned the Network Pool to.

10. Use an Isolated vApp Network in this vApp.

11. You need to choose the same IP range you placed the physical device in.

12. You should now have access from the VM in the isolated vApp to the physical device.

How it works...

We are using the vSphere port group that is mapped to a VLAN inside the vApp, as shown in the following diagram:

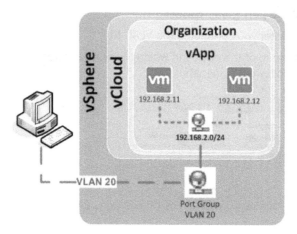

The really huge drawback is that you have a 1:1:1 relationship between a VLAN, a Network Pool, and the OvDC. By choosing more than one port group for the Network Pool, you would not be able to define which port group is used for which vApp Network.

Sharpening the Edge

We have now used the Edge (organization and vApp router) a lot, and in some cases, the Edge is too resource-starved to provide a fast service. Let's do something about that.

Getting ready

We will need a deployed Edge, either an organizational Edge or a vApp router. You could use the vApp router out of the *Deploying a vApp with vApp router* recipe in this chapter.

How to do it...

If you use an organizational Edge, perform the following steps:

1. Go to your organization.

2. Click on **Administration**.

3. Double-click on the OvDC you created the Edge in.

4. Select **Edge Gateways**.

5. Right-click on the Edge and select **Upgrade to Full Configuration**.

6. Answer the warning message and the Edge will now be upgraded.

If you want even more power for the organizational Edge or want to want to give more power to a vApp router:

1. Log into the vCNS as an Administrator.

2. Click on **Datacenters**.

3. Click on your datacenter.

4. From the right side, now click on **Network Virtualization** and then on **Edge**.

5. Look at the naming; the Edge you're looking for has the same name as your Organization Network (organizational Edge) or vApp Network (vApp router):

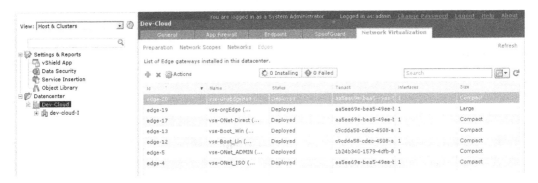

6. Double-clicking on this Edge will open up all the configuration items.

7. In the Edge, click on **Settings**. You should see the following screen:

8. Click on **Actions** and select **Large** (same as **Full** in vCloud) or **X-Large**.
9. The Edge will now be redeployed.

How it works...

We are using vCNS to use all the functions that it is capable of. This will enable you to upsize a vApp router. However, please be aware that VMware will not support this.

In the following table you can see the amount of resources that a given size of an Edge requires:

	Compact	Large (Full)	X-Large
CPU	1 vCPU	2 vCPU	2 vCPU
Memory	256 MB	1024 MB	8192 MB
Storage	539.1 MB	1.28 GB	12.37 GB

A huge drawback is that if you redeploy the Edge (or the vApp router), vCloud will make vCNS go back to the original size.

There's more...

Please note that you can also activate HA for a vApp router. You can switch HA on by performing the following steps:

1. Follow the steps from the previous section.

2. Click on **HA Configuration** and select **Change**. You should see the following screen:

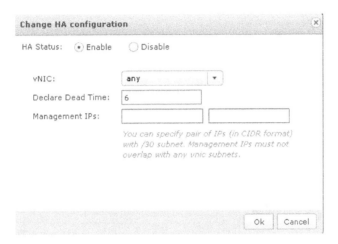

3. Choose **Enable** and click on **OK**.

4. This will deploy a second Edge device on a different ESXi host. Please be aware of the additional resources used.

Using vApp Network fencing

In this recipe, we will explore vApp Network fencing. We will see how we can use this feature.

Getting ready

To play with fencing, we need to have a Direct Organization Network (or isolated, but that's not as much fun) and some VM templates.

How to do it...

1. Create a new vApp using the ⬚ button.

2. Add two VMs to the vApp and name them.

3. Connect the VMs to the Direct Organization Network using the **Static - IP manual** option.

4. Set the manual IPs outside the range of the Static IP Pool for each VM.

5. In the **Configure Networking** section, click on **Fence vApp**, as shown in the following screenshot:

6. Finish the vApp creation.

7. Deploy the vApp.

8. After the vApp is deployed, double-click back into it and go to **Virtual Machines**:

9. See that the VMs now have an internal and external IP. To communicate with the VMs, use the external IP.

10. Now stop the vApp.

11. Right-click on the vApp and choose **Copy to...**.

12. Name the vApp and click on **OK**.

13. After the vApp has been copied, start both vApps (the original and the copy).

14. Check the IPs of all VMs in all vApps.

How it works...

You may know vApp Network fencing from VMware Lab Manager, but the vCloud implementation is different.

Fencing allows you to re-use the same IPs and MAC addresses in multiple vApps. This is rather different from using an isolated network, as fencing allows full connection to the fenced VMs just with different IPs, as you can see in the following diagram:

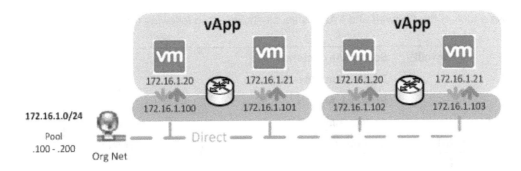

The VMs inside the fence communicate using the internal IPs (.20 and .21), but appear to be using the external IPs (.100 and .101) for any communication to the outside. Communication is allowed out, but not in.

Fencing allows one to deploy a vApp with the same content multiple times and still use them without changing their IP or MAC addresses. However, you need to understand that the VMs inside are the same, meaning that if you have an Active Directory inside the vApp, things will go wrong. The AD will advertise itself with its internal IP that is not accessible via the outside; also, it will receive AD advertising from the original AD outside the vApp (the AD you copied it from) with the same IP.

What happens in the background is that for each fenced vApp, a new Edge device is deployed and configured. The Edge has the same name as the network; however, the HREF (the number behind the name) is different; refer to the following screenshot (compare the Names):

There's more...

Because we are again using a vApp router (Edge), we can have a look at the settings by performing the following steps:

1. Right-click on the Organization Network in the vApp.

2. Choose **Configure Services**.

3. Click on **Firewall** and then on **NAT**.

Have a look at the **Firewall** and **NAT** values, as shown in the following table:

Firewall	Source: Any, Internal
	Destination: Any, External
	Protocol: ANY
	Action: Allow
NAT	IP Translation: VM mapped automatically to external IP

As we can see, the firewall rules allow that all traffic from the inside is allowed outside; however, outside traffic is not allowed in.

We could now change this setup by adding an additional firewall rule as shown in the following table:

Firewall	Source: Any, External
	Destination: Any, Internal
	Protocol: ANY
	Action: Allow

This setting allows the VMs in the fence (.20 and .21) to be reached from the VMs on the outside using the public IPs (.100 and .101). However, you should be rather careful with a configuration like that. Maybe opening up only certain ports for the inbound connection is a better idea.

In addition to all this, you can configure the external IP (DNAT) of each VM by performing the following steps:

1. Right-click on the Organization Network in the vApp.

2. Choose **Configure Services**.

3. Click on **NAT**.

4. Click on the DNAT rule and click on **Edit**. You should see the following screen:

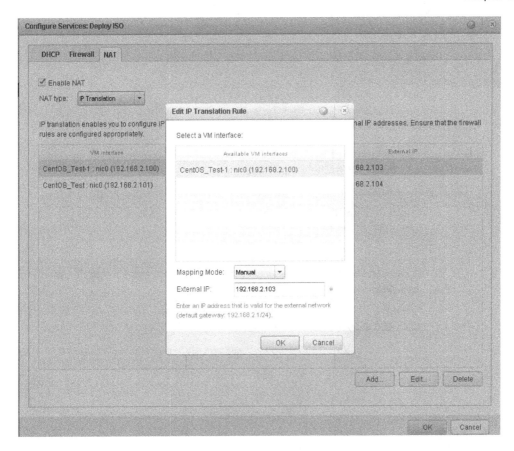

5. Change the **Mapping Mode** value to **Manual** and enter the IP under **External IP**.

6. Click on **OK** and again on **OK** to activate these settings.

Creating multitiered vApp Networks

Having multiple networks inside the same vApp is not straightforward, at least not if it comes to easy-to-connect ability.

Getting ready

We need a VM template that we can add multiple times to build the vApp.

If you want to follow my instructions to build your own router, you will need a virtual router and you need to know how to configure it. If you would like to use my example, have a closer look at the *There's more...* section of this recipe.

How to do it...

Let's work through the two different options we have.

Perform the following steps for using the vApp router:

1. Create a new isolated Organization Network, call it `App Net`, and assign it a **192.168.2.0/24** network with an IP Pool.

2. Create a new vApp.

3. Add at least three VMs to the vApp.

4. When it comes to connecting the VMs to the network, we do the following:

    1. Create a vApp Network, call it `DB Net`, and assign it a 192.168.1.0/24 network with an IP pool.

    2. Connect one VM to the **DB** network.

    3. Connect one VM to the previously created Organization Network called the **App** network.

    4. Create another new vApp Network, call it `Web Net`, and assign it a **192.168.3.0/24** network with an IP pool.

    5. Connect one VM to the **Web** network, as shown in the following screenshot:

5. Finish the vApp creation.

6. Double-click on the vApp and choose **Networking**.

7. Connect both vApp Networks to the Organization Network and unselect both the **Firewall** and **NAT** options, as shown in the following screenshot:

 This will allow the traffic to flow between all networks.

8. Right-click on each of the vApp Networks and choose **Configure services** and perform the following:

    1. Click on **Static Routing**.

    2. Check **Enable static routing**:

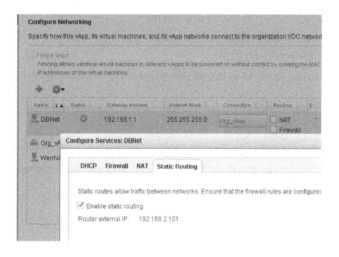

    3. Note down the **Router external IP** value.

9. Click on **Apply** to save the network configuration.

10. Power on the vApp.

11. Log into the OS of the VM that is deployed in the **App** network, and enter the following to add a route to its routing table:

| **For Linux** | `route add -net [network] netmask [subnet mask] gw [gateway ip]` |
| **For Windows** | `route ADD [network] MASK [subnet mask] [gateway ip]` |

The `[gateway ip]` value is the IP that you noted down as **Router external IP**. For example, `route add 192.168.1.0 MASK 255.255.255.0 192.168.2.101`.

12. Now all networks can communicate with each other. You might like to improve this with your own firewall rules.

Perform the following steps to create your own router:

1. Create a new vApp.

2. Add at least three VMs to the vApp.

3. When it comes to connecting the VMs to networking, we do the following:

    1. Create a vApp Network, call it `DB Net`, and assign it a 192.168.1.0/24 network with an IP pool.

    2. Connect one VM to the **DB** network.

    3. Create a vApp Network, call it `App Net`, and assign it a 192.168.2.0/24 network with an IP pool.

    4. Connect one VM to the **App** network.

    5. Create a vApp Network, call it `Web Net`, and assign it a 192.168.3.0/24 network with an IP pool.

    6. Connect one VM to the **Web** network.

4. Finish the vApp creation.

5. Double-click on the vApp and choose **Virtual Machines**.

6. Add the router VM (see the *There's more...* section for more details).

7. Make sure that you add a network card for each of the three networks and set it to **DHCP** as show in the following screenshot:

8. Click on **Guest Customization** and then switch off Guest Customization.

9. Finish the router VM integration.

10. Deploy the vApp.

11. Now the only thing left to do is configuring the router VM (see the *There's more...* section). Make sure that you assign the IPs for each network card as the one set as a gateway in the network settings.

How it works...

Using the vCloud solution, you can make use of the vApp routers, and therefore, make the configuration a bit faster; however, using a software router (for example, m0n0wall) is a bit more complicated in the initial setup, but is a much better solution as it gives more configuration freedom. In addition to this, using a virtual router will allow you to use this configuration as a template and redeploy it without too much hassle. The following diagram shows the network configurations for the two configurations we have been discussing:

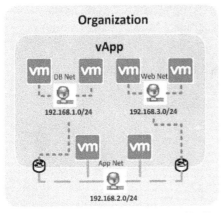
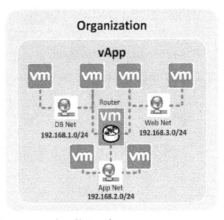

Creating multitiered vApps makes sense for development as well as for production deployment. It helps in testing the communication between different application layers and configuring the hardening of the applications.

Both solutions need you to understand how routing/firewalling/NATing works, but that's not a bad skill for any admin to learn in the first place. We don't have the space in this book to go into it.

There's more...

In this section I will give you a fast introduction to a virtual router. The following instructions will show you how to base configure the m0n0wall virtual appliance. In this example, I will refer to the previous configuration. Please note that VMware will not support the configuration of third-party routers. However, using a third-party router is actually quite a common occurrence.

Downloading and importing a virtual router into vCloud

Perform the following steps for downloading and importing a virtual router into vCloud:

1. Go to `http://m0n0.ch/wall/` and click on **Download**.
2. Download the `.zip` version **(generic-pc-vm)**.
3. Unzip and upload the content to a vSphere datastore.
4. Add the `.vmx` file to your vCenter.
5. Power on the router VM and wait until you see a menu on the screen (or wait for two minutes).
6. Power off the router VM. We have to perform this step to create all the other files that are needed for a proper VM.
7. Import m0n0wall as a template into vCloud.
8. Deploy the VM into your configuration (add as many network cards as the number of interfaces you need; m0n0wall comes with two network cards).
9. Power the m0n0wall VM on.
10. Open the Remote Console as shown in the following screenshot:

```
*** This is m0n0wall, version 1.34
    built on Mon Nov 12 13:17:22 CET 2012 for generic-pc
    Copyright (C) 2002-2012 by Manuel Kasper. All rights reserved.
    Visit http://m0n0.ch/wall for updates.


    LAN IP address: 192.168.1.1

    Port configuration:

    LAN   -> em0
    WAN   -> em1


m0n0wall console setup
***********************
1) Interfaces: assign network ports
2) Set up LAN IP address
3) Reset webGUI password
4) Reset to factory defaults
5) Reboot system
6) Ping host

Enter a number: em0: watchdog timeout -- resetting
```

Setting up the networking

Perform the following steps to set up the networking:

1. Type 1 and press *Enter*.
2. You probably don't use VLANs inside the vApp, so let's skip this by selecting **No**.
3. All the network devices and their MACs are now listed.
4. Assign a network card to the LAN side (DB network) of the router. Choose **em0**.
5. Assign the WAN side (the **App** network) of the router a network card. Choose **em1**.
6. Now assign the third interface (the **Web** network) a network card. Just type in em2.
7. Just press *Enter* and accept the reboot (**y**).

Setting up the web interface

Perform the following steps to set up the web interface:

1. After reboot, you will come back to the menu; now press *2* to set up the LAN interface IP.
2. Enter an IP and Network mask (192.168.1.1/24) that is consistent with the LAN network you set up.
3. Don't use a DHCP server in that LAN (choose **n**).
4. You are now able to use the web interface of m0n0wall. Just go to one of your VMs in the DB network, open a browser, and enter the IP of the m0n0wall you configured in the previous step.

5. The default credentials are admin and mono. After login you will see the following screenshot:

Configuring the WAN interfaces with the correct network settings

Perform the following steps to configure the WAN interfaces with the correct network settings:

1. Navigate to **Interfaces | WAN**.

2. Change the **Type** value to **Static**.

3. Enter under **Static IP configuration** the IP (192.168.2.1) in both the IP and gateway.

4. Uncheck **Block private network** (at the bottom of the page).

5. Click on **Save**.

Configuring the OPT1 interfaces with the correct network settings

Perform the following steps to configure the OPT1 interfaces with the correct network settings:

1. Navigate to **Interfaces | OPT1**.

2. Check **Enable Optional 1 interface**.

3. You can change the name to `Web` if you like.

4. Enter under **Static IP configuration** the IP (`192.168.3.1`).

5. Configure the firewall rules to allow the traffic to flow.

6. Navigate to **Firewall | Rules**.

7. Create/edit a rule for every network with the following settings:

	LAN	WAN	OPT1
Action	Pass	Pass	Pass
Interface	LAN	WAN	OPT1
Protocol	Any	Any	Any
Source	Any	Any	Any
Destination	Any	Any	Any

8. Click on **Apply Changes**.

Configuring static routing

Perform the following steps to configure static routing:

1. Navigate to **System | Static routes**.

2. Add a rule for all networks as follows:

	LAN	WAN	OPT1
Interface	LAN	WAN	OPT1
Destination Network	192.168.1.0/24	192.168.2.0/24	192.168.3.0/24
Gateway	192.168.1.1	192.168.2.1	192.168.3.1

3. Click on **Apply Changes**.

4. It is best to reboot the router VM now. You can do this by going to the console and choosing from the menu option **5**.

5. This completes the unsecure, rudimentary setup for a router interface.

See also

▸ An easy-to-use and very small (128 MB memory, 26 MB disk) router is mOnOwall, which is available at `http://m0n0.ch/wall/`.

 Please note that there is a VM ready for deployment in the *Downloads* section.

Ensuring no change in IP after redeployment

When you undeploy a vApp and then redeploy it, the IP of the vApp router or the NAT addresses might change (or even the MAC for that matter). Let's see what we can do about that.

Getting ready

If you would like to create a new vApp, you just need an External Network and a vApp template; we will create a vApp in this recipe.

If you like to retrofit a vApp, you need a vApp with a vApp Network that is attached to an Organization Network.

For testing purposes, use a second vApp or make a copy of the existing one. Leave the second one undeployed.

How to do it...

The following sections show how to ensure no change occurs in IP after redeployment by setting up the vApp and retrofitting an existing vApp.

Ensuring no change occurs in IP after redeployment by setting up the vApp

Perform the following steps:

1. Go to your organization and click on **My Cloud**.
2. Click on the green icon (**+**) to create a new vApp.
3. Select a vApp and **Next** until you come to the **Configure Networking** section.
4. Check **Switch to the advanced networking workflow** (bottom of the window).
5. Make sure that the VMs are still configured to a vApp Network.
6. In the **Advanced Networking** window, connect the vApp Network to an Organization Network:

7. Check **Retain IP/MAC resources**.

8. Close the wizard and deploy the vApp.

Ensuring no change occurs in IP after redeployment by retrofitting an existing vApp

Perform the following steps:

1. Double-click on the vApp to enter it.

2. Click on **Networking**.

3. Click on the vApp Network that is connected to an Organization Network.

4. Check the checkbox in **Retain IP/MAC Resources** as shown in the following screenshot:

5. Click on **Apply** to save the changes.

6. Your vApp is now configured and should not lose its IP/MAC settings when redeployed.

How it works...

While using a Static IP Pool, vCloud automatically takes over management of the IPs configured within the pool, meaning that, whenever a vApp router (Edge gateway) is deployed (when the vApp is powered on), an IP out of the IP pool will be allocated to it. When the vApp is undeployed (the vApp is powered off), the IP gets released back into the pool. You can access the IP allocation for each network by right-clicking on it and selecting **IP Allocation**. This also means that if you undeploy and then redeploy vApps that are connected to an External Network, you might get a different IP. This can be very tiresome, especially if you are using the IP for an RDP/SSH forward.

The setting for the default time for an IP release is set in **Administration | General | IPaddress release timeout.** The default value is **0** seconds. Increasing this setting to a higher value makes sure that vApps and VMs that are redeployed only for a short time keep their IP setting.

Please be aware that when you use this setting, you will deplete the available IPs in the Static IP Pool and you won't be able to deploy additional VMs until you have added more IPs to the pool or deleted VMs or vApps that are no longer required.

There's more...

If you would like to test these settings, follow the ensuing instructions:

1. Double-click on your vApp to enter it.
2. Click on **Networking**.
3. Right-click on the vApp Network that has a vApp router configured, and select **Configure Services**.
4. Click on **NAT**. Note down the IPs that are configured there.
5. Exit with **Cancel**.
6. Click back on the vApp folder, so you will see all the vApps you are currently having access to.
7. Undeploy the vApp by clicking on the **Stop** button.
8. Make sure you wait about a minute (or more depending on your **IPaddress release timeout** setting in **General**).
9. Now deploy the other vApp.
10. After deployment, check the IPs again.
11. Now deploy the first vApp (that we switched off to retain the IP settings).
12. Notice that the IPs are the same as before.

I might like to encourage you to test the reverse. However, you might need to reduce the number of IPs available in the pool to force the reallocation.

Automatic IP management for External Network Pools

Using vCloud to manage the IPs in an External Network Pool is quite efficient; however, only the IP is being managed, DNS settings are not. There are several other ways to do this.

Getting ready

We need a vApp with VMs attached to an External Network that get their IPs from a Static Network Pool.

In this example, we will focus on a Windows solution. We will need an Active Directory Server that has an integrated DNS (enable Active Directory Integrated DNS). You will need all the credentials ready for establishing connectivity to the Active Directory.

We also need a vApp that should contain Windows VMs that are able to join an Active Directory Domain. The vApp Network should be able to connect the VMs inside to the Active Directory, so it probably should be an Organization Network that connects to an External Network.

How to do it...

1. Double-click on the VM you want to use for this testing.

2. Follow the *Joining VMs automatically to domains* recipe in *Chapter 3, Better vApps*, to enable the automatic joining of the AD domain.

3. Log into your organization.

4. Start the vApp. If you have already switched on the vApp before you made the AD changes to it, you might need to force the Guest Customization. To do this, right-click on each VM and select **Power On** and **Force Guest Customization**.

5. Check what IPs have been assigned to the VMs by either entering the vApp and clicking on **Virtual Machines** or by right-clicking on the External Network and selecting **IP Allocation**.

6. Go back to your AD Server.

7. Now check on your DNS server and the AD Server for the configuration update.

How it works...

We are actually just combining multiple recipes together and using a common AD function. By using the Windows Active Directory automatic updating function, we can automatically add a VM to the Windows-based DNS server. Unfortunately, there is a drawback. When you delete the vApp or the VM, the DNS entry will not be released. This can lead to some problems, and needs to be addressed with appropriate procedures or scripts.

There's more...

There are several more ways to deal with this. We will have a quick look at each method; however, a complete discussion is beyond the scope of this book.

Static DNS Pool

One method to deal with the DNS problem is to use preassigned DNS entries. This means that you will create an External Network and assign it an IP pool. When you are done, you assign in the DNS server *a* entries for each IP using a naming standard that uses increasing numbers.

The drawback here clearly is that the hostnames that have been used in DNS must be used in the vApps, and also that the naming standard cannot contain a reference to the operating systems.

Preallocated DNS pool with a manual IP

This solution again uses a predefined DNS pool. However, we will not use an External Network Pool (we still have to configure at least one IP to create an External Network Pool), but we will use manually assigned IP addresses while creating the VMs.

The benefit is that you can now preallocate hostnames that contain operating system references (or even application references). The drawback, however, is that you do not have any automated system. You still need to know what hostname is already in use.

Automated setup

Using vCenter Orchestrator or Puppet, you could define a workflow that creates a VM and automatically updates the DNS server.

Linux and Guest Customization

With Linux, the Guest Customization is a bit different; we will have to use the command `nsupdate` to update the DNS server; however, you will have to create trust between the client and the DNS server. See the following *See also* section.

See also

- Microsoft Dynamic DNS update at `http://technet.microsoft.com/en-us/library/cc784052(v=ws.10).aspx`
- Puppet IT Automation at `http://puppetlabs.com`
- Linux nsupdate at `http//:www.linuxcommand.org/man_pages/nsupdate8.html` and `http://caunter.ca/nsupdate.txt`

Creating load-balanced VMs in an organization

We will now use the Edge to create load-balanced VMs.

Getting ready

You will need a deployed organizational Edge with a suballocation of at least one IP.

Please also create an Organization Network that connects to the Edge device (if you have problems, have a look at the *Giving your networks an Edge* recipe in *Chapter 1, Setting Up Networks*).

Create a vApp with two VMs in it. You will need two VMs (Windows or Linux) with a web server installed (IIS or Apache). The VMs should have IPs from the Organization Network (pool or manual). Make sure your web server is prepared and tested for load balancing. Due to the limited space, I cannot go into details on how to configure IIS or Apache for load balancing. But Google will have the answers for you.

The VMs in this vApp should be connected to the Edge via the Organization Network you created. You might like to either use manual IPs or fix the IP allocation (as shown in the *Ensuring no change occurs in IP after redeployment* recipe in this chapter).

With regards to licensing, the load balancing (as well as VPN and HA) features of vCNS require advanced licensing. vCNS Advanced comes with vCloud Suite Advanced or a better edition.

How to do it...

1. Enter the organization you have created the Edge and the vApp in.
2. Click on **Cloud Resources** and then double-click on the OvDC you have created.
3. Click on **Edge Gateway**.
4. Right-click on the Edge and select **Edge Gateway Services**.
5. Click on **Load balancer**.
6. Configure the pool servers by performing the following steps:
   1. Click on **Add**.
   2. Name the pool, for example, `Webserver`.
   3. Check **HTTP** (and if you want, check **HTTPS**; however, I will not cover this in detail).

4. In the drop-down menu, you can select the method that shows how the connection should be distributed between the pool members, as shown in the following screenshot:

5. In the **Configure Health-Check** step, we can configure what the load balancer should monitor to know if a resource is unavailable. For the moment, we can just click on **Next**.

6. Now add the member servers to the pool by clicking on **Add**.

7. Add the server by its IP from the Organization Network it's connected to.

8. You can add different **Port** and **Monitor Port** values instead of the default. We are configuring HTTP so the **Port** value 80 is fine:

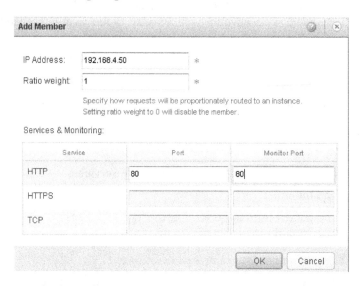

9. After adding a second member server to the pool, review the settings and finish the wizard.

7. Configure the **Virtual Servers** (also called **Virtual IP (VIP)**) by performing the following steps:

    1. Click on **Add**.

    2. Give the VIP a name.

    3. Choose whether the IP should be used from the Edge network or from the External Network (for this example, we choose the External Network).

    4. Enter the IP you want. It has to be part of the suballocation you specified for the Edge.

    5. Select the service you would like to load balance and the **Persistency Method** (stickiness).

    6. Finally, do not forget to check **Enabled**, as shown in the following screenshot:

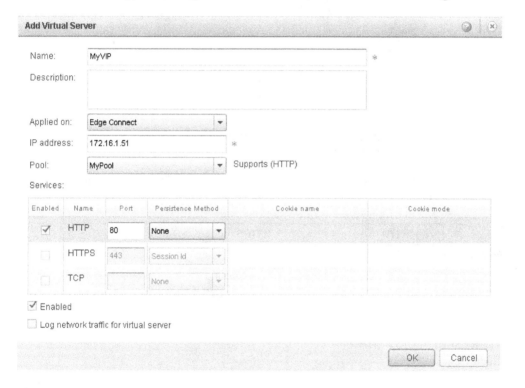

8. Click on **OK** to finish the setup and then exit the Edge configuration with **OK**.

9. The Edge will now be configured. After the configuration is finished, you should be able to try an HTTP connection to the VIP you have specified.

How it works...

The Edge contains a load balancing function. This function is accessible via vCloud; however, the amount of configuration that can be done is limited. We will later show how we can configure more using vCNS. The configuration from the previous example is reflected in the following diagram:

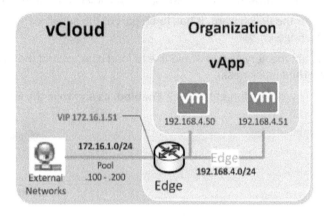

The VIP **172.16.1.51** (from the external network) is used to load balance the HTTP (TCP port 80) service to the VMs that are configured on the Edge network.

What really happens in the background is that vCloud uses the Edge to configure the load balancing. The options for the load balancer that vCloud can set are as follows:

	HTTP	**HTTPS**	**TCP**
Balancer mode	▸ IP Hash ▸ Round Robin ▸ URI ▸ Least connected	▸ IP Hash ▸ Round Robin ▸ Least connected	▸ IP Hash ▸ Round Robin ▸ Least connected
Heath-Check mode	▸ HTTP ▸ TCP	▸ SSL ▸ TCP	▸ TCP
Persistency method	▸ None ▸ Cookie	▸ Session ID ▸ None	▸ None

If you are using the HTTP cookie method, you have some additional configuration items. You can define the cookie name as well as the mode. The cookie modes available are **Insert**, **Prefix**, and **App**.

One of the things that vCNS doesn't do is SSL offloading; only SSL pass through is supported at this stage.

There's more...

Instead of using the vCloud/vCNS load balancer, you can also use any load balancer that is available as a VM, such as F5 and Cisco provide. If you would like to play with a load balancer, you can get 30-day trial versions from most vendors. Using other virtual load balancers gives you some more flexibility as you can insert them directly into the vApps. The disadvantage is that they may incur additional licensing.

Load balancer methods

The following load balancing methods exist:

Round Robin	In this method, connections are passed to the next server in line.
IP Hash	In this method, connections are passed to the severs based on the hash of the source IP address of each packet.
Least Connected	In this method, connections are sent to the server with the least connections.
URI	In this method, connections are distributed based on the URL and the available server. This is possible only with HTTP.

See also

▶ URI is explained at `http://en.wikipedia.org/wiki/Uniform_resource_identifier`

▶ Free load balancers that can be virtualized can be found at the following links:

  ❑ Ha-Proxy: `https://haproxy.1wt.eu`

  ❑ Nginx: `https://nginx.org/en`

Creating a secure connection between organizations (which can be in different vClouds)

Connecting one vCloud Organization Network to another isn't easy, and most of the time, rather impossible. However, this is how it works, the *easy* way.

Getting ready

We need two organizations, each with an Edge configured as well as an Organization Network that connects to the Edge. Make sure that the Organization Networks have different IP ranges (for example, 192.168.2.0/24 and 192.168.4.0/24).

For testing, we need vApps in both organizations that have VMs that are connected to the Edge.

How to do it...

1. Enter the organization (either one).
2. Click on **Cloud Resources** and then double-click on the OvDC you have created.
3. Click on **Edge Gateway**.
4. Right-click on the Edge and select **Edge Gateway Services**.
5. Click on **VPN**.
6. Check **Enable VPN** as shown in the following screenshot:

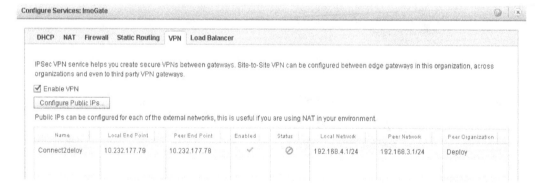

7. Click on **Add** to add a new connection. You should now get the following screen:

8. Name the connection and select **a network in another organization** under **Establish VPN to**.

9. Now click on **Login to Remote VCD**. You should get the following screen:

10. Fill out the remote connection with a user that has Org Admin rights.

11. After login, the rest of the mask is filled out. We now need to select the end point of the VPN:

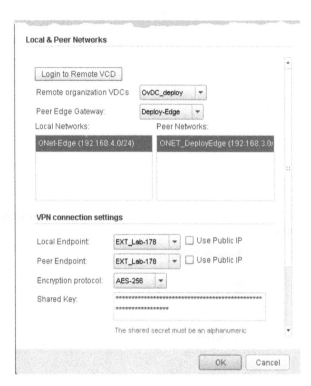

12. We can leave the rest alone. Just click on **OK**.

13. The VPN connection is now ready, and by clicking on **OK**, we let the Edge to configure itself.

14. After the Edge has been configured, we now need to configure the firewalls in both Edges to actually let some traffic through. The following instructions have to be done on both Edge devices in each organization:

    1.   Click on **Edge Gateway**.

    2.   Right-click on the Edge and select **Edge Gateway Services**.

    3.   Click on **Firewall**. You should see the following screen:

4. Click on **Add** and add the following two firewall rules:

vpn1	Source: 192.168.2.0/24:Any
	Destination: 192.168.4.0/24:Any
	Protocol: ANY
	Action: Allow
vpn2	Source: 192.168.4.0/24:Any
	Destination: 192.168.2.0/24:Any
	Protocol: ANY
	Action: Allow

5. Click on **OK** to exit the configuration.

15. The firewalls on both Edges are now configured to allow the traffic between the networks. You should now be able to deploy a VM on both sides and perform a simple PING test.

How it works...

With this method you can connect two different environments, which can not only be in the same vCloud but could also be a physically separate vCloud, making a VPN an easy way to connect two vClouds, for example, client-based disaster recovery.

The following diagram shows such a setup:

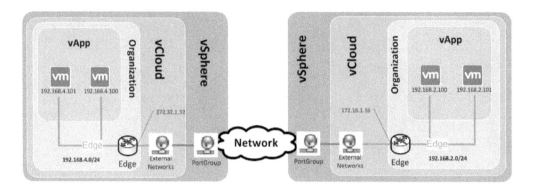

Here vCloud creates an IPSec VPN in vCNS. vCloud not only creates the VPN on one Edge but also on both sides, sharing the encryption key between them and setting up the connection. That's why we also need to configure the firewall on both sides of the IPSec VPN tunnel. Please note that the previous firewall rules are extremely relaxed, therefore, you might want to consider a more secure approach.

The VPN is a tunnel that starts and ends with an Edge device (or if you are connecting to an outside network the end would be a VPN-capable device). vCloud/vCNS supports the following encryption standards:

- AES-NI
- SSL VPN
- AES256-SHA

There's more...

There's more we can do with the VPN network, which is explained in this section.

Connecting to other networks in the same organization

Another VPN you can open up is between two Edge devices in the same organization. To do this, we need two Edges deployed in the organization, and each should have an Organization Network attached. Perform the following steps for connecting to other networks in the same organization:

1. Navigate to **Edge Gateway Services** | **VPN**.
2. Click on **Add**.
3. Choose **a network in this organization** in **Establish VPN to**:

4. Select the Edge you want to connect to.

5. Select the networks you would like to attach to each other.

6. Click on **OK**.

Connection to the outside

You can connect to a remote network that is not a vCloud but just a common VPN endpoint (for example, your business network). This is done by performing the following steps:

1. Navigate to **Edge Gateway Services | VPN**.

2. Click on **Add**.

3. Choose **a remote network** in **Establish VPN to::**

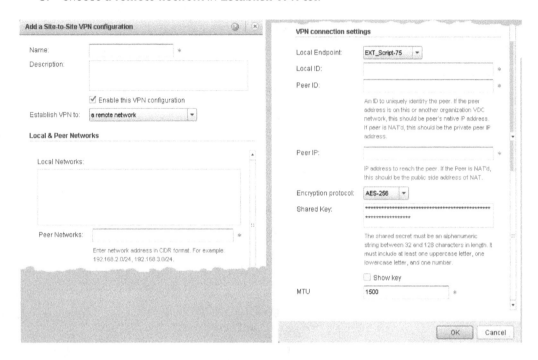

4. Enter the peer network definition you want to connect to (for example, `172.16.0.0/16`).

5. The **Peer ID** value is the IP of the VM that you want to reach.

6. The **Peer IP** value is the public IP you are connecting to; if the peer VM is behind a NAT, this IP is the NAT's public IP.

7. The **Shared key** value has to be the one you configured on the remote network.

8. Don't forget to set the firewalls.

Public IPs

Instead of using the IPs' Edge received from the External Network, you can define your own public IPs. This is mostly needed if your External Network is connected through NAT to the Internet. To configure public IPs, perform the following steps:

1. Navigate to **Edge Gateway Services** | **VPN**.

2. Click on **Configure public IPs**. You should see the following screen:

3. For each External Network that has been configured with the Edge, enter one **Public IP** value.

More VPN possibilities

When you log into the vCNS and have a look at the VPN settings, you will see that you can also use SSL plus VPNs. You don't have to use vCloud's VPN configurations to connect two (or more) organizations; you can use the vCNS directly to set up an SSL VPN.

Depending on the size of the vCNS, a certain number of simulations of SSL VPN connections are supported, as shown in the following table:

	Compact	**Full (Large)**	**X-large**
VPN connection	25	100	Not supported

Monitoring which network resources have been used where

After we have devoted this chapter to creating vApp and Organization Networks, you might really like to know how you can keep track of all this mess.

Getting ready

Not much, just a whole bunch of vApp and Organization Networks and the will to figure it all out.

How to do it...

1. Log into your vCloud as `SysAdmin`.

2. Click on **Manage & Monitor**.

3. Click on **External Networks**. You should see the following screen:

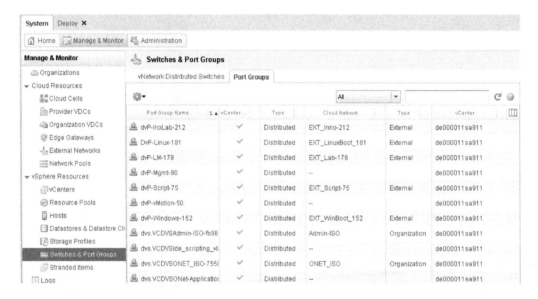

Here you will find all External Networks, how much of the allocated IP pool is already used, and an overview of their VLAN ID, vCenter, and port group associations.

4. Click on **Switches & Port Groups**. You should see the following screen:

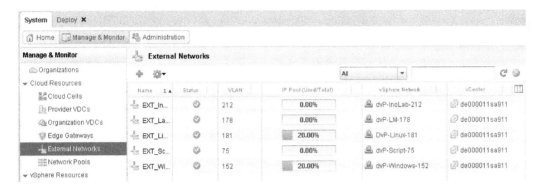

Now you will find an allocation of what port groups in vSphere are assigned to which cloud network, and of what type, as well as on which vCenter they live.

5. Now open up an organization.

6. Click on **Administration** and then on any of the OvDC.

7. Now select **Org VDC Networks**. You should get the following screen:

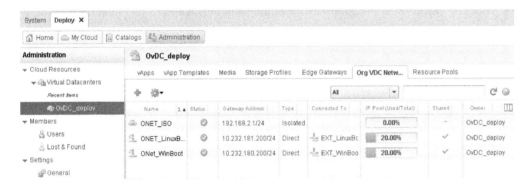

Here you will find all the Organization Networks that have been deployed for this OvDC as well as how much of their IP pool has been used up.

How it works...

Every network item in vCloud is associated with an item in vSphere or vCNS. The following is an overview:

vCloud item	Item in
External Network	Port group in vSphere
Network pool	Port group with VLAN
	VXLAN network in vCNS
Edge gateway	Edge gateway in vCNS
Isolated Organization Network	Edge gateway in vCNS
Isolated vApp Network	Edge gateway in vCNS

One of the things you should really never do is delete the underlying infrastructure of vCloud. This means that if you delete an Edge device in vCNS that is representing an Organization Network, you won't be able to delete the Organization Network from vCloud, leading to the fact that you can't delete the organization.

 Most other things are less dramatic, but still keep this rule in mind:
First delete objects in vCloud and then you can delete them anywhere else.

What it means is that vCloud stores its objects in its own database; if you delete an object in vSphere or vCNS, you may not be able to delete it in vCloud anymore.

See also

▶ Please have a look at *Chapter 8, Troubleshooting vCloud*, to understand more on how to spot and resolve problems.

3
Better vApps

In this chapter, we will be looking more closely at vApps by covering the following recipes:

- ▸ Proper vApp start-up and shutdown
- ▸ Adding a VM to a vApp
- ▸ Importing a vApp into vCloud
- ▸ Exporting a vApp from vCloud
- ▸ Creating a sandbox environment
- ▸ Using Guest Customization with pre and post deploy
- ▸ Using PowerShell or Perl to perform Guest Customization tasks
- ▸ Sharing a vApp
- ▸ Joining VMs automatically to domains
- ▸ Using vApp maintenance mode

Introduction

One thing that needs to be said about vApps is that they actually come in two completely different versions: the vSphere vApp and the vCloud vApp.

vSphere and vCloud vApps

The vSphere vApp concept was introduced in vSphere 4.0 as a container for VMs. In vSphere, a vApp is essentially a resource pool with some extras, such as the starting and stopping order and (if you configured it) network IP allocation methods. The idea is for the vApp to be an entity of VMs that build one unit. Such vApps can then be exported or imported using **OVF** (**Open Virtualization Format**). A very good example of a vApp is VMware Operations Manager. It comes as a vApp in an OVF and contains not only the VMs but also the startup sequence as well as setup scripts. When the vApp is deployed for the first time, additional information such as network settings are asked and then implemented. A vSphere vApp is a resource pool; it can be configured so that it will only demand resources that it is using; on the other hand, resource pool configuration is something that most people struggle with. A vSphere vApp is only a resource pool; it is not automatically represented as a folder within the **VMs and Template** view of vSphere, but is viewed there as a vApp, as shown in the following screenshot:

The vCloud vApp is a very different concept. First of all, it is not a resource pool. The VMs of the vCloud vApp live in the OvDC resource pool. However, the vCloud vApp is automatically a folder in the **VMs and Template** view of vSphere. It is a construct that is created by vCloud, and consists of VMs, a start and stop sequence, and networks. The network part is one of the major differences (next to the resource pool). In vSphere, only basic network information (IP's assignment, gateway, and DNS) is stored in the vApp. A vCloud vApp actually encapsulates the networks. The vCloud vApp networks are full networks, meaning they contain the full information for a given network including network settings and IP pools (for more details see *Chapter 2, vCloud Networks*, where we use this feature in various recipes). This information is kept while importing and exporting vCloud vApps, as shown in the following screenshot:

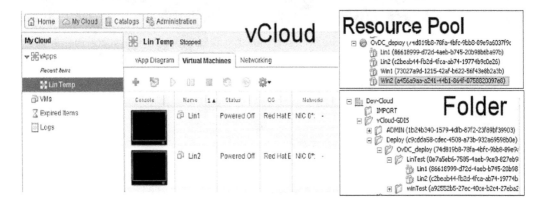

While I'm referring to vApps in this book, I will always mean vCloud vApps. If vCenter vApps feature anywhere in this book, they will be written as vCenter vApp.

Roles and rights

We will have a closer look at the influence of roles and what you can do with them in vCloud in *Chapter 6, Working with vCloud Roles*. However, I will mention in each recipe what default role you have to be a part of to execute the recipe.

Proper vApp startup and shutdown

If you have a vApp with VMs that depend on each other, for example, an application and a database, we can now make sure they start and shut down in the proper sequence as we can make sure that they are shut down instead of being powered off.

Getting ready

You will need a vApp with VMs (of any flavor). At least one VM must have VMware tools installed.

You can do this as `SysAdmin`, `OrgAdmin`, `vApp Author`, or a vApp user.

How to do it...

1. Right-click on the vApp and select **Properties**.
2. Click on **Starting and Stopping VMs** and perform the following steps:
   1. For the VMs that are configured with VMware tools, select **Shutdown** from the pulldown under the column **Stop Action**, and leave VMs without VMware tools on **Power Off (default)**, as shown in the following screenshot:

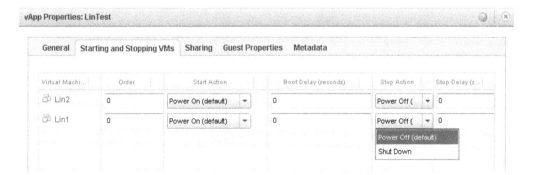

2. Adjust the startup order for the VMs depending on their dependencies.

3. Add time delays to make sure that after the VM is booted, the system has enough time to start the services (for example, a database) before starting the next system that depends on it.

3. Click on **OK**.

4. Power on the vApp by clicking on the play button (green triangle).

5. Monitor the boot sequence and note problems and timing changes.

6. Shut down the vApp by clicking on the stop button (red square).

7. Monitor the shutdown sequence and note problems and timing changes.

How it works...

While working with vSphere vCenter, you will know that there are two different options to stop a VM, **Power Off** and **Shut Down Guest**. Selecting the **Power Off** option shuts the VM down as if you would pull the power cord on a physical device, while selecting the **Shut Down Guest** option will pass a command to the OS in the VM to shut down gracefully.

vCloud doesn't have the same power selections as vSphere does. The shutting down of a vCloud vApp will depend upon the method you have specified in the vApp properties. The default option set for a new vApp is **Power Off**. Be aware that **ShutDown** *only* works with VMs that have VMware tools installed. If you are trying to shut down a VM that has no VMware tools installed, you will receive an error, and the VM and the vApp will not power off. VMs that don't have VMware tools capability (for example, appliances) must always be set to **Power Off**.

vCloud's default action for VMs in vApps is **Power Off**. This can be changed by configuring each VM for the appropriate power action. In addition to this, you can configure a starting sequence as well as boot delay timing.

What this means is that when vCloud powers on a VM, it then waits for the configured amount of time before powering on the next VM. vCloud will start with the lowest numbered VM in the sequence and then work its way up. If you want to have VMs boot at the same time, just configure them with the same sequence number.

Let's have a closer look at the delay timing. Consider the following example:

Virtual machine	Order	Boot delay	Stop delay
VM1	1	60	60
VM2	2	120	120
VM3	3	30	30

When the vApp gets started, VM1 powers on, and then the system waits for 60 seconds before powering on VM2. Again, the system waits for 120 seconds before powering on VM3. After VM3 is powered on, vCloud will wait for 30 seconds until it defines the start task as `finished` and will then release the lock on the vApp.

The reverse is true for the stop sequence.

Important changes in vCloud 5.5

In vCloud 5.5, we now have an additional right-click option for VMs (not vApps): **Power Off**. In addition to that, the right-click option **Stop** has been renamed to **Shut Down Guest OS**, as shown in the following screenshot:

There's more...

Let's take a closer look at the power options and how vApp templates deal with these settings.

Power Off

One of the little problems in vCloud 5.1 is that it's actually hard to issue a shutdown signal (not **Power Off**) to a single VM. If you right-click on a VM, you will see that only the **Power Off** option is present, but not the **Shut Down Guest** option; even if you have configured the vApp to shut down this VM, the command will still issue a power off signal to VM. The only options you have are to use the vCloud API (which has a VM `shutdown` command) or to use the VM operating system to issue a shutdown signal.

There is a way to power off a vApp that has its VMs configured for shutting it down.

After right-clicking on a running vApp, choose **Force Stop**.

This will issue a power off signal to all VMs, bypassing all the time delays configured in the vApp.

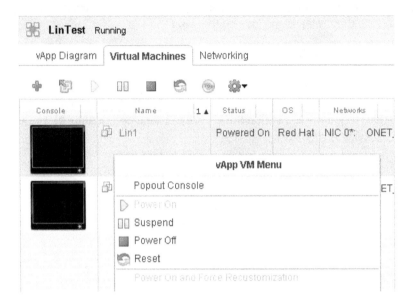

 If you are using vSphere to shut down the VM, vCloud will not recognize this and will think the VM is still powered on.

Templates

Configuring the startup and shut down of a VM is very important if you are creating vApp templates. The startup and shut down options will be inherited by all vApps that are made from configured vApp templates.

Adding a VM to a vApp

It is easy to add a new vApp; however, how does one add just *one* VM to an existing vApp?

Getting ready

We obviously need a deployed vApp as well as some vApp templates in the catalog.

You have to be a vApp Author or an Org Admin to be able to do this. As a vApp Author, you can only add VMs from your own catalog; as an Org Admin, you can also add VMs from a public catalog from a different organization.

How to do it...

1. Double-click on the vApp to enter it.

2. Click on the green (**+**) button to add a single VM to the vApp.

3. Select the VM(s) you want to add from the catalog and click on **Add**, or create a completely new VM by clicking on **New Virtual Machine**:

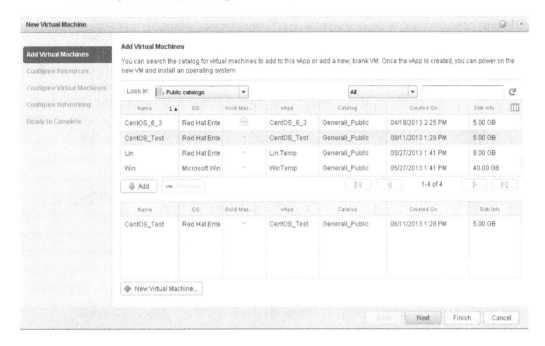

4. Choose the storage profile you want the new VMs to be placed on.

5. Now choose their network connectivity.

6. In vCloud 5.5, we can now also customize the hardware of the VM before adding it to the vApp.

7. After clicking on **Finish** in the wizard window, the VM(s) will be added to the current vApp.

8. Now that you have added the VM to the vApp, you should consider the following options:

   - The new VM's **Guest Customization** settings

   - The new VM's startup and shut down configuration (see the *Proper vApp start up and shut down* recipe in this chapter)

How it works...

Adding a single VM to a vApp is different from adding additional vApps to your vCloud, as you may need to make sure that the VMs you are adding are actually working with the vApp you choose. The issue starts with Guest Customization settings in the VM, special operating system configurations, or hardening scripts that exist in this VM, and so on.

Any VM you might add to an existing vApp will need some aftercare, such as setting its power off / shut down settings or checking the Guest Customization settings.

To understand what VMs you are going to import, it is important to create a naming standard for a VM inside a vApp template. This will clearly mark them as nonspecific VMs, by adding words such as, vanilla, base, or pure. A very typical problem I see is that a lot of people do not rename the VMs inside a vApp template; this means that when you open the dialog, you will see various VMs with the same name, making it harder than it should be to find a reliable source. We will talk more about naming standards in *Chapter 6, Creating a Naming Standard*.

There's more...

If you choose to create a new VM, you have the normal options to do so by performing the following steps:

1. Double-click on the vApp to enter it.
2. Click on **Virtual Machines**.
3. Click on the green (**+**) button to add a single VM to the vApp.
4. Then click on the button **New Virtual Machine...**, and the following window will appear:

Don't forget to install VMware tools on it later. Be aware that the hardware version of the VM depends on the maximal virtual hardware setting of the underlaying PvDC, which again depends on the version of your ESXi servers.

Importing a vApp into vCloud

Adding an existing vApp into vCloud is more or less straightforward, but there are some things I would like to point out. This recipe will help you import an existing vApp into vCloud.

Getting ready

Obviously we need a vApp or a VM. The vApp can contain one or more VMs. The VM must be in vSphere; it can come out of VMware Workstation/Fusion or can be in an OVF (vCloud 5.5 supports OVA as well). All of this works without the vCloud Connector.

You can import an OVF template as an Org Admin, but you must be a Sys Admin to import a VM from vSphere.

How to do it...

There are two ways to import a VM or vApp into vCloud: directly from vSphere or as an OVF/OVA.

Importing a VM from vSphere

A VM that is already in vSphere can be added to any existing vApp or to a catalog using the following steps. However, you must be a system administrator to do this.

1. Log into vCloud with a SysAdmin role.
2. Open the organization you want to import the VM into.
3. Click on **Catalogs** and then click on **vApp Templates**.
4. Click on the ⬚ button, and you should see the following window:

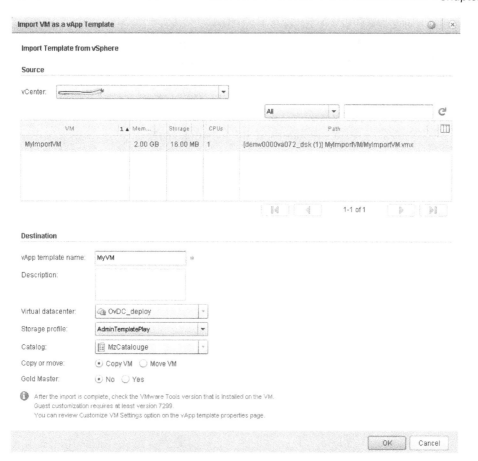

Perform the following steps once you enter the previous page:

1. Select the vCenter you want to import the VM from.

2. Select the VM you would like to import (only powered off VMs are visible).

3. Give the new VM a name.

4. Select the OvDC and the storage profile.

5. Select the catalog you would like the VM to be part of.

6. Choose if you would like to move the VM (delete it from vSphere) or if you want to copy it.

7. Lastly, choose if you want the VM template to be **Gold Master**.

8. Select **OK**.

Importing an OVF/OVA into a catalog

Importing a VM in OVF/OVA format can be done by the Org Admin role, as shown in the following steps. OVA can only be imported with vCloud 5.5.

1. Log in to the organization you want to import the VM into.

2. Click on **Catalogs** and then on **vApp Templates**.

3. Click on the 🖳 button and perform the following steps:

    1. Click on **Browse** to browse to the OVF file on your desktop.

    2. Give the VM a name.

    3. Select the OvDC and the storage profile.

    4. Select the catalog you would like to deploy the VM into.

    5. Click on **Upload**:

4. The Java client will now show an upload window of the files that are being uploaded.

5. Wait until the upload is finished.

6. vCloud will now take some additional time until the OVF is imported into it; just wait until it finishes the waiting.

Import an OVF/OVA into My Cloud

This is a new feature of vCloud 5.5.

Importing a VM in OVF/OVA format can be done by the Org Admin role using the following steps:

1. Log in to the organization you want to import the VM into.
2. Click on **My Cloud**.
3. Click on **Add vApp from OVF**.
4. Select the source of the vApp; this can be on your local client disk or it can be a URL.
5. You are now shown some details of the vApp we are importing, for example, the upload size as well as how much space the vApp will take up.
6. If needed, accept the licensing agreement.
7. Select the vApp name and on what OvDC it should be stored on.
8. Now, configure the computer name (hostname) and the storage profile for each VM.
9. Configure the network adapters for each VM.
10. If there are any custom properties defined in the OVA, you will need to fill them in now.
11. You are now able to customize the hardware (vCPU, memory, and storage) for all VMs, as shown in the following screenshot:

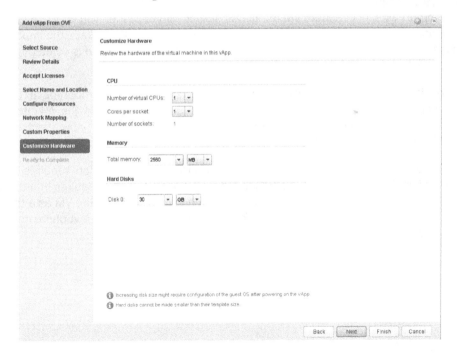

12. Click on **Finish** in the wizard and wait until the upload and import has finished.

Importing from Workstation/Fusion

The importing of a VM from Workstation/Fusion (MAC version of Workstation) is a two-step process:

1. Export the VM either as an OVF or into vSphere:

    ❑ Export VM as an OVF using the following steps:

    ▸ Power off the VM.

    ▸ Navigate to **File | Export to OVF**.

    ▸ Choose a folder to export it to.

    ❑ Export VM to a vSphere using the following steps:

    ▸ Power off the VM.

    ▸ Right-click on the VM and navigate to **Manage | Upload**.

    ▸ Now choose where to put the VM.

2. Import it into vCloud using the two import methods (as shown before).

How it works...

Importing a VM from vSphere is basically making a clone of a VM. Unfortunately, vCloud can only import VMs, not vSphere VM templates or running VMs. When you import a VM via vSphere, you can choose if you want to create a copy or move the VM. In fact, the import works the same way, just that when you move the VM, the vSphere source is deleted from the disk after the import is finished.

Although it is possible to import a VM directly from vSphere into a vApp, importing an OVF will create a vApp template. After the vApp template is created, you can import the VM into a vApp as was shown in the recipe *Adding a VM to a vApp*. In vCloud 5.5, you can now directly import an OVF/OVA into My Cloud.

The import of a vApp as OVF involves a Java-based application and therefore requires a Java client to be installed on the client. In addition to this, uploading an OVF requires that the transfer directory on the vCloud Cell is large enough to contain the entire VM as a thick format. The following diagram shows the difference between an OVF and a vSphere import with regards to storage:

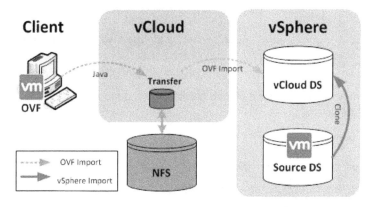

The vCloud `transfer` directory should be shared (NFS mount) among all vCloud Director Cells. It can be a local hard disk if a single-cell vCloud is used; however, this is not really a recommended setup.

The Java client uploads the OVF files or the OVA files into the vCloud `transfer` directory (`/opt/vmware/vmware-vclouddirector/data/transfer`). When the import is finished, vCloud imports the OVF into vSphere, deploying it onto a vSphere data store. The upload status that is displayed shows the time and percentage of the upload of the OVF files into the `transfer` directory. It does not show the time that vCloud will take to import the OVF into vSphere.

This is done to proxy the upload. Consider that someone would like to upload the OVF through the Internet. This design allows for exposing only the vCloud HTTPS interface to the Internet, and hides the vSphere environment.

Important changes in vCloud 5.5

There were two changes introduced in vCloud 5.5 that impact the import. The first is that now, templates can be imported not only in the OVF format but also in the OVA format. The difference between an OVF and an OVA format is that OVA is a single file that contains all the files that make up an OVF.

The second change is that vCloud has stopped using a Java client for upload. It now uses the **VMware Client Integration Plugin**. The Integration plugin can be downloaded when you click on the **Add vApp from OVF** button.

There's more...

There are some other things we should have a look at when we import a vApp into the vCloud.

Aftercare

After you have imported a VM into a vCloud catalog, it's a good idea to deploy it immediately and then adjust its settings.

Things you should consider doing:

- Configure the startup and shut down sequence
- Configure the Guest Customization settings
- Adjust the hostname
- Update the virtual hardware version
- Check the operating system to see if there is anything you need to configure, for example, domain settings.

Migrating running VMs

A typical challenge in a productive environment is that one wants to import production VMs that are currently running. This is easily done; however, it may take some time and one has to be a bit careful with data consistency.

A typical scenario where such an approach is required is to test an update of a production system.

Follow the ensuing steps to do this:

1. Log in to vSphere.
2. Find the VM you would like to import.
3. Right-click on the VM and choose **Clone** and perform the following steps:
   1. Choose a new name for the VM.
   2. Choose **Host or Cluster**, **Resource pool**, and **Datastore** to put the VM into.
   3. When it comes to Guest Customization, choose **NONE**.
4. Wait until the clone is finished (this can take quite a while).
5. Import the clone into vCloud as shown previously.

See also

▸ More information on OVF can be found at `http://en.wikipedia.org/wiki/ Open_Virtualization_Format`.

▸ To read up on Java client troubleshooting, refer to *Chapter 8, Java Client*

▸ To read up on cloning running vApps, refer to *Chapter 7, Cloning-Running vApps*

Exporting a vApp from vCloud

Exporting a vApp from vCloud is simple and straightforward; just let me say a few words on the specifics.

Getting ready

Obviously we will need a vApp with at least one VM. You have to be an Org Admin to be able to export a VM.

How to do it...

In vCloud 5.1 you can only export from the library, using vCloud 5.5 you can also export a vApp from My Cloud.

Exporting a vApp from a catalog

Perform the following steps to export a vApp from a catalog:

1. Navigate to the organization you want to export from.
2. Click on **Catalogs**.
3. Click on **vApp Templates**.

4. Right-click on the VM that you wish to export, and select **Download…** as shown in the following screenshot:

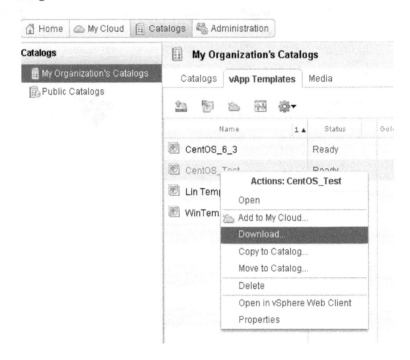

5. Click on **Browse**, and select a folder and a name to store the OVF export.
6. If you select the **Preserve identity information** checkbox, the exported VM will keep its UUID, MAC, and network settings.
7. Wait until the VM is exported.

Exporting a vApp from My Cloud

This is a new function in vCloud 5.5. Follow the ensuing steps to export a vApp from My Cloud:

1. Navigate to the organization you want to export from.
2. Click on **My Cloud**.
3. Right-click on the vApp you want to export and select **Download…**.
4. Enter a name for the vApp and browse to the location on the local disk where you would like to store it.
5. Select the format as either OVF or OVA.

6. If you select **Preserve identity information**, as shown in the following screenshot, the exported VM will keep its UUID, MAC, and network settings:

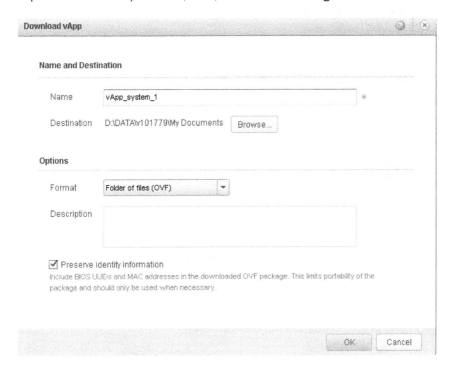

7. Wait until the export has finished.

How it works...

The export follows the same principle as the OVF import. First, the vApp is exported as an OVF to the vCloud `transfer` directory and then transferred from there to the local desktop.

The ability to preserve the identity (UUID, and so on) of a VM is rather critical, as it allows the transfer of VMs between clouds and cloudless systems, like a normal vSphere system. The OVF format is able to transfer VMs not only among VMware systems but also among various tools that already allow the import of OVF-formatted VMs to other hypervisors, such as Citrix and Microsoft.

See also

> ▸ To know more about UUID issues with vCloud, refer to *Chapter 7, Making the VM BIOS ID (UUID) Unique*

> ▸ To know more about Java client troubleshooting, refer to *Chapter 8, Java Client*

Creating a sandbox environment

Let's create a test environment that cleans up automatically after its users.

Getting ready

We will be creating a new organization and OvDC. So, we need a PvDC with some spare CPU usage, memory, and disk space (the best option would be an own storage profile) for this organization.

In addition to this, a network pool is useful, as it allows users to create their own little isolated networks.

If you would like to allow users access the Internet or the corporate network, you might like to add an External Network into the mix. Alternatively, you may like to create an isolated OrgNet to make inter-vApp connection possible.

How to do it...

We will now create all the parts we need for a sandbox environment.

Creating an organization for the sandbox

We should create an organization to cater for the sandbox:

1. Log into vCloud as `SysAdmin`.
2. Click on **Manage & Monitor** and then click on the green icon (**+**).
3. Give the organization a new name (for example, `Sandpit`) and decide on its LDAP binding.
4. Don't allow for catalog publishing, as we won't create one.

5. The **Policies** page is where we will start configuring the organization for being a sandbox. Choose a short runtime and a slightly larger storage lease. The vApp template's storage lease time will have no consequence as we don't allow for a catalog. Make sure you set the **Storage cleanup** option to **Permanently delete** as shown in the following screenshot:

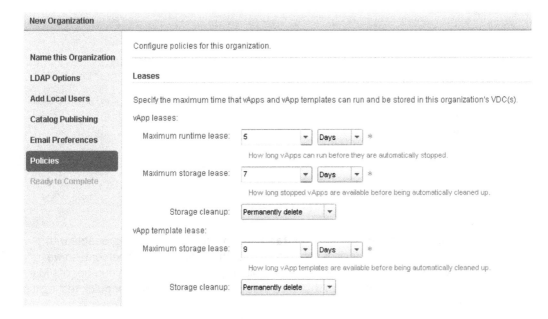

You also want to reduce the impact of the sandbox environment on your other productive environments by setting a limit on the number of intensive operations as well as the simultaneous connections (remote console).

6. Click on **OK** to finish the creation of this organization.

Creating an OvDC for the sandbox

The next thing we need to do is give some resources to the organization:

1. Click on **Organization VDCs** and then click on the green icon (**+**).

2. Select an the organization we have just created and then assign it to a PvDC.

3. The Allocation Model is another thing that needs some thought. **Pay-As-You-Go** is the model of choice (see the explanation in the *How it works* section of this recipe):

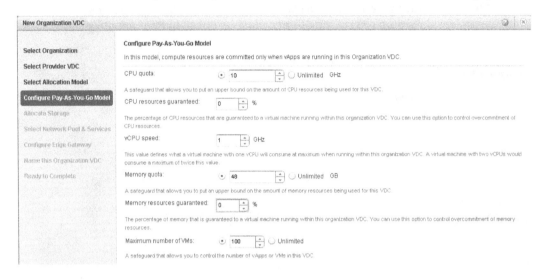

4. Set the **CPU quota** and **Memory quota** values to a top limit that is agreeable with your PvDC's other usages. It is important to set the guarantee to **0** percent, so we actually do not reserve any resources for this organization. Limit the number of VMs as well as set the vCPU speed to **1** GHz. This isn't terribly fast, but for quick testing it's enough.

5. The storage profile should be either an own storage profile or should be a part of one with clear limits on its usage. Thin provisioning and fast provisioning make it easier to use the sandbox.

6. Assign it a network pool, but limit the number of networks to a reasonable number. I mostly go for something like 20 networks. If that's not enough, you can always increase it.

7. We don't want an edge so skip the next step.

8. Give the OvDC a name and finish the creation.

Adding networking

Now we need some networking attached to the organization by performing the following:

▶ I normally do not allow a sandbox access an External Network as I believe there should be no way in which a tester in the sandbox can access any real networks.

▶ I *do* normally add an isolated Organizational Network to make it easier for developers to connect vApps with each other.

How it works...

vCloud is one of the best tools to create test environments with. It allows for the creation of isolated networks, easy-to-configure routers, firewalls, and so much more. With vCloud, users are able to deploy small to complex test environments reducing the time and cost in development. The downside is that users quickly fill up vCloud with vApps and VMs, and for a system administrator, it is often hard to know what can be deleted and what cannot. This is why we create a sandbox environment that cleans up after the user automatically.

Lease time

Creating a test environment that cleans up after the user is quite cool and reduces the demand on resources. The secret is to use leases. Leases come in three categories:

- ▶ **vApp runtime leases**: This type of lease defines how long a vApp will be running before it is powered off. vCloud will power off VMs using the method and sequence defined in the vApp. Every time a vApp is powered on, the vApp runtime lease starts to tick.

- ▶ **vApp storage leases**: The vApp storage lease is the time until a vApp is either deleted or moved to a holding area. If the vApp is still running, it will be stopped.

- ▶ **vApp template storage leases**: This type of lease affects only vApp templates, and starts running when a vApp is added to a catalog. When the vApp template time has run out, the vApp template either gets deleted or moved to a holding area.

When you deploy a vApp, you can reset the lease time. However, you cannot exceed the predefined maximum lease times.

Users will get notified before and after their lease expires.

Allocation model

The other important point is the *resource allocation* model we are using and the reservations we are setting. The Pay-As-You-Go model is ideal for a sandpit, as it doesn't reserve any resources, creating a low-impact organization. The only important thing is to limit the top number of resources that this organization can consume. The limit should be determined by how much of more important work is done on the same PvDC and what maximal resources can be spared. Also, it is always possible to just disable the OvDC so that users cannot create new vApps.

 For more information, see the *Choosing the right allocation model* recipe in *Chapter 6, Improving the vCloud Design*.

Networking

The network pool can also contribute to a higher workload of the base system. For every isolated network, a vApp router (which is an Edge device, as shown *Chapter 2, vCloud Networks*) is created, therefore increasing the amount of resources that the system resource pool consumes. On the other hand, isolated networks can really improve some testing environments. This leads to the point of limiting the number of networks that one can create so that not too many vApp routers are created.

There's more...

Let me point out a couple of things in regards to the sandpit environment.

Fair warning

Each user can set the warning time for expiring leases on their own. To do so, click on **Preferences** (upper-right corner of the main GUI screen). The default is **5 days before expiration**, as shown in the following screenshot:

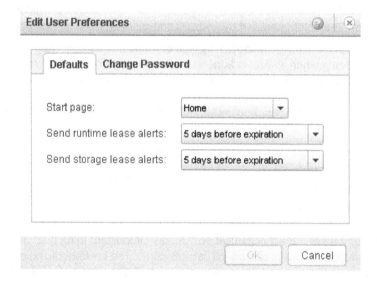

Using an Edge gateway to give access to the play infrastructure

If you would like to give your test user some basic infrastructure to play with, such as e-mail, DNS, and Active Directory, the best way is to put it into a different organization. The reason to do so is twofold. Firstly, all vApps (even ones that a system administrator creates) are following the lease time set in the organization, so creating permanent infrastructure isn't possible. Secondly, if deployed in a different organization, testers can't damage your infrastructure directly. If someone were to damage it, a quick use of the **Revert to Snapshot** option can rectify the problem.

To create such a concept, follow the ensuing instructions:

1. Create your sandbox.
2. Create a vApp in a different organization that holds your infrastructure.
3. Create a snapshot of that vApp to secure it.
4. Create a VPN between the sandbox and this Infrastructure vApp (see the *Creating a secure connection between organizations (which can even be in different vClouds)* recipe in *Chapter 2, vCloud Networks*).

This will allow you to have full control over your infrastructure, while testers can go nuts in their little organization that actually cleans up after them.

Using Guest Customization with pre and post deploy

When you use Guest Customization Scripts, it's important to define when they are running.

Getting ready

We will need a vApp with VMs in it. To test the results in this recipe, it is good if you have a Linux and a Windows VM so that you can test the results better.

How to do it...

1. Double-click on the vApp to enter it.
2. Select a VM that you want to configure with Guest Customization.
3. Right-click on the VM and select **Properties**.
4. Click on **Guest OS Customization**.
5. Make sure you have enabled Guest Customization and then scroll down to the end of the page.
6. In the large textbox, enter the following scripts depending on your operating system:
   - The following is the Linux script:
     ```
     #!/bin/sh
     if [ x$1 == x"precustomization" ]; then
     /bin/date > /tmp/VMStatus
     echo VM Precustomization >> /tmp/VMStatus
     Hostname >> /tmp/VMStatus
     elif [ x$1 == x"postcustomization" ]; then
     /bin/date >> /tmp/VMStatus
     ```

```
echo postcustomization >> /tmp/VMStatus
Hostname >> /tmp/VMStatus
fi
```

❑ The following is the Windows script:

```
@echo off
if "%1%" == "precustomization" (
echo %DATE% %TIME% > C:\VMStatus.txt
echo VM Precustomization >> C:\VMStatus.txt
echo %Hostname>> C:\VMStatus.txt
)
else if "%1%" == "postcustomization" (
echo %DATE% %TIME% > C:\VMStatus.txt
echo VM Precustomization >> C:\VMStatus.txt
echo %Hostname >> C:\VMStatus.txt
)
```

7. Click on **OK** to exit the properties.

8. You may like to configure another VM.

9. Now click back on the vApp.

10. Either power it on, if this vApp has not been deployed before, or right-click on it and select **Power On and Force Recustomization** if the vApp has been run before.

11. Wait until Guest Customization has run and the VM is closed.

12. Now log into the same VM by clicking on the screen of the VM.

13. Check out the `C:\VMStatus.txt` or `/tmp/VMStatus` file.

How it works...

When we talk about Guest Customization, we talk about a VM that changes its setting automatically when it is first booted. In Windows, Guest Customization is nothing other than running Sysprep, and in Linux it's a script that runs when the VM boots.

Guest Customization is used in vSphere, and can be triggered there when one deploys a VM template. In vSphere, Guest Customization settings can be stored in vCenter to be used together with deployment. These contain settings such as licensing, network settings, and especially custom scripts that are run when the VM is deployed. There is even an alarm setting that allows one to check when Guest Customization has finished. Sadly, vCloud doesn't use vCenter to create and trigger a Guest Customization; it uses its ESXi plugin to do so. vCloud sends all required data to the plugin, and the plugin facilitates the rest. This means that you can't use vCenter to monitor when Guest Customization has finished.

One of the really exciting features of vCloud with regards to Guest Customization is that a VM can be forced to re-run Guest Customization. Normally, Guest Customization only runs the first time the VM boots; with vCloud, you can force a VM to start and run Guest Customization. This can be triggered by right-clicking on a stopped VM and choosing **Power On and Force Recustomization**:

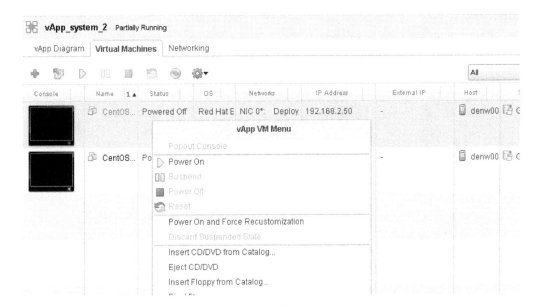

This feature allows VMs to join different networks or AD domains just by right-clicking, reducing the effort of adjusting their settings in the operating system.

The most important fact to know is that, Guest Customization requires VMware tools to be installed on the VM—no VMware tools, no Guest Customization. This means that VMs without VMware tools cannot get IPs allocated (or any other Guest Customization setting) from IP pools.

There's more...

The following section explains some things that you need to know.

Limits

There can be a maximum 1500 characters in a Guest Customization script that is used in a VM. Therefore, it is sometimes simpler to have a Guest Customization script stored on the operating system of the VM, and the Guest Customization script then calls it, and after running it, deletes it from the OS.

Old bugs

Until Version 5.1.2, there was a bug with Guest Customization. If you created a vApp template, the **Change SID** button as well as the **Change Password** button would be deactivated. Check out VMware KB 2038286.

Logfiles

When Guest Customization has been run, logfiles are written to the operating system.

For Windows, these files are stored at:

- ▶ `C:\WINDOWS\TEMP\vmware-imc\toolsDeployPkg.txt`
- ▶ `C:\WINDOWS\TEMP\customize-guest.log`

For Linux, it is:

- ▶ `/var/log/vmware-imc/toolsDeployPkg.txt`
- ▶ `/var/log/messages` (grep for customize-guest)

Actually, this is quite a problem, as the whole customization script is displayed there, which could include things such as clear text passwords and IPs/hostnames of important systems. Think about that when writing your customization script next time.

Template Guest Customization

With vCloud 5.5, you are now able to change the Guest Customization settings of a VM template. You need vSphere 5.5 deployed for this to work. Perform the following steps to do so:

1. Navigate to **Catalog | vApp Templates**.
2. Double-click on a vApp template.
3. Right-click on a VM and select **Properties**.
4. Select **Guest Customization**.
5. You now can change all the Guest Customization settings.

See also

- ▶ More information on Microsoft Sysprep can be found at: `http://technet.microsoft.com/en-us/library/cc783215%28v=ws.10%29.aspx`

Using PowerShell or Perl to perform Guest Customization tasks

Guest Customization can use only DOS commands (Windows) or Bash commands (Linux) natively. The following section describes how to get higher language scripts going.

Getting ready

We need a vApp with at least one VM in it.

How to do it...

There are two ways of using PowerShell or Perl to perform Guest Customization tasks. They are described in the following section.

Using PowerShell or Perl to perform Guest Customization tasks via the VM Properties

Perform the following for using PowerShell or Perl to perform Guest Customization tasks via the VM Properties:

1. Write wrapper around the program (see the *How it works...* section).

Using PowerShell or Perl to perform Guest Customization tasks via an OS script

1. Create a script on the local VM.
2. Start the local script via Guest Customization in the VM properties.
3. Wait until the script finishes running.
4. Delete the local script on the VM via a command line in Guest Customization.

How it works...

The Guest Customization script is forwarded from the VM properties to the vCloud ESXi plugin. It is then inserted into the VM using VMware tools. VMware tools will then act differently depending on the operating system.

In a Windows system, it will trigger Sysprep and insert the script into the Sysprep configuration. Windows will then initiate Sysprep and execute the script.

In a Linux system, VMware tools will generate a script that makes all the changes and will be started with the next boot.

In both cases, the scripting can only use the native capabilities of the operating system's command line, namely DOS or BASH. If you would like to use another language, you need to make sure it's installed, and you will need to write a wrapper. A wrapper is a little program or piece of code that starts the program in another language.

For most wrappers, it is extremely important to get the paths right, so it always pays to be expressive with it.

Windows PowerShell wrapper

The following is a wrapper to start a PowerShell script that is stored on the operating system:

```
start /wait C:\Windows\System32\WindowsPowerShell\v1.0\powershell.exe
-File [powershell file] [parameter1] [parameter2] [..]
```

To run a single PowerShell command, use the following wrapper:

```
start /wait C:\Windows\System32\WindowsPowerShell\v1.0\powershell.exe
[powershell command]
```

The `start/wait` command is used to make sure that the system waits until the command has finished before continuing.

Linux Perl wrapper

When you are using Linux, things are a bit more relaxed. All you need is the header (see the following code) that tells BASH where to find the executable for the language. You might also need to supply the correct path to the libraries you need:

```
#!/usr/bin/perl
print "Hello World";
```

To run a single Perl command use the following wrapper:

```
/usr/bin/perl -e 'print "Hello World";'
```

There's more...

Which user is actually running Guest Customization?

Under Windows, it is basically the user who installed VMware tools, which is typically `nt authority\system`; however, it's a bit more complicated if you change the user. If you set up VMware tools with a different user, pre-customization scripts will run as the user you set VMware tools up with. Post-customization scripts will always run as `nt authority\system`.

In Linux, things are easier as Guest Customization runs as *root* for both pre- and post-customization scripts.

However, sometimes it is important to use a different user to run tasks or to include a password into a command line. The problem with this is that the password will be stored in the VM properties as well as in the logfiles of this VM. Systems have been easily hacked this way.

See also

▶ Perl command-line options `http://www.perl.com/pub/2004/08/09/commandline.html`

▶ PowerShell command-line options `http://technet.microsoft.com/en-us/magazine/ff629472.aspx`

Sharing a vApp

So your colleague created a vApp and you can't see or use it? You can use the sharing option to share vApps with other users or groups.

Getting ready

We need one or more vApps as well as two users. The users can be local users or LDAP users, and one must at least be a vApp Author.

How to do it...

1. Navigate to your organization.
2. Right-click on the vApp you would like to share and select **Share**.
3. The properties of the vApp open up on the Share page.
4. Now click on **Add Members**.
5. You can now share this vApp with everyone in this organization or just a specific group or user. Take note that there is a search field.

6. Choose the **Access Level** option you want to give this user, as shown in the following screenshot:

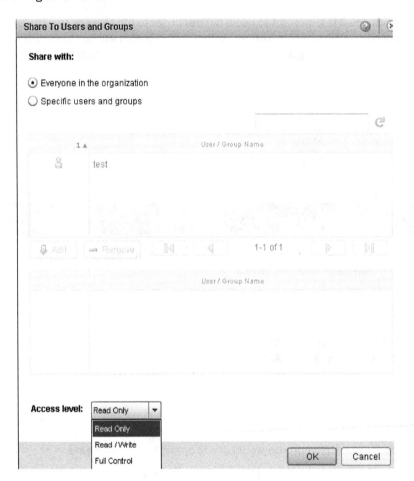

7. Select the user and click on **Add**.

8. Click on **OK**.

9. You can still change the access level of the user or group.

10. Click on **OK** to close the properties' window.

11. Now log in as the other user. You should now see and have access to the vApp:

How it works...

By default, only the creator and the Org Admin have access to a vApp. Using the sharing options, we can make vApps accessible to other users.

There are three access levels that can be assigned to users for any given vApp:

Access level	Explanation
Read Only	The users only have access to the vApp but cannot change it
Read/Write	The users can access the vApp, start and stop it, add it to a catalog, copy it, and change the properties
Full Control	The users can access the vApp, start and stop it, add it to a catalog, copy it, change the properties, and change the owner

A common problem is that in one organization, there are multiple sub-organizations or projects that need to share space but don't really want to share all their vApps with each other. The typical solution is to create two LDAP (AD) groups that are part of the organization. Users will then share their vApps only with their group, separating what is visible for users in this organization. Also, users of both groups will be able to see all the vApps.

There's more...

Sharing also works for catalog items. The following is a list of what the different access levels mean:

Access level	Meaning
Read Only	Open, add to My Cloud, download, and copy to catalog
Read/Write	Open, add to My Cloud, download, copy to catalog, publish, move to catalog, and delete
Full Control	Open, add to My Cloud, download, copy to catalog, publish, move to catalog, delete, and share

Joining VMs automatically to domains

The following section explains how to automatically make VMs join an Active Directory.

Getting ready

Understandably, we need a Windows VM in a vApp. But we also need an Active Directory that we can join. Last but not least, we need a network in which the VM is connected so it can talk to the Active Directory. A good test is to create a VM and manually join it to the AD, to make sure that the VM can connect directly to the AD.

In this example, we assume that you have an AD server in your organization (isolated org network) or one that you can connect to via an external network (direct connect org network).

For this example, we need all the credentials to be able to add a VM to AD.

How to do it...

Any vApp Author can perform this task. Follow the ensuing steps:

1. Double-click on the vApp to open it up.
2. Right-click on a Windows VM (powered off) and select **Properties**.
3. Click on **Guest OS Customization**. You should get the following screenshot:

Virtual Machine Properties: CentOS_Test

| General | Hardware | **Guest OS Customization** | Guest Properties | Resource Allocation | System Alerts | Metadata |

General

☑ Enable guest customization

The computer name and network settings configured for this VM are applied to its Guest OS when the VM is powered on. The following settings a the VM is powered on or if "Power on and Force Recustomization" is performed: Change SID, Password Reset, Join Domain and Customization Sc Guest customization should not be enabled if the VM uses Guest Properties for customization.

☑ Change SID

Applicable for Windows VMs and will run Sysprep to change Windows SID. On Windows NT, VCD uses Sidgen. Running sysprep is a prerequisite

Password Reset

☐ Allow local administrator password

   ◯ Auto generate password

   ◉ Specify password   [   ] ✳

☐ Require administrator to change password on first login

Join Domain

☑ Enable this VM to join a domain

   ◯ Use organization's domain ◉ Override organization's domain

Domain name:	myDomain.local	✳
User name:	MyDomAdmin	✳
Password:	*********	✳
Account organizational unit:		

4. Make sure the **enable Guest Customization** checkbox is ticked.

5. Make sure the **Change SID** checkbox is ticked.

6. Make sure the **Enable this VM to join a domain** checkbox is ticked.

7. Enter all the AD domain settings and make sure that the user has the right to join computers to the domain.

8. Click on **OK**.

9. Power on the VM (or if you had it running before, right-click on it and select **Force customization**).

10. The VM will power on and will now join the domain.

How it works...

Actually it's pretty simple. vCloud just uses the built-in function of Windows (Sysprep) to join a domain.

There's more...

Instead of configuring every single VM to be able to join a domain, we can just configure the organization to be ready to join an AD.

Configuring the organization

Perform the following steps to configure the organization:

1. Log into the organization as an Org Admin.

2. Click on **Administration**.

3. Click on **Guest Personalization**. You should now see the following screen:

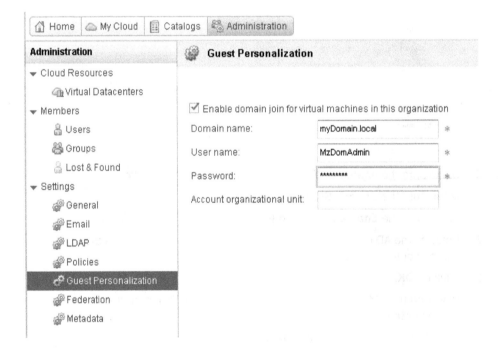

4. Add the required credentials for the AD you want VMs to connect to in this organization.

5. Click on **Apply**.

Configuring the VM

Perform the following steps to configure the VM:

1. Double-click to open the vApp.

2. Right-click on the VM you want to configure and select **properties**.

3. Select **Guest OS Customization**. You should now see the following screen:

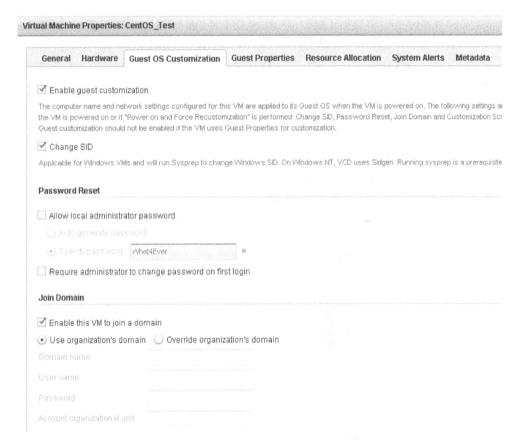

4. Select the checkboxes **Enable Guest Customization** and **SID change**.

5. Select the **Enable this VM to join a domain** checkbox.

6. Select **Use organizational domain**.

7. Click on **OK**.

8. Proceed as normal.

Using vApp maintenance mode

The vApp maintenance mode helps you control the state of VMs in your vCloud system. The following section shows how to use it as well as gives some examples.

Getting ready

We just need a vApp with VMs in it and two users. One is `SysAdmin` and the other can be `OrgAdmin` or the owner of this vApp.

How to do it...

1. Log into vCloud as `SysAdmin`.
2. Open the organization you want to work in.
3. Click on **MyCloud** to see all the vApps.
4. Right-click on a vApp and select **Enter Maintenance Mode**.
5. Agree to the change by clicking on **OK**.
6. You will now see that the vApp is marked as being in maintenance mode:

7. Now log out and log into the organization using the other user.
8. If you now try to change the vApp or its VMs, you will find that you can't.
9. Log in back as `SysAdmin`.
10. Right-click on the vApp again and select **Exit Maintenance Mode**.
11. The vApp is now back to normal.

How it works...

Maintenance mode blocks a vApp from being changed. The idea behind it is that a system administrator or an automation user (using the API) can block changes to the VM. The user then can, for example, make a backup, create an export, or resolve a problem, without an organizational user being able to impact the process.

 Third-party backup programs might use vApp maintenance mode.

See also

▸ The *Updating vCloud* recipe in *Chapter 7, Updating without Interrupt.*

4
Datastores and Storage Profiles

We will cover the following recipes in this chapter:

- ► Adding a new storage profile to vCD
- ► Using a specific datastore for templates
- ► Using storage profiles for storage tiering
- ► Making operations on NFS-datastores faster
- ► Working with vApp templates and their Shadows
- ► Reducing the chain length of Linked Clones
- ► Configuring storage alarms
- ► Monitoring storage
- ► The problems associated with the backup and restore of vCloud

Introduction

Datastores are the foundation that all VMs are based on, so we should take a closer look at them. Since Version 5.1 of vCloud Director, we can use not only datastores but also storage profiles and datastore clusters for VM storage.

Datastores, profiles, and clusters

Datastores probably don't need to be explained in detail, but here is a short introduction to cover the basics. A datastore is a VMware object that exists in ESXi. This object can be a hard disk that is attached to an ESXi server, an NFS, or iSCSI mount on an ESXi host, or a fiber channel disk that is attached to an HBA on the ESXi server.

A storage profile is a container that contains one or more datastores. Storage profiles don't have any intelligence implemented in them; they just group datastores together. However, they are extremely beneficial in vCloud. If you run out of storage space on a storage profile, you can just expand the storage by adding another datastore to the same storage profile.

Datastore clusters again are containers for datastores, but intelligence is now included. A datastore cluster can use Storage DRS, which allows for VMs to automatically use Storage vMotion to move from one datastore to another. This can be configured depending on the I/O latency or the storage space left. Depending on your storage backend system, this can be extremely beneficial.

vCloud Director doesn't know the difference between a storage profile and a datastore cluster. If you add a datastore cluster, vCloud will pick it up as a storage profile, but that's ok.

Be aware that storage profiles are part of the vSphere Enterprise Plus licensing. If you don't have Enterprise Plus, you won't get storage profiles, and the only thing you can do in vCloud is use the storage profile ANY, which doesn't contribute to productivity.

Thin provisioning

Thin provisioning means that the file that contains the virtual hard disk (`.vmdk`) is only as big as the amount of data written to the virtual hard disk. For example, if you have a 40 GB hard disk attached to a Windows VM and have just installed Windows on it, you are using around 2 GB of the 40 GB disk. When using thin provisioning, only 2 GB will be written to the datastore, not 40 GB. If you don't use thin provisioning, the `.vmdk` file will be 40 GB in size. Please note that thin provisioned .vmdk files do not shrink. There are quite a few methods to shrink them manually; however, if you are using fast provisioning (linked clones), it is not recommended to manually shrink them.

If your storage vendor's storage APIs are integrated into your ESXi servers, thin provisioning may be offloaded to your storage backend, making it even faster.

Fast provisioning

Fast provisioning is similar to the linked clones that you may know from Lab Manager or VMware View. However, in vCloud, they are a bit more intelligent than in the other products. In the other products, linked clones can *not* be deployed across different datastores, but in vCloud they can.

Let's talk about how linked clones work. If you had a VM with a 40 GB hard disk and you cloned that VM, you would normally have to spend another 40 GB (not using thin provisioning). With linked clones you will not need another 40 GB, but a lot less. In layman's terms, what happens is that vCloud creates two snapshots of the original VM's hard disk. A snapshot contains only the differences between the original and the snapshot. The original hard disk (.vmdk file) is set to read-only and the first snapshot is connected to the original VM so that one can still work with the original VM. The second snapshot is used to create the new VM. Not only does using snapshots make deploying a VM using fast provisioning fast but also it saves a lot of disk space.

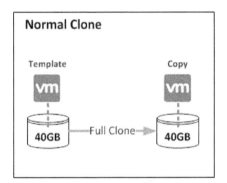

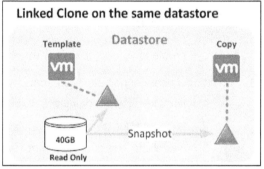

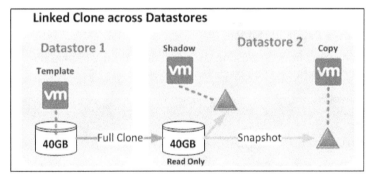

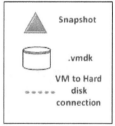

The problem with linked cloning is that a snapshot must be on the same datastore as its source. So if you have a VM in one datastore, its linked clone cannot be in another. vCloud has solved that problem by deploying a Shadow VM. When you deploy a VM with fast provisioning onto a different datastore than its source, vCloud creates a full clone (a normal full copy) of the VM onto the new datastore and then creates a linked clone from the Shadow VM.

If your storage vendor's Storage APIs are integrated in your ESXi servers, fast provisioning may be offloaded to your storage backend making it faster. Refer to the *Making operations on NFS-based datastores faster* in this chapter.

Adding a new storage profile to vCD

You have just created a new storage profile in vSphere but now need to add it to an OvDC. Here is how it's done.

Getting ready

First, we need a datastore that has been added to the ESXi hosts. We also need an organization as well as an OvDC, to which we can add it.

How to do it...

To add a storage profile to vCloud, there are three major steps involved.

1. Creating a user-defined storage capability:

    1. Log in to vCenter using the WebClient.

    2. Click on **vCenter** and then on **Datastores**.

    3. Select the first datastore that should be part of the new storage profile.

    4. Click on **Manage** in the tabs and then on **Profiles**.

    5. Now we add user-defined storage capability to a datastore; click on the **Assign Storage Capability** button.

    6. Now you can select from an existing **User-defined Storage Capability** datastore or create a new one by clicking on **New**.

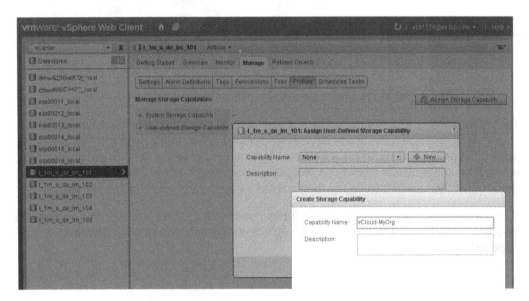

7. If you click on **New**, give the capability a name and a description, for example, `vCloud-MyOrg`.

8. Click on **OK**, and then again **OK**. Now the datastore should show the name you entered under **User-defined Storage Capability**.

9. If you want, you can now assign the same or other capabilities to more datastores.

2. Creating a storage profile:

   1. Log in to vCenter using WebClient.

   2. Click on **Rules and Profiles** and then on **VM Storage Profiles**.

   3. Click on the green **+** button (**Create a new VM Storage Profile**).

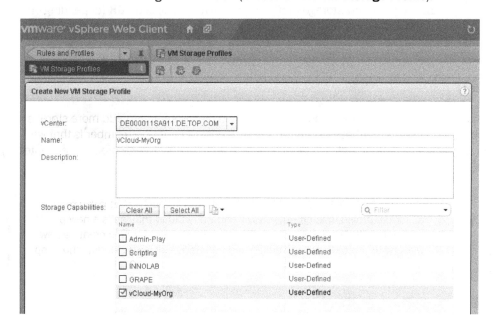

   4. Give the storage profile a name and select the user-defined storage capability you defined earlier.

   5. Click on **OK**.

   6. If this is the first time you have created a storage profile, you need to enable storage profiles on the cluster (refer to the *There's more...* section).

3. Adding a storage profile to vCloud:

   1. Log in to vCloud as `SysAdmin`.

   2. Click on **Manage & Monitor** and then on **vCenter**.

3. Right-click on the vCenter you have added the storage profile to and click on **Refresh Storage Profiles**.

4. Wait until the task is finished.

5. Click on **Provider VDCs** and double-click on the PvDC you want the storage profile to be added to.

6. Now click on the green **+** button.

7. Add the new storage profile to the PvDC and click on **OK**.

8. We now need to add it to an OvDC. Click on **Organization VDCs** and double-click on the OvDC you want to add the storage profile to.

9. Click on **Storage Profiles** and then click on the green **+** button.

10. Add the new storage profile to the OvDC and click on **OK** (depending on your OvDC allocation model you need to assign the storage to this OvDC).

11. The new storage profile is now ready to be used.

How it works...

Storage profiles make your life much easier in vCloud as it is simple to add more storage capability to the system without too much bother. The only thing to remember is that we need to sync vCloud with vCenter to be able to pick up the new storage profiles we created in vCenter.

 One of the smaller but annoying problems with vCloud is that if you rename a storage profile in vSphere, you will find that vCloud thinks it's a new profile and you can't delete the old one. The only solution so far is to create a new OvDC with the new storage profile and then move all vApp, Media, and vApp templates to the new OvDC and then delete the old OvDC.

There's more...

Some typical problems with storage profiles and why they don't show up in vCloud are:

▸ Storage profiles are not enabled. To enable them perform the following steps:

1. Log in to vCenter WebClient.

2. Navigate to **Rules and Profiles | VM Storage Profiles**.

3. Click on the second button (**Enable VM Storage Profiles**).

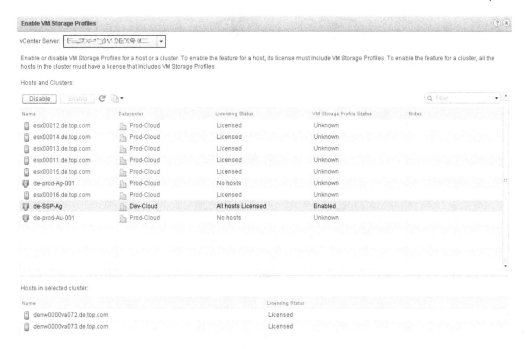

4. Select your cluster and click on **Enable**.

▶ **Profile with no capability**: You have created a profile, but you haven't assigned it a user-defined storage capability. Refer to Step 1 of this recipe to assign it.

▶ **Profile-Driven Storage isn't running**: All the previous checks out, but the storage profile still doesn't show up. Check whether the VMware Storage Profile Service is running by performing the following steps:

1. Log in to your vCenter server.

2. Navigate to **Start | Administrative Tools | Services**.

3. Check the status of VMware vSphere Profile-Driven Storage service.

See also

▶ The *Creating and using a Naming Standards* recipe in *Chapter 6, Improving the vCloud Design*

Using a specific datastore for templates

Templates are inactive most of the time, so putting them on expensive storage is a waste. Here is how you make sure that the templates and media are stored on inexpensive storage.

Getting ready

We need a vApp or a vApp template and two storage profiles. One storage profile is the profile the vApp or vApp template currently sits on, and the other one is the one we want to dedicate to vApp templates and media. You should choose some inexpensive disks for this storage profile.

How to do it...

1. Refer to the *Adding a new storage profile to vCD* recipe in this chapter to add the new storage profile to your organization.

2. Give it a good name that makes it clear that it is only used for templates and media.

3. Creating a new vApp template:

    1. Navigate to the vApp that you want to make a vApp template.

    2. Right-click on **vApp** and then select **Add to Catalog**.

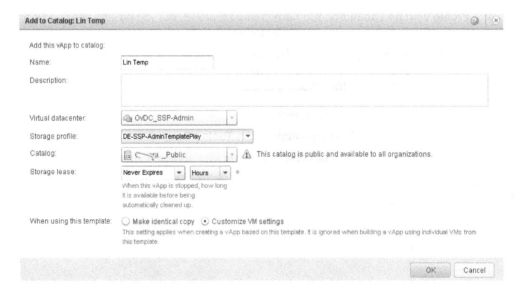

    3. Now select the new storage profile for templates and media.

    4. Click on **OK**.

4. Moving an existing vApp template or media:

    1. Navigate to the vApp template or media in your catalog that you want to move to the inexpensive template storage.

    2. Right-click on the vApp template or media and select **Move to Catalog**.

    3. Now select the new storage profile for templates and media.

    4. Click on **OK**.

How it works...

vApp templates and media are typically things that are stored once and then mostly read. So storing them on fast and expensive storage is a bit of a waste. Creating a storage profile that uses inexpensive disks can save you money.

There is another thing you need to take into consideration: linked clones (or in vCloud talk, fast deployment). If you are using linked clones and the VMs are staying in the same datastore as their templates all the time, you will save space and time. However, you might need a very large datastore to accommodate everything. Large datastores (especially using vSphere storage extends) can become slow in performance or create problems with backup and restore. This is something to consider for your design.

I personally use an admin organization where all my templates are staged and stored. We have discussed this before and I will go into more detail in the *Keeping your templates under control* recipe, *Chapter 6, Improving the vCloud Design*.

See also

▶ The *Working with vApp templates and their Shadows* recipe

Using storage profiles for storage tiering

Selecting the right kind of storage can be challenging, but there is a way of making it easier.

Getting ready

We need some kind of tiered storage; this could be SSD, SAS, and SATA disk, or mirrored disk, normal disks, and slow disks. We also need an organization that we can host this tiering in.

How to do it...

1. Create a storage profile for each of the storage tiers in vSphere; refer to the *Adding a new storage profile to vCD* recipe in this chapter.

2. Make sure to name the storage profile so that it makes sense to customers. The classic example is using Gold, Silver, and Bronze to indicate how good or expensive the storage is for customers. Refer to upright the *Creating a Naming Standards* recipe in *Chapter 6, Improving a vCloud Design*.

3. Import the storage profile into vCloud.

4. Add the storage profile to the OvCD.

5. Make sure that you publish the details of the storage tiering and provide the details for the customer who uses it.

How it works...

The recipe is extremely easy; however, it is astounding how many people don't use it. Most people think that storage comes in a multitude of combinations; however, if you invest some time and effort, you will find that 80-90 percent of all VMs will be on the same storage, and it makes sense to formalize a storage standard. Using a storage standard can save a lot of money. When you realize how much money each storage tier costs and what the actual gain for the customer is, people will automatically redefine their requirements. You don't necessarily need a charge model to make this work; from my experience, a show-back model works quite well. A show-back model means that you show the customers how much money has been spent on their VMs, making them realize that storage—or virtualization, for that matter—isn't free.

See also

► The *Using OvDCs for Compute tiering* recipe in Chapter 6, Improving a vCloud Design

Making operations on NFS datastores faster

When using NFS storage, you need to know how to activate the offload, which is what we will be doing in the following sections.

Getting ready

We need an NFS datastore. What is more important is that you inserted the Storage APIs of your storage vendor into your ESXi servers for making operations on NFSdatastores faster, (refer to the *See also* section).

How to do it...

1. Log in to vCloud as `SysAdmin`.
2. Navigate to **Manage & Monitor | Datastores and Datastore clusters**.
3. Right-click on the NFS datastore and select **Properties**.

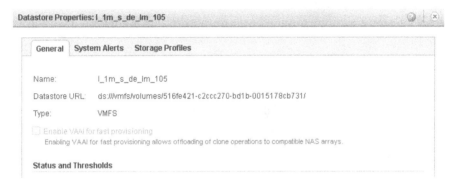

4. Check the box next to **Enable VAAI fast provisioning**.
5. Click on **OK**.

How it works...

vStorage APIs for Array Integration (**VAAI**) is basically part of the storage API of your Storage vendor and lets you offload certain operations from the ESXi host onto the storage backend. This all works only if your storage array also supports VAAI.

For instance, if you are using NetApp, you can integrate your NFS storage with ESXi. Operations such as creating snapshots or creating full clones are processed by the storage backend, not ESXi, which is much quicker. What happens, for example, is that if you offload a clone operation, a NetApp backend actually doesn't create a copy of the .vmdk file (as ESXi would do) but creates a pointer that points to the original file, taking only seconds instead of several minutes.

There's more...

Check with your storage vendor about VAAI and Storage APIs.

See also

> ► There is a very good knowledge-base article that explores VAAI. VMware knowledge base 1021976 vStorage APIs for Integration FAQ.

Working with vApp templates and their Shadows

We've learned how fast provisioning creates Shadow VMs; in the following sections we will cover how to work with them and what to do when there are problems.

Getting ready

We need a vApp template that has been deployed to OvDC that is configured with fast provisioning.

How to do it...

1. Log in to vCloud as `SysAdmin` or `DomainAdmin`.

2. Navigate to the organization you have deployed the vApp templates from.

3. Click on **Catalogs** and then on **vApp Templates**.

4. You will now see that the vApp template has a number greater than 0 in the column **Shadow VMs**. If this is not the case, you have not deployed the vApp template onto an OvDC that has fast provisioning enabled.

5. Double-click on the vApp template; you now see some details about the vApp template.

6. Click on **Shadow VMs**. This will show you where the Shadow VM is deployed and what its vSphere name is.

7. Double-click on one Shadow VM and you will see even more details.

8. Now log in to vSphere using WebClient.

9. Click on **vCenter** and then on **Hosts and Clusters**.

10. Navigate to **Resource Pools | System vDC**.

11. In System vDC you will find the Shadow VMs stored in vSphere.

How it works...

Shadow VMs are automatically created by vCloud. Shadows are not automatically destroyed, so additional copies of vApps are faster. Another important point is that if you are using VMware Chargeback, you will find that the storage for Shadow VMs is not charged to the organization but to the system, which is good news for the customer.

There's more...

You normally don't have to worry about Shadow VMs. However, what can happen is that you lose a Shadow VM for some reason. Typically, this is due to storage breakdowns or wrongful deletion. If this happens, it is not very tragic. Looking back at the initial introduction to fast provisioning, you will remember that the Shadow VM's link to its hard disk is a snapshot in itself, so if the Shadow is deleted, the linked clone VM will still be working. However, if you try to deploy another copy of the vApp template, it will fail with an error message (as seen in the next screenshot) informing you that a VM doesn't exist. If you look at the Href ID (the long number in the next screenshot) you will find that it's one of the Shadow VMs.

What you need to do is delete the reference of the Shadow VM. You can safely delete the Shadow VM in vSphere to try this out; however, it is not a recommended procedure for production.

1. Log in to vCloud as `SysAdmin` or `DomainAdmin`.

2. Navigate to the organization you deployed the vApp templates from.

3. Click on **Catalogs** and then on **vApp Templates**.

4. Double-click on the vApp template.

5. Click on **Shadow VMs**.

6. Right-click on the Shadow that is compromised and select **Delete**.

7. Ignore all error messages, refresh and delete until the Shadow VM is gone from the list.

When you are deploying a new vApp from this template, it will automatically create a new shadow.

Reducing the chain length of Linked Clones

When you are provisioning and copying VMs, the chain length of linked clones goes up and performance goes down. Here is how to shorten the chain.

Getting ready

We need a vApp that has been copied from a vApp or a vApp template.

How to do it...

1. Log in to vCloud.

2. Navigate to the vApp that has been copied.

3. Double-click on the vApp to get to the VMs.

4. Right-click on a VM and select **Properties**.

5. Click on **General**.

6. Scroll down to **Chain Length**. The value should now be **2** or more. If that's not the case, make a copy of the vApp and enter the copy.

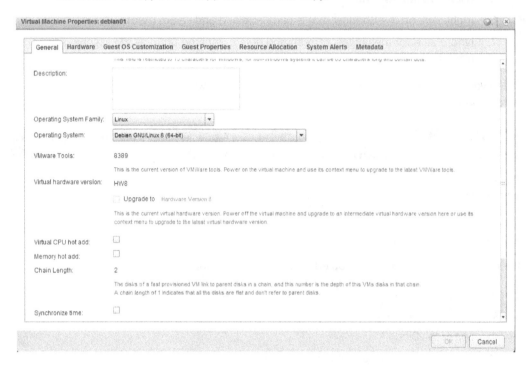

7. Click on **Cancel**.
8. Right-click again on the VM, but now select **Consolidate**.
9. Click on **Yes** if you want to collapse the disks.
10. Depending on the size of the hard disk attached to the VM, this operation can take a while. In some cases, hours.
11. Then right-click on the VM again and select **Properties**.
12. In **General**, scroll down to **Chain Length**. The value should now be **1**.

How it works...

Have a quick look at the introduction of this chapter to review how linked clones work.

What happens is that when VMs are fast provisioned, snapshots of snapshots are created. The more we do that, the more we are exchanging storage performance for storage space. As a snapshot contains only the changes between the original disk and the current state, every time a change is read it must either come from the snapshot or from the original disk. The longer the chain between the VM and its original disk, the more the files that must be read to find the data.

Consolidation takes all the information from all the snapshots and the original disk and creates a full copy of the VM. Thus, the VM is not a linked clone anymore.

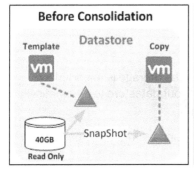
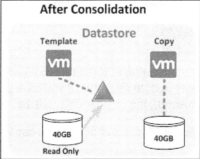
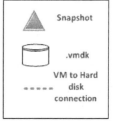

When you use linked clones across datastores, a Shadow VM is created and the chain starts afresh at the Shadow VM as it is a full clone of the original VM.

Another problem is that snapshots of VMs keep adding to the chain length. When one creates a snapshot of a VM that has a chain length of 1, the result is a VM with a chain length of 2. Another snapshot would make the chain length 3. And it goes on in this manner.

Be aware that consolidation can take a long time and will add quite some stress to the storage system—and even the network—if you are using NFS or iSCSSI without an offload. Therefore, doing a consolidation during peak business hours should be avoided.

 You can always schedule a consolidation task with vCenter Orchestrator, PowerShell, or any other API access for a weekend or at night time (beware of backup!).

Configuring storage alarms

vCloud sets an alarm automatically, reminding you about storage capacity. In the following sections we will cover setting it manually.

Getting ready

We just need one datastore that is already used in vCloud.

How to do it...

1. Log in to vCloud as `SysAdmin`.
2. Click on **Manage & Monitor** and then on **Datastores & Datastore Clusters**.

3. Select one datastore and double-click on it.

4. You can now configure here the two disk space thresholds, yellow and red.

5. Set the required amount and click on **OK**.

How it works...

vCloud automatically sets the yellow and red threshold when the Storage is imported into vCloud. However, it doesn't update its status. If you have set your datastore to automatically grow (via the storage backend), the original value will be kept.

The yellow threshold is set at 25 percent of the total capacity and the red at 15 percent of total capacity.

There's more...

Notifications and alarms can not only be used to get someone's attention but also to start scripted actions. As an example, you could run a script that creates a new datastore on a storage array, adds it to a storage profile in vCenter, and then refreshes the storage profiles in vCloud.

Monitoring storage

How do you know how much storage is used, how much is thin provisioned, and how much is free on a given profile? This recipe will show you how to answer these questions.

Getting ready

We need some datastores and profiles that have been used.

How to do it...

1. Log in to vCloud as SysAdmin.

2. Click on **Manage & Monitor** and then on **Datastores & Datastore Clusters**. Here you will find a general overview of all storage available in vCloud.

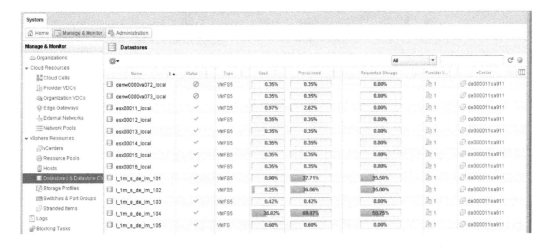

3. Double-click on a datastore and you get more detailed information. Before, you saw only percentages of the storage used, while now you also get the GB value.

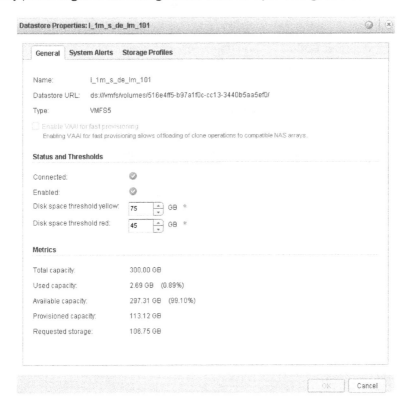

4. Click on **Storage Profiles**.

   You see a similar overview, but now all the datastores of a storage profile or the Datastore clusters are added up. You also see an overview of how many datastores a storage profile or Datastore cluster contains as well as how many PvDCs and OvDCs they are used in.

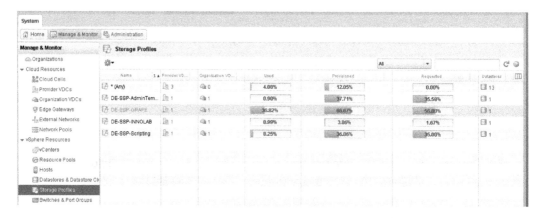

5. Click on **Provider VDCs** and then double-click on a PvDC.

6. Now click on **Datastores**. Here you find an overview of all datastores that belong to this PvDC.

7. Click on **Storage Profile**. Here you find an overview of all storage profiles that belong to this PvDC.

As `OrgAdmin` or `SysAdmin` you can also view the OvDC storage profile consumption by performing the following steps:

1. Enter the organization you would like to check out.

2. Click on **Administration** and then on **Virtual Datacentres**.

3. Double-click on the OvDC you want.

4. Click on **Storage Profile**. Here you see how much space has been requested for this storage profile. Please be mindful that it says **Requested** in the last column, but it actually means provisioned (see the next screenshot):

How it works...

In the storage overviews you see three values; here is what they mean:

- ▶ **Used**: This is the space that is used by the VMs in the datastore, including their snapshots and logfiles. This shows the amount that is currently physically allocated; if thin provisioning is used, only the amount of space used by the VM is shown.

- ▶ **Provisioned**: This is the amount of space that is reserved for VMs and shows the amount of storage that would be used if no thin provisioning were used or all the VMs were to fill up.

- ▶ **Requested**: This is the amount of storage used by the vCloud object on the datastore. These objects are all the items that are created by vCloud, such as Shadow VMs and Edge devices.

Storage can be monitored with a lot of different systems. The method shown in this recipe is one of the possible options. You may want to check the monitoring of your storage backend; however, it would only know about the storage that is committed. It also depends on whether you are using the storage offload or not. If you are using the storage offload, vCloud would not know the full story.

All this adds up to the point of really checking what you want to monitor and what systems are used.

The problems associated with the backup and restore of vCloud

You have probably been thinking of how to back up and restore your vCloud content; here are some thoughts on this.

How it works...

Surprisingly, it actually doesn't work well at all (at the time of writing this book). Most backup vendors can currently back up VMs from the vCloud quite well; however, they don't have a clear concept about restores yet.

For backups there are basically two methods. The first is to use a backup agent inside the VMs that transfers the data to be backed up via the network. Software examples would be Symantec NetBackup and IBM Tivoli. The second method is to integrate the backup with the storage backend. A software example would be CommVault. What happens here is that the backup is done by backing up the VM directories directly on the datastores.

Let's consider the downside of the storage-integrated backups first. Most backup vendors have no problem when dealing with thin-provisioned VMs, but you may want to check that first. However, linked clones (fast provisioning) can become a major problem. Have a quick look at the introduction to this chapter and you will see that VMs are actually provisioned on snapshots. So when you perform the restore, you will restore the snapshot but will also need the original source disk that the snapshot was made from. Some backup vendors are not able to do that. So it's best to check.

When we consider backing up from inside the VM, we don't have many problems with thin provisioning or linked clones as the OS itself wouldn't know about it. However, the downside is that we put an additional load onto the VM network as well as onto the CPU and memory of the VM.

The major problems arise when you restore the snapshot. To understand the problem, we need to make a small detour into how ESXi, vCenter, and vCloud store objects.

Each of the systems uses a unique identifier for each object. In ESXi, it's the UUID that is embedded in the .vmx file. In vCenter, it is the MoRef value that can be accessed via the HTTPS interface. In vCloud, it's the Href value that is accessible via the REST interface or is visible as the long number that is attached to each vCloud object in vCenter. A vCloud VM is identified by its Href in vCloud, and vCloud binds this Href to the VMs MoRef in vCenter.

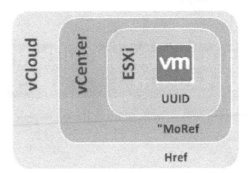

Now back to restoring. When we back up a VM from vCenter, we back up its content or its files. When the VM is restored in vCenter, the VM automatically receives a new MoRef. You can probably already see the problem. Because most backup programs interface with vCenter to recreate the VM, the Href of vCloud points to a non-existent MoRef in vCenter. As there is currently no way in the vCloud API to link an existing Href to a different MoRef, all this doesn't work. There is also currently no way to create new objects in vCloud using an existing MoRef. The only way to import a VM that has been restored in vCenter is to import it into vCloud, which is another clone action and may take quite some time.

So this leaves most backup vendors having to restore a VM back into vCenter and leaving the rest up to the admins. Most backup vendors are working on the problem and should come forward with a solution soon.

Backing up vApp templates is easier as we can just export them to vCenter or to OVF. Refer to the *Exporting a VM from vCloud* recipe in Chapter 3, *Better vApps*.

 Please see your storage and backup vendor. However, I would advise you to let him show you how a restore works.

5
Working with the vCloud API

In this chapter, we will cover topics that will introduce us to accessing the vCloud API using the most common languages. We will look at the following recipes:

- Using PowerShell with vCloud Director
- Accessing REST with Firefox
- Accessing vCD via PHP
- Using vCenter Orchestrator to automate vCloud
- A scripted cell shutdown
- Adding ISO files to vCD automatically

Introduction

The API interface of vCloud is an HTTPS-based REST interface. This is a major improvement over the vSphere API, which is SOAP-based. Most of the newer developments of VMware now come with a REST-based interface, adopting and standardizing on modern standards. The main difference between SOAP and REST is that REST can be accessed very easily and without much overhead, while SOAP advertises to clients how it needs to be addressed and what return is to be expected.

Saying that, vCloud uses REST to talk to vCNS, and SOAP to talk to the vSphere API.

The next diagram shows all the connections of the full vCloud Suite. It shows all the API interactions between the various vSphere, vCloud, and vCNS components.

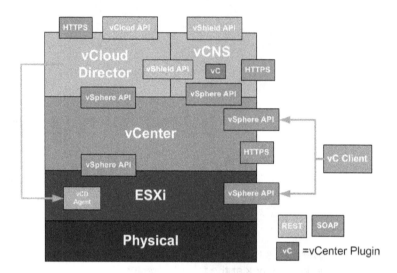

The focus of this chapter is to get you started with the different ways to access the vCloud API. It is not intended to teach you the full set of possibilities of each language or tool, but to make your first steps easier. At the end of each recipe, I will give you links that will help you get to the next level.

 One thing you really need to understand is that the vCloud web interface (the GUI) you have used until now is not using the API. This means that you can't always follow the same way in programming as you do clicking though the GUI.

You can use almost any language to automate vCloud, but there are a few ready-made solutions that make your life easier. Such ready-made solutions are provided for Microsoft PowerShell, PHP, Perl, vCenter Orchestrator, and for using direct REST calls.

For each of these methods, we will investigate:

- What we need and where to get it from
- Some install and config tips
- How to connect to vCloud
- How to get base information out of vCloud

- ▶ How to deploy a new vApp from a vApp template
- ▶ How to start a vApp

Logging in to the System organization

When you log in to vCloud using the vCloud API, you can log in to the System organization or a different organization. When you log in to vCloud, you must choose the organization in which you want to log in to by adding the organization to your username. For example, MyUser@System would log me in to the System organization (mind the capital S) and MyUser@MyOrg would log me in to the organization MyOrg.

The System organization is the highest level in vCloud and you have to be SysAdmin to successfully log in to it. In the System organization, you can do everything that you can do in vCloud and across all other organizations.

When logged in to another organization, you can only do things your role allows you.

One thing I would always do is create a user for any automation tool that accesses vCloud. This makes sure that you can easily track what the automation does in the logs, as well as shut down the access to the vCloud very fast. This is especially true when logged in to the System organization.

To successfully follow the recipes in this chapter, you need to have access to the System organization.

Gathering prerequisites and information gathering

For all our recipes we need:

- ▶ A dedicated user for the API who is SysAdmin in vCloud
- ▶ An organization and OvDC with an Organization Network that we can use
- ▶ A vApp template that we can use for deployment

In each recipe, we will have four main themes: connecting to vCloud, gathering information, creating a vApp, and powering the new vApp on.

In the section where we gather information, we will collect the information that we need in order to deploy a new vApp. To create a new vApp, we need the following information:

- ▶ The OvDC that the vApp will be deployed to
- ▶ The vApp template we want to deploy from
- ▶ The network we want to connect the new vApp to

Please note that square brackets [ ] will be used to indicate that you need to enter something into the code at this stage.

So if I write `get-Org -name [Name of Org]`, you should be writing something like `get-org -name MyOrg`.

Project Onyx

I would also keep a lookout on the Onyx project. Onyx creates automation code based on mouse clicks; however, it currently works only with vSphere Client (not the Web Client) and not with vCloud. But you should keep tabs on it. More on Onyx can be found at:

`http://communities.vmware.com/community/vmtn/automatiotools/onyx`

Using PowerShell with vCloud Director

This is how you can access vCloud using Microsoft PowerShell.

Getting ready

Please note that the vApp template we will be using should not have a network attached.

Installing PowerCLI

You need to install vSphere PowerCLI; you can download it from `www.vmware.com/go/powercli`.

When you install PowerCLI, make sure that you install it with the vCloud Director PowerCLI option, which is not installed by default. You can always reinstall PowerCLI with the correct settings. If you already have PowerCLI installed, you can re-run the installer to add the vCloud PowerCLI.

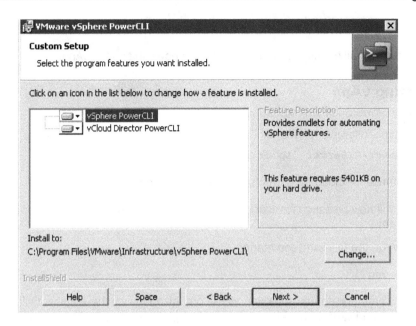

After you have installed PowerCLI, you have to run the following command in PowerShell to make it work:

```
Set-executionPolicy remotesigned
```

A PowerShell editor

A really good program to use with PowerShell is the free software PowerGUI. It helps with exploring the API and its objects. You can download it from www.powergui.org.

After you have installed PowerGUI, you need to activate the VMware libraries by performing the following steps:

1. Open the PowerGui script editor.
2. Navigate to **File | PowerShell Library**.
3. Select all VMware libraries.
4. Click on **OK**.

When you now type in the script editor pressing *Tab*, it will show all the available commands.

How to do it...

We now go through all the steps, from connecting to powering on the vApp.

Connecting vApp

1. Open PowerShell or PowerGUI Script Editor.

2. Run the following command:

   ```
   Connect-CIServer [ip or name of vCD]
   ```

   CI stands for Cloud Infrastructure; most vCloud comments begin with CI

3. You will now be asked for your credentials. Enter the user you created for accessing the API.

4. Now run the following command:

   ```
   get-Org
   ```

   This command should show you all the organizations you have currently in your vCloud and verifies that everything is working as it should

Gathering information

Now that we are logged in, let's get the information we need to deploy a vApp.

1. We will store everything in variables, so we can use it again later. Now let's get the OvDC we want. Run the following command:

   ```
   Get-OrgVdc
   ```

   It will display all the OvDCs that you currently have

2. We now select one and store it in a variable. If you like, you can just copy and paste the name of the organization in the following command:

   ```
   $OvDC = Get-OrgVdc -Name [name of the Org]
   ```

   If you are using PowerGUI, you will see that the variable $OvDC has been added to the right side. You can now use your mouse to expand the content, showing all attributes and child elements of the OvDC you stored in the variable

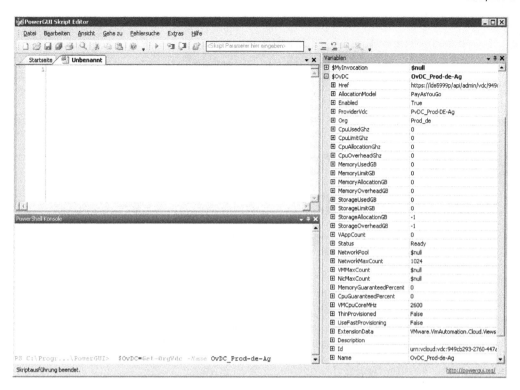

3. Let's get the Organization Network by using a pipe. The pipe we will be using is the |
symbol and it means that the result from the last command will be forwarded into the
next command as shown in the following command:

```
Get-org -Name [Org name] | Get-OrgNetwork
```

The next command shows only the Organization Networks that exists in the
organization you specified:

```
$Onet = Get-org -Name [Org name] |Get-OrgNetwork -Name [OrgNet
name]
```

4. We now get the vApp template. This time we will use a filter; however, you can still use
the direct method using the name of the template. The `where` filter is quite good for
that; playaround or look up the difference between `-like` and `-contains`. The `$_`
variable is very important in Powershell as it stores the values of the last used output.
In the next example, we basically loop through all vApp templates and look if any of
them (`$_`) have name attributes that are similar to the vApp template names.

```
$Tvapp=Get-CIVAppTemplate |where {$_.name -like "[template name]"}
```

We have now collected all the information we need, so let's deploy a new vApp.

Creating vApp

1. To create a new vApp, run the following command:

   ```
   $vApp =New-CIVApp -Name MyTest -VAppTemplate $Tvapp -OrgVdc $OvDC
   ```

   As you see, we have captured the new vApp directly in a variable to be reused later.

2. After the vApp is deployed, we now need to add a network to it. It can be done by running the following command:

   ```
   $vappNet=New-CIVAppNetwork -ParentOrgNetwork $Onet -VApp $vapp -
   Direct
   ```

3. The vApp now has a network, but we still need to attach the VM in the vApp to the network. That is easily done by running the following command:

   ```
   $vapp|Get-CIVM|Get-CINetworkAdapter|Set-CINetworkAdapter
   -VAppNetwork $vappnet -Connected $true -IPAddressAllocationMode
   Pool
   ```

   Have a look at the command. It is rather fancy. We take the vApp, get its VMs, get the VMs' network card information, and then set the same card with the new settings. This works not only for one VM inside a vApp but for all VMs and all their network cards. The pipe | here acts like the `for each` command.

You now have created a vApp and connected it to a network.

Powering on vApp

▶ The last step of powering on the vApp is very simple. It can be done by running the following command:

```
$vapp|Start-CIVApp
```

How it works...

PowerShell connects to the REST API of vCloud. This means that even if a command currently doesn't exist or doesn't do all that you expected it to do, you can always build the command by using variables. The VMware community is a big help and PowerCLI is improving fast for vCloud use.

Not all options are exposed to PowerCLI at the moment; however, if you use the command GET-CIVIEW, you will get all the arguments. As an example, have a look at the difference between the content of the two objects:

```
$temp  = get-org -name [name of an org]
$temp2 = get-org -name [name of an org]  | get-ciview
```

See also

▸ There is quite some help online in the VMware community at
http://communities.vmware.com/community/vmtn/automationtools/
powercli/vcdpowercli

▸ You can see all the PowerShell commands at http://www.vmware.com/
support/developer/PowerCLI/PowerCLI51/html/ or by navigating to
Windows on Start | **VMware** | **PowerCLI**; there you find a help file as well as
other documents

Accessing REST with Firefox

We will now access vCloud using REST directly as explained in the following sections.

Getting ready

Please note that the vApp template we will be using should have a network attached.

We first need to download and install a REST client we can play with. I prefer the Firefox
plugin, which you can download from https://addons.mozilla.org/en-US/firefox/
addon/restclient/.

After downloading and installing the client, we are ready to go.

How to do it...

We will now use the REST API to work with vCloud.

The first connection

1. Open Firefox and go to the Add On **RESTClient**.

2. Click on **Authentication** and select **Basic Authentication**.

3. Enter your vCloud username and password. The username should be in the format
myuser@System, to make sure you authenticate to the System organization of
vCloud. You may also want to check the **Remember me** box.

4. Click on **Headers** and select **Custom Header**.

5.   Enter `Accept` under **Name** and `application/*+xml;version=5.1` under Value. Check **Save to favorite** as we need this constantly and then click on **Okay**.

6.   Set **Method** to **POST** and **URL** to `https://[vcloud ip or hostname]/api/sessions`.

7.   Click on **SEND**.

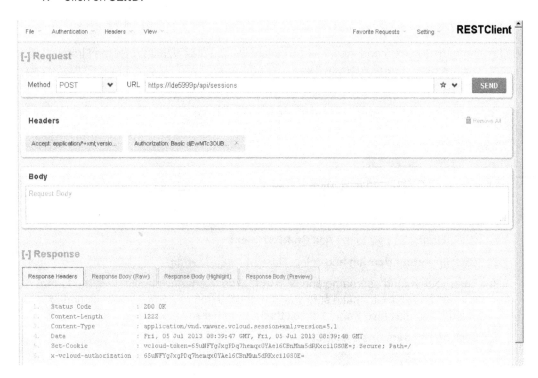

8.   You should now get a response displaying **200 OK**.

9.   When you click on the little star next to the **SEND** button, you can save this URL for later use.

10. Click on the field **Response Body (Preview)** to see the child elements that exist. We will be using this view from now on as it gives us the links to follow.

Gathering information

Now that we are logged on, let's get the information we need to deploy a vApp by performing the following steps:

1. Set the **Method** to **GET** and **URL** to …/`api/org`.

2. Click on the Href for the organization we want to deploy in. It will now be put into the **URL** window above. Notice the long number? That's the unique reference for any object.

3. Click on **SEND** and you should now see in **Response** the OvDCs and Organization Networks that are part of the organization. Under each object, you will always see all its child objects.

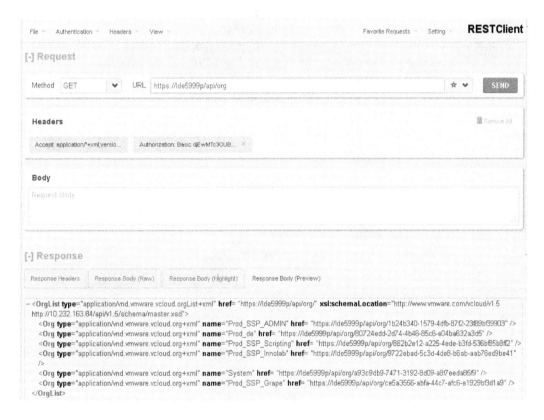

4. Copy the Href for the OvDC you want to deploy the vApp in onto a Notepad. We need that link to create the new vApp.

5. Copy the Href for the Organization Network you want to use with the vApp onto a Notepad.

6. If your vApp template is in the same organization as the one you want to deploy it in, you need to find the catalog item in the response. If not, go back to the start (`/api/org`) and click on the catalog where your vApp template is located.

7. Click on the blue Href link from the catalog and it will be automatically put into the URL, then just click on **SEND**. Work your way down to the object you want.

8. The Catalog contains the catalog items. Choose the one that contains your vApp template.

9. Copy the Href of the vApp template object onto a notepad.

10. Now, we just need to get the name of the network the vApp template was constructed with. Click on the Href for the vApp template and press **SEND**.

11. The response is a long XML message; you need to find `<NetworkConnection network=`.

12. Behind `network=` is the name of the network you created the template with; copy it to a Notepad. The name is rather important as vCloud just substitutes the original network the vApp deploys with the new one. Therefore, we need the old name and the new network reference.

Creating a new vApp

Now that we have collected all the information, let's create a new vApp. For that we need to build up the XML for the REST post.

1. Copy the Href of the OvDC into the URL and click on **SEND**.

2. Now set **Method** to **POST** and add `/action/instantiateVAppTemplate` at the end of the existing URL. It should now read like **https://myCloud/api/vdc/[href code]/action/instantiateVAppTemplate**.

3. Click on **Headers** and select **Custom Header**.

4. Enter `Content-Type` as the name and `application/vnd.vmware.vcloud.ins tantiateVAppTemplateParams+xml` as the value.

5. The header section should now contain three headers: **Authentication**, **Accept**, and **Content-Type**.

6. Now we need to add the following XML to the body. I have highlighted the lines that need to be changed.

    ```
    <InstantiateVAppTemplateParams
      xmlns="http://www.vmware.com/vcloud/v1.5"
      name="[MyNewvApp]"
      deploy="true"
      powerOn="false"
      xmlns:xsi="http://www.w3.org/2001/XMLSchema-instance"
    ```

```
xmlns:ovf="http://schemas.dmtf.org/ovf/envelope/1">
<Description>[My New vApp]</Description>
<InstantiationParams>
<NetworkConfigSection>
        <ovf:Info>Configuration parameters for logical
          networks</ovf:Info>
        <NetworkConfig
          networkName="[Old vApp Template Network NAME]">
          <Configuration>
            <ParentNetwork
              href="[href of the OrgNe]" />
            <FenceMode>bridged</FenceMode>
          </Configuration>
        </NetworkConfig>
    </NetworkConfigSection>
  </InstantiationParams>
 <Source href="[href of the vApp Template]" />
    <AllEULAsAccepted>true</AllEULAsAccepted>
</InstantiateVAppTemplateParams>
```

7. When all the preceding code is put in, click on **SEND**.

8. If you did anything wrong, a long error message appears as the response; scroll to the very end to see what is wrong.

9. If everything is correct, the response you get back is a vApp. The new Href is in the <VApp> object. Copy the vApp Href onto a Notepad; we will need it to power it on.

Powering on

1. Set **Method** to **Post**.

2. Delete the content type from the header and the content from the body.

3. Copy the new vApp Href from the last step into the **URL** field and add /power/action/powerOn at the end. The URL should now look something like **https://myCloud/api/vApp/[href code]/power/action/powerOn**.

4. Alternatively, you could start with /api/org and click through to the vApp you created, and then look for power on. There is a Href with the action attached to it.

5. Click on **SEND**.

How it works...

It is clear that the example we saw on how to use the vCloud REST API is not really the best way to automate vCloud. What is shown here is how the REST API works and how objects are constructed. Every language that connects to the vCloud must use the API and the way it works. If you can do something in REST, you can use the same methods to recreate it in any of the languages. Have a look at the way PHP creates a new vApp; it is quite similar.

As I mentioned before, the vCloud GUI doesn't use the REST interface. This means that you can't always follow the way the vCloud API does things. Create a new vApp via the GUI and you will see that you can define the VM name and the VM hostname, as well as the network IP. Using the REST API, you will need to perform all the previous steps in this recipe after the vApp is created.

See also

▶ *vCloud Director API Reference* at `http://pubs.vmware.com/vcd-51/index.jsp`. After the website opens, click on vCloud API Schema Reference

▶ vCloud API Community at `http://communities.vmware.com/community/vmtn/developer/forums/vcloudapi`

Accessing vCD via PHP

This is how you use PHP to work with vCloud.

Getting ready

Download the PHP vCloud API for vCloud from `http://www.vmware.com/go/vcloudsdkforphp`.

I assume you will use PHP on Linux, so you might need a Linux VM with PHP libraries and the PHP base configuration. You probably need the `HTTP_Request2` and `Net_URL2` libraries.

Untar the download into the directory from where you would like to use the files. Place the new script in the main directory (`vCloudPHP-5.1.2`). You can move them; however, that requires you to reconfigure the pointer to the libraries.

If you are playing on a Windows environment, the base install might be different and you will need to follow the instructions that come with the Windows installer.

How to do it...

In this section, we will create a program that will deploy a new VMs from a command line. We will put some variables inside the program and some to use via the command line. The script we are using is an adapted and simplified version of the base `hellovcloud.php` script that ships with the vCloud API in the sample folder.

Also, it might be interesting to compare the REST approach (see the previous recipe) to the PHP approach as they are rather similar.

Base PHP skeleton

1. First we create the skeleton of the PHP script:

```php
<?php
// add library to the include_path
set_include_path(implode(PATH_SEPARATOR, array('.','/library',
                          get_include_path(),)));

require_once 'VMware/VCloud/Helper.php';
require_once dirname(__FILE__) . '/config.php';
 [put script here]
?>
```

2. Then we need to define the input options from the command line. Put everything that follows from now on between `<?php ?>` tags.

```php
// Define the input paramaters
$longs   = array(
     "vm:", //the vApp name
     "vdc:",   //the OvDC we are deploying to
     "onet::",   //the ONet we will be connecting the VM to.
);
$shorts  = "";
$opts = getopt($shorts, $longs);

// loop through command arguments
foreach (array_keys($opts) as $opt) switch ($opt)
{
    case "vm":
         $vAppName = $opts['vm'];
         break;
    case "vdc":
         $vdcName = $opts['vdc'];
         break;
    case "onet":
         $OrgNetName= $opts['onet'];
         break;
}
```

Because we don't want to define everything through the command line, we are making some variables static. If you wonder about the $TNet, the name of the vApp template network, have a quick look at the REST section, where it is explained.

```php
//Connection variables
$server = "[vCloud Server]";
$user= '[username]@System';
```

```
$pswd= '[Password]';

//initialize some other variables
  $vAppTempName = "[vapp template name]";
  $TNet="[name of the network the template was build with]";
  $vdcRef=null;
$vAppTemplateRef=null;
```

Connecting to vCloud

1. Let's connect to the vCloud.

```
$httpConfig = array('ssl_verify_peer'=>false,
    'ssl_verify_host'=>false);
$service = VMware_VCloud_SDK_Service::getService();
$service->login($server, array('username'=>$user,
    'password'=>$pswd), $httpConfig);
```

Gathering information

Now, let's gather all the information we still need to create a new vApp.

We need to get the object reference (called SDK Object) for the OvDC. I will explain all the steps as comments (//) in the following code:

```
//get ovDC ref
$OrgRefs=$service->getOrgRefs();
//get all Orgs from vCloud
foreach ($OrgRefs as $OrgRef) {
//loop thought all Orgs to find OvDC
  $sdkOrg = $service->createSDKObj($OrgRef);
//make Org SDK object out of Org Reference
  $vdcRefs = $sdkOrg->getVdcRefs($vdcName);
//get all the OvDCs in the Org that match the name $vdcName
  if (1 == count($vdcRefs))
  {
      $vdcRef=$vdcRefs[0];
//Found!
    break;
  }
}
if (!$vdcRefs){
//not found
    exit("No OvDC $vdcName found\n");
}
$sdkVdc = $service->createSDKObj($vdcRef);
//make a OvDC SDK object out of OvDC ref
```

Now that we found the SDK Object of the OvDC, let's get the Organization Network.

```
//get ONet Ref
$netRefs = $sdkOrg->getOrgNetworkRefs($OrgNetName);
//as we know what we are looking for we can search directly for it
if (0 == count($netRefs))
{
    exit("Onet $OrgNetName not found\n");
}
$netRef = $netRefs[0];
$pnetwkRef = VMware_VCloud_SDK_Helper::createReferenceTypeObj(
                                    $netRef->get_href(),
'ParentNetwork');
//to connect the Network directly we need to get the parent network
reference.
```

Last but not least, we need the template `Ref`. We use the same method we used in the OvDC. We loop through all Orgs and all OvDCs to find the vApp template.

```
//get Template
$TOrgRefs=$service->getOrgRefs();
foreach ($TOrgRefs as $TOrgRef) {
  $TsdkOrg = $service->createSDKObj($TOrgRef);
  $TvdcRefs = $sdkOrg->getVdcRefs();
  foreach ($TvdcRefs as $TvdcRef) {
    $TsdkVdc = $service->createSDKObj($TvdcRef);
    $vAppTemplateRefs = $TsdkVdc-
  >getVAppTemplateRefs($vAppTempName);
    if ($vAppTemplateRefs)
    {
        $vAppTemplateRef = $vAppTemplateRefs[0];
      break 2;
    }
  }
}
if (!$vAppTemplateRef){
    exit("No vAppTemplate with name $vAppTempName is found\n");
}
```

Creating a new vApp

Now it is time to create a new vApp. I would recommend having a look at the REST section and to spot the similarities.

```
$info = new VMware_VCloud_API_OVF_Msg_Type();
$info->set_valueOf("Configuration parameters for logical
  networks");
```

```
$conf = new VMware_VCloud_API_NetworkConfigurationType();
$conf->setParentNetwork($pnetwkRef);
$conf->setFenceMode('bridged');

$netconf = new VMware_VCloud_API_VAppNetworkConfigurationType();
$netconf->set_networkName($TNet);
$netconf->setConfiguration($conf);

$section = new VMware_VCloud_API_NetworkConfigSectionType();
$section->setInfo($info);
$section->setNetworkConfig(array($netconf));

$iparams = new VMware_VCloud_API_InstantiationParamsType();
$iparams->setSection(array($section));

$params = new
  VMware_VCloud_API_InstantiateVAppTemplateParamsType();
$params->set_name($vAppName);
$params->setDescription("Something");
$params->setInstantiationParams($iparams);
$params->setSource($vAppTemplateRef);

$vApp=$sdkVdc->instantiateVAppTemplate($params);
```

Powering on the vApp

After we instantiated the vApp, we need to find it and then power it on. Between the instantiate command and the `powerOn` command, there should be enough time for vCloud to finish creating the new vApp; we will wait until the task of instantiating has finished.

```
$tasks = $vApp->getTasks()->getTask();
    if ($tasks)
    {
        $task = $tasks[0];
        $service->waitForTask($task);
    }
```

Now we need to get the SDK object of the new vApp.

```
$vAppRefs = $sdkVdc->getVAppRefs($vAppName);
$vAppRef = $vAppRefs[0];
$sdkVApp = $service->createSDKObj($vAppRef);
```

Now we just need to power the vApp on.

```
$params = new VMware_VCloud_API_DeployVAppParamsType();
$params->set_powerOn(true);
$params->set_deploymentLeaseSeconds(null);

$sdkVApp->deploy($params);
```

How it works...

PHP is one of the easy ways to get vCloud automation going from Linux; however, it works just as well in Windows. The main reason for using PHP is that you could put the program directly into a web server and create your own little web server that provisions VMs automatically.

See also

▸ The help files come with the download, go to the directory `[download location]/vcloudPHP-5.1.2/docs/`

▸ PHP Language reference at `Php.net`

▸ VMware PHP vCloud community at `http://communities.vmware.com/community/vmtn/developer/forums/vcloudsdkphp`

Using vCenter Orchestrator to automate vCloud

We now look into automation using vCenter Orchestrator (vCO).

Getting ready

You need to download the vCO appliance (version 5.1 or better) from VMware. vCO is part of the normal vSphere software bundle. The appliance is preconfigured with an internal DB and LDAP and makes getting started with vCO easier. If you are already using vCO as a Windows install, that's fine.

After downloading, installing, and configuring vCO, we are ready to go. If you need some help with configuring, refer the *See also* section of this recipe.

How to do it...

The first connection

First we need to connect the downloaded vCO to our vCloud by performing the following steps:

1. Open a web browser and go to `https://[vCO URL]`.
2. Click on **Orchestrator Configuration**.
3. Log in to the configurator.
4. Click on **Network** and then on **SSL Trust Manager**.
5. Enter the URL of your vCloud Director in **Import from URL** and then click on **Import**. This will add the SSL cert of your vCloud Director to the vCO-accepted SSL certs.
6. Now click on **vCloud Director (5.1)**.
7. Click on **New vCloud Director Connection**.

8. Fill out the form:
    1. Enter the URL for your vCloud into **Host**.
    2. Put `System` (capital S) into **Organization**.
    3. Choose **Basic Authentication** in **Authentication strategy**.
    4. Check **Shared session**.
    5. Enter your API users' credentials.

9. Click on **Apply changes**.

10. You should now have a new entry in the vCloud Director settings and vCO should now be ready to connect to this vCloud.

Gathering information

We will depart from the pattern we have established as vCO doesn't work that way. Instead, we will have a quick look at how vCO works.

We will now create a new workflow that will create a new vApp and power it on. This is a longer recipe, but it will teach you a lot.

1. Log in to vCO:

    1. Open a web browser and go to `https://[vCO URL]`.

    2. Click on **Start Orchestrator Client**.

    3. Log in to vCO.

    4. On the top is the drop-down menu; enter it and select **Designer**.

2. Create a new workflow:

    1. Right-click on your user name and select **New Folder**. Give it a name (for example, `MyStuff`) and click on **OK**.

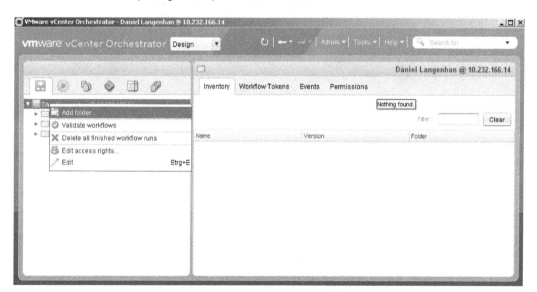

    2. Right-click on the folder and select **New workflow**.

    3. Give it a name (for example, `MyFistWorkFlow`).

    4. You now see the editor window of the workflow.

3. Add elements to the workflow:

   1. Click on **Schema**.

   2. Select **Workflow element** from the **Generic** elements and drag it between the green arrow (at the start of the workflow) and the grey circle (at the end of the workflow). A window will appear; enter into the search text `Instantiate`. As you type, you will see that you get fewer choices. Select the **Instantiate a vApp Template** workflow and click on **Select**.

   3. Choose the workflow element again and drag it between the instantiate and end markers.

   4. Select the **Power on a vApp** workflow.

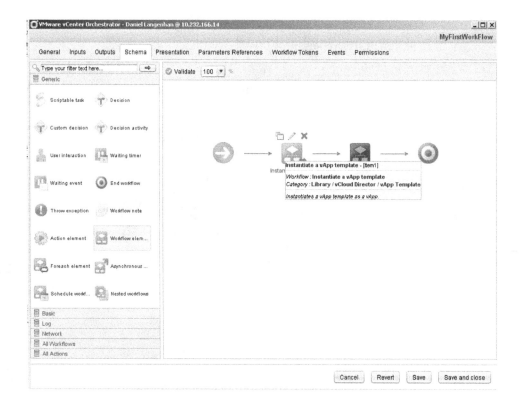

4. Deal with the IN and OUT attributes of workflows:

   1. Now, we need to define the variables (in vCO language attributes). Move your mouse over the **Instantiate** workflow and then click on the pencil icon that appears.

   2. In the window that opens, click on **IN**. Here are all the attributes that the Instantiate workflow needs in order to work. We will now go and define them.

3. Each attribute has **Not set** in the column **Source Parameter**. Click on the first **Not set**; another window opens.

4. Click on **Create parameter/attribute in workflow**.

5. In the next window that appears, just click on **OK**. It will create this attribute with the default name in our workflow.

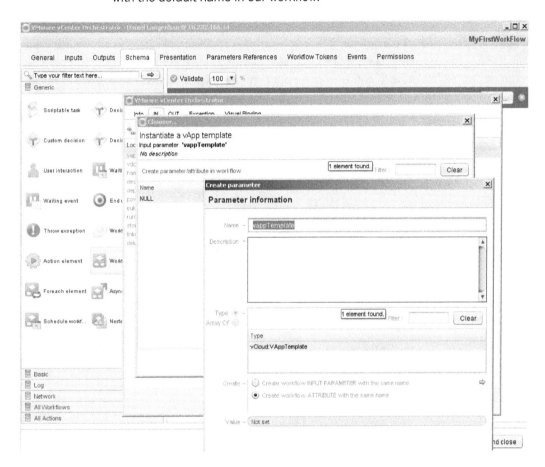

6. Repeat the process with all the inputs.

7. Now move on to the **OUT** section. There is only one attribute, vappOut; repeat the above process.

8. Click on **Close**.

9. Now move on to the **Power On** workflow. In the **IN** section, there is only one variable called **vApp** and you will see that it is now already automatically mapped to **vappOut**. **vappOut** is the reference of the new vApp we will create with the Instantiate workflow. You can click on **Close** as this element has already been configured by vCO.

5. General, input, and output attributes:

1. Click on **General**. You will find that all the variables you created are collected here. We will now configure some static variables and move the others to the **Inputs** section. Attributes in the **Inputs** section will prompt the user for an input. Attributes in the **General** section are static.

2. We will ask the user for the name of the new vApp. Move it to the **Inputs** section by right-clicking on the **Name** attribute and selecting **move as the INPUT** parameter.

3. We will select a static template, meaning we will not ask the user for it. But we still have to define what we put into it, so click on **Not set** next to the attribute.

4. A new window will open showing you the content of your vCloud. Navigate to the vApp template you want to use to deploy and click on **Select**.

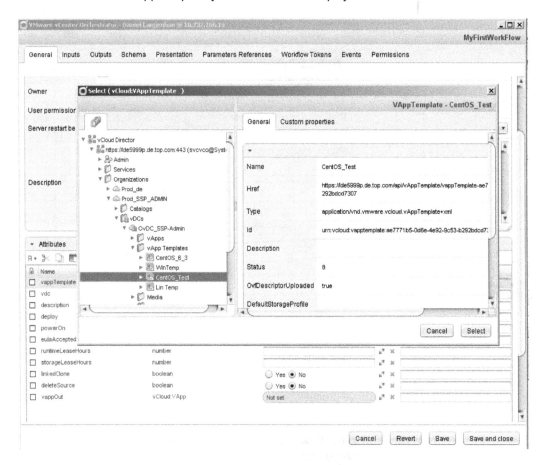

5. Continue to choose what input you will ask the user for and what you define yourself static.

6. Verify the workflow:

    1. Click on **Save and Close**.

    2. A window will pop up telling you that the workflow isn't validated. That's expected at this stage and I wanted to show this to you. Click on **See details**.

    3. The validation will show you that the **vAppOut** attribute of the **Power On** workflow element has not been set properly. Click on **Bind Attribute** and then select **vAppOut**.

    4. Select the **vappOut** attribute and bind it to the output.

    5. Click on **OK**.

    6. Click again on **Save and Close**.

7. Version control:

    1. Now a window will appear asking you if you would like to increase the version number; do so.

    2. You are back in the workflow folder. You can now explore your workflow without editing. Go explore a bit.

Creating a new vApp and powering it on

Now that we created a complete new workflow, let's run it.

1. Right-click on the workflow we created and select **Start Workflow...**.

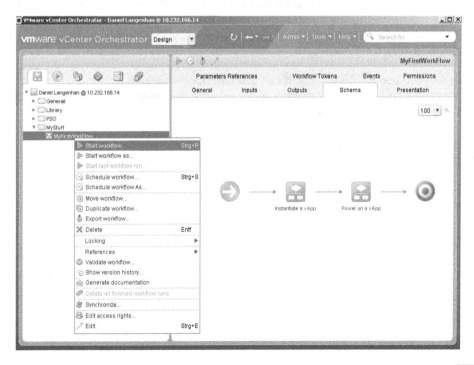

2. vCO will now pop up a window that asks you for your input. Answer all the questions.

3. Watch the workflow execute; see how it goes into subworkflows and starts filling up the log.

4. After the workflow has run, you will see that it keeps the runs stored under the workflow. You can go back into the run and have a look at the attributes and logs.

How it works...

vCenter Orchestrator is quite a powerful tool to use. It can not only interact with vCloud but also with vCenter. In addition to that, you can download and install plugins that allow you to use SSH, PowerShell, REST, or SQL to communicate with other systems.

Each of the plugins need to be installed via the vCO configuration tool, but can then also be accessed via vCO. Each of the plugins bring pre-created example workflows as well as a lot of small useful scripts (called Actions in vCO).

There's more...

vCenter Orchestrator not only lets you build workflows but also allows you to create webviews. Webviews are small web pages where workflows are displayed and can be started from. This allows for automation using a web browser. You should have a look at it as it is rather cool.

Last but not least, you can call vCO workflows via HTTPS, start them, check on their status, and get the result. This makes it very easy to add vCO as the domain-scripting solution for all things VMware. Remember that you can script vCenter via vCO directly and vShield via the REST plugin for vCO.

Not only can vCO use HTTPS but also it can use AMPQ, which allows for a more modern approach on the subject of automating a whole VMware, Windows, Linux, Storage, and Network environment.

See also

▶ VMware vCenter Orchestrator at `http://www.vmware.com/support/pubs/orchestrator_pubs.html`

▶ A brief document on how to get vCO working at `http://communities.vmware.com/docs/DOC-20368`

▶ If you would like to learn more about vCO, I recommend the book *Automating vSphere with VMware vCenter Orchestrator* by *Cody Bunch, VMware Press Technology*

A scripted cell shutdown

We will now create a more controlled shutdown of vCloud.

Getting ready

This script that you create will be running on the vCloud Director VM itself, so we need to be able to log in to the VM and become a root user.

You also need a user account, that is `SysAdmin` in order to execute the script.

How to do it...

There are two ways to get the script into the vCloud VM:

- Copy/paste via SSH:
    1. Log in to the vCloud Director VM via a SSH Client (for example, Putty).
    2. Gain root access, if you haven't already.
    3. Type the command `vi /sbin/vCloud-Shutdown`.
    4. The text editor vi opens. Press the *i* key.
    5. Copy and paste the code into vi.
    6. Press the keys *w* and *q* to save and quit vi.
    7. Run the command `chmod 744 /sbin/vCloud-Shutdown`.

- Copy via SCP or SFTP:
    1. Open up a connection to the vCloud Director VM with an SCP (WinSCP).
    2. Copy the program to `/sbin/`.
    3. Close the connection.
    4. Log in to the vCloud Director VM via an SSH Client (for example, Putty).
    5. Gain root access, if you haven't already.
    6. Run the command `chmod 744 /sbin/vCloud-Shutdown`.

The script

The script is given as follows:

```
#!/bin/bash

VCLOUD_HOME=/opt/vmware/vcloud-director/bin
VCDUSER="vcdadmin"
```

```
VCDPASS="mypassword"
#
# check if cell is running
#
STATUS=$($VCLOUD_HOME/cell-management-tool -u $VCDUSER -p $VCDPASS
  cell -status 2>&1 |  grep -i "is active = ")
echo "STATUS :: $STATUS"

case $STATUS in
  *true)
    $VCLOUD_HOME/cell-management-tool -u $VCDUSER -p $VCDPASS cell
  -quiesce true

    while [[ true ]];do
      ACTIVE=$( $VCLOUD_HOME/cell-management-tool -u $VCDUSER -p
$VCDPASS cell -status | sed -n 's/Job count = \([0-9]*\)/\1/p')
      if [[ ACTIVE -eq 0 ]];then
                  break
          fi
          sleep 60
    done
    RESULT=$($VCLOUD_HOME/cell-management-tool -u $VCDUSER -p
$VCDPASS cell -shutdown)

    service vmware-vcd status

    while [[ true ]];do
            count=$(service vmware-vcd status | grep "is not
            running" | wc -l)
          if [[ $count -eq 2 ]];then
                  break
          fi
          sleep 10
      echo -n .
      RESULT=$($VCLOUD_HOME/cell-management-tool -u $VCDUSER -p
        $VCDPASS cell -shutdown)
    done
    echo $(service vmware-vcd status)
    ;;
  *false)
    ACTIVE=$( $VCLOUD_HOME/cell-management-tool -u $VCDUSER -p
      $VCDPASS cell -status | sed -n 's/Job count = \([0-
      9]*\)/\1/p')
    if [[ ACTIVE -ne 0 ]];then
      echo "JOBS active ($ACTIVE), wait ..."
```

```
$VCLOUD_HOME/cell-management-tool -u $VCDUSER -p $VCDPASS
  cell -quiesce true

while [[ true ]];do
  ACTIVE=$( $VCLOUD_HOME/cell-management-tool -u $VCDUSER -p
    $VCDPASS cell -status | sed -n 's/Job count = \([0-9]*\)/\1/
p')
  if [[ ACTIVE -eq 0 ]];then
              break
        fi
        sleep 30
    echo -n .
  done
  RESULT=$($VCLOUD_HOME/cell-management-tool -u $VCDUSER -p
    $VCDPASS cell -shutdown)

  service vmware-vcd status

  while [[ true ]];do
            count=$(service vmware-vcd status | grep "is not
              running" | wc -l)
            if [[ $count -eq 2 ]];then
                    break
            fi
            sleep 10
    echo -n .
    RESULT=$($VCLOUD_HOME/cell-management-tool -u $VCDUSER -p
      $VCDPASS cell -shutdown)
    done
    echo $(service vmware-vcd status)
  fi
  ;;
*)
  echo "Status :: $STATUS :: don't know what to do"
  ;;
esac
```

How it works...

Let's see why we have built the preceding program in the first place. We can shut down the vCD VM using vCenter, by using the command `service vmware-vcd stop`.

Using the `service` command to shutdown vCD has a disadvantage: it just stops vCD regardless of operations that are currently under way. In the user manual of vCloud, the proper shutdown of a vCloud cell is shown using the `cell-management-tool` tool.

The `cell-management-tool` tool is found in the `/opt/vmware/vcloud-director/bin/` directory. You require a vCD `SysAdmin` account to operate it. To shut down vCD properly, you first have to quiesce the cell by using the command `cell-management-tool -u VCLOUDUSER -p VCLOUDPASS cell -quiesce true`.

Where VCLOUDUSER is your vCD `SysAdmin` account, just the account no `@System` is required and VCLOUDPASS is the corresponding password. After you quiesce the cell, you should check if any jobs are still running by using the command `cell-management-tool [user and pass] cell -status`.

When the Job Count reaches zero, you can shut down the cell by running the command `cell-management-tool [user and pass] cell -shutdown`.

Now, you can check the status of the vCD cell with the command `service vmware-vcd status`.

After the cell is shut down, you can do the maintenance of the VM or shut down the VM.

Starting vCD is always via the command `service vmware-vcd start`.

However, if you have just updated vCD or recovered from an error, it is advised to monitor the messages log; the best command for that is `Tail -f /opt/vmware/vcloud-director/log/vcloud-container-debug.log`.

For more information refer to *Chapter 8, Troubleshooting vCloud.*

There's more...

Another slightly annoying problem with scripts is that they contain the `SysAdmin` password of vCD in clear text. There are a lot of ways around that; here is one of the easiest while not the most secure:

1. Create a text file with the vCloud `SysAdmin` password in clear text. Save it in the `/opt/vmware/vcloud-director` directory. Give it permissions that only root can read (700 root:root); you can also hide it by using . at the beginning of the filename.

2. Then add the following lines at the beginning of the preceding script:

   ```
   PWFILE=/opt/vmware/vcloud-director/.pwfile
   if [[ ! -f $PWFILE ]];then
           echo "No pwfile found"
           exit
   fi
   ```

3. Now, replace every occurrence of -p $VCLOUDPASS with -p 'cat $PWFILE'.

Adding ISO files to vCD automatically

Here is a good programming idea that you can now create. It's not easy, but a neat challenge and a very useful little program to have a go at.

Getting ready

Choose a language or tool of your choice. If you don't have a preferred one, think about which system will interact with the program or which platform you will be running the script under.

How to do it...

First, we need to define what the program should do:

▸ We want to upload a .iso file from the local disk of your desktop

▸ We want to add the .iso file to a catalog in vCloud

Here are the programming steps you need to do:

1. Create an object that contains the media filename and location as well as the type ISO.

2. Get the OvDC reference where the catalog we want to upload is stored.

3. Get the catalog reference.

4. Upload the media to the catalog.

5. Wait for the task to finish.

How it works...

To learn a programming language and an API is hard. The first reference you should consult is the API reference of vCloud. I normally start with the REST API as it shows me what is possible, whereas the specific language references show me only what has been implemented as methods so far.

I found people who posted programs that uploaded media in Powershell and PHP. Doing it in vCO isn't that difficult because there is already a workflow you can use as a base.

> Why do I think this is a useful little program? Think about a loop you could put in there and upload all the ISOs into one library; then go home while everything is being automated.

6
Improving the vCloud Design

In this chapter, we will focus on some quick and simple recipes that let you develop a deeper understanding of how to design a vCloud. We will look at the following recipes:

- ▸ Creating a naming standard
- ▸ Using service accounts in the vCloud environment
- ▸ Setting up networks for the vCloud VM
- ▸ Working with vCloud roles
- ▸ Keeping your templates under control
- ▸ Choosing the right Allocation Model
- ▸ Using OvDCs for compute tiering
- ▸ Understanding how the different vCloud types impact the design
- ▸ Retrofitting a shared directory into an existing vCD Cell
- ▸ Connecting more than one vCloud Cell to the same infrastructure
- ▸ Creating multiple vCD Cells for the same vCloud
- ▸ Load balancing vCD
- ▸ Working with catalogs in vCloud 5.5

Introduction

VMware vCloud is quite a complex application as you have already found out; therefore, it is extremely important to create a stable, simple, and expandable design.

Design is one of the most important things of a vCloud deployment; it can have long-lasting financial implementation. To explain what is going on, I will use the following example:

When you plant an apple tree, you can see it grow and it will bear fruit; this fruit will be small to start with, but will grow with the tree. As time passes by, the tree grows more leaves and branches, and then the apples start to shrink.

A design is like a guide for pruning, fertilizing, and the poles that guide the tree growth. It makes sure the apples stay big and juicy.

A design specifies how and why things are done, how things fit together, and specifies concepts that need to be adapted. Some typical features one should look for in a vCloud design are:

- How is vCloud integrated with vSphere?

- How many Cells are used and where load balancing is done?

- How does the underlying vSphere infrastructure influence the vCloud (for example, cluster settings)?

- How and with what other systems does vCloud interact (for example, vSphere and vCNS)?

- What is your default decision when it comes to storage or compute tiering? What about the OvDC allocation models?

Another important part of a complete design is that multiple documents are created. I personally go for a layered solution, meaning that I have at least three different document types (or sections in one document) as follows:

- **Design document**: The design document captures general decisions and how things work.

- **Configuration document**: The configuration document contains all the settings for a specific system. These include specialized settings such as IPs, Allocation Model settings, and Organization settings.

- **Build document**: The build document shows how to build a system using the settings from the configuration document. This can be as easy as a screenshot collection to more deceptive versions.

These documents are layered as you have different kinds of information that overlay over one another, creating a complete picture.

Designing a vCloud system isn't a task that can be done in a hurry. For example, if you choose the wrong allocation model for your OvDCs, you will have to shut down all already deployed vApps and move them to a new OvDC (and maybe even storage profile), which can take quite some time. While you do that, you interrupt (in the worst case) a production environment or block developers doing their work. The worst-case scenario ever can be when you choose the wrong vSphere layer below and have to lift or recreate everything. You may be able to imagine the financial impact on a business or on your own job.

Creating a naming standard

One of the things that most people forget is to create a good naming standard.

Getting ready

You need something where you can publish the naming standard for people to read. The other important point is to make sure and to enforce that the naming standard is followed. A standard is not worth creating if it's not followed.

How to do it...

This recipe is a bit different from all the others as it doesn't contain step-by-step instructions. A naming standard is something that needs to be developed. I will give you all the pointers that you should look out for.

vSphere naming standard

It is important to have a naming standard not only for your vCloud object but also for the underlying vSphere objects.

- **ESXi hostname**: You probably already have a working naming standard for hostnames; however, you might like to rethink it a bit. With blade centers such as HP c7000s or Cisco UCS, it might actually make sense to consider an ESXi Server as a resource that can be redistributed. As ESXi Servers can be added quickly and moved easily between clusters (using vSphere Host Profiles). A good naming standard would be to number the ESXi Server instead of individually naming them.

- **vSphere cluster naming**: Clusters have multiple purposes, and the naming standard should explain what they are for. Clusters in vSphere and clusters in vCloud have different purposes. In vCloud, they are normally the source of a PvDC, and each PvDC has different purposes. For example, you want a production PvDC to use HA, while a development PvDC doesn't need it. So consider HA and its settings, location, and purpose as well as the ESXi Servers that are deployed in this cluster.

- **Resource pools**: Resource pools should not impact vCloud, as vCloud creates them themselves. The exception, however, is that if you don't have enough ESXi Servers for several clusters and you want to use resource pools as a source for PvDCs, then it's a good idea to create a naming standard for them.

- **Port group naming**: Port groups (that you create yourself) are directly responsible for External Networks that we need a lot. But mostly the normal naming standard is enough. Something that contains the VLAN ID works well. As you can name the External Network in vCloud, whatever you want, it is not such a problem. However, think about something that your network team will understand.

- **Storage profile or Datastore cluster**: The storage profile naming is important, as when you import the storage profile, you *cannot* create a vCloud object with a different name. So, the vSphere name is the vCloud name. You might want to choose something that helps users decide where they should store their VMs. You should probably include storage tiering in the naming standard. See also the *Using storage profiles for storage tiering* recipe in *Chapter 4, Datastores and Storage Profiles*.

- **User-defined storage capability**: As in most cases, there is a one-to-one relationship between storage capability and storage profile/cluster, and people normally use the same naming convention as for the profiles/clusters.

- **Datastore naming**: The Datastore naming again isn't so important for vCloud, but it should be something that your storage team understands so that you can communicate easily with them.

> Don't forget that vCloud creates its own objects on vSphere using its own naming standard.

vCloud naming standard

The vCloud objects are basically split into two categories: objects that can be seen only by admins and objects that are visible to customers. The customer-facing objects can be seen by admins too; however, it's the customers who need to be able to understand what these objects are. Let us discuss the objects that are visible to the admins first:

- **vCloud Director Cell**: A vCloud Cell is one installation of vCloud Director on one VM; therefore, it is the VM hostname and cannot be changed.

- **Provider vDC (PvDC)**: PvDCs are a bit easier as they can be coupled with the clusters or resource pools that are the source of the PvDC. However, you might like to contemplate a different approach and name the PvDC after its purpose or location.

▶ **External Networks**: As already mentioned, External Networks are direct links to the port groups in vSphere. You can use the already existing naming standard for port groups or add more information about their purposes. As you can easily figure out which port group belongs to which External Network, communicating with your network team isn't an issue. However, you might like to add more information about the network specifications.

▶ **Network Pools**: Network Pools come in only three varieties that you can name. VXLAN Network Pools are named automatically by vCloud and cannot be renamed. You may like to create a naming standard that contains information regarding what kind of pool it is and what its capacity is. Also, I would recommend putting the VLAN ID in the pool name.

Now let's move on to the objects that are visible to the customers. Be aware that a customer might also create some of them himself, and therefore they may have their own standards:

▶ **Organization**: When you name an organization, you should think about what an organization represents in your vCloud. It comes down to the design and whether organizations are used for projects, departments, or external customers. Think about easy-to-access links for the customers as well as if anyone will actually log in or if the organization is only for automation purposes.

▶ **Organization vDC (OvDC)**: OvDCs are all about allocation models. Remember that an organization can have multiple OvDCs and that each is part of a PvDC. So computer-tiering is mostly done here and should be represented in the naming standard. When users deploy a vApp, they need to choose an OvDC, so making it something that people understand easily is the key. You could also put information about the allocation model in the name.

▶ **Organization Networks**: Organization Networks come in three varieties, and a naming standard helps in understanding what one connects a vApp or VM to. It should contain the type and maybe the purpose and to what it connects.

▶ **Catalog**: A catalog, especially a published one, needs a name that lets customers understand what they are looking at. You could probably include the publishing organization, the content one would expect, and maybe the level of access the customer will have.

▶ **vApp**: Naming vApps can be interesting. A customer might just like something simple such as `MyTest2` or something more complex. vApp naming must be unique in the same organization. Also, remember that vApps can contain multiple VMs, and therefore, naming it after the VM is not such a good solution. Also, be aware that there is a limit of 3,000 vApps per organization in vCloud 5.1.

▶ **vApp template**: Templates should have a clear naming that conveys what they are for and what they do. It even makes sense to introduce a version number into the naming standard. Typical things I use are words such as vanilla to indicate that the template is a plain OS installed without any extra configuration. See also the *Working with catalogs in vCloud 5.5* recipe in this chapter.

> ▸ **Edge gateway**: The naming for Edges is not easy as they can contain a lot of options that are also susceptible to change. Good names contain an idea where the Edge connects to and for the purpose it was set up.

> ▸ **vApp Networks**: vApp Networks are again as bad as vApp names; they come in two varieties and one vApp can have multiples of each. Typical names have a relation to what they are used for and what their purposes are.

> ▸ **Roles**: Last but not least, we have roles. Roles are customer-facing, but are defined in the system. Think about the fact that you might have different organizations that require different roles, and that Org Admins would see *all* the roles that are created in the system.

Example of a naming standard notation

The following is an example of how I note down a naming standard; you don't need to follow it, but it may get you started to find your own notation:

```
OvDC_<CountryCode>_C<Compute tier>
   <CountryCode>
      de = Germany
      au = Australia
   <Compute tier>
      G = Gold
      S = Silver
      B = Bronze
```

How it works...

One of the reasons a naming standard is extremely good is automation. Have a look at *Chapter 5, Working with the vCloud API*, where we needed to know the name of the object to find it. If we don't need to know its specific name but could construct it out of the naming standard, it makes programming much easier. For example, instead of looking for the OvDC `MyCoolClusterWithHA`, we could be looking at the OvDC that is the `Gold` tier on the cluster for `Germany`, whose name is `OvDC_de-Gold`. Much easier, right? Also, you can use the API to query for all objects that follow a naming. So, if all your OvDCs start their name with `OvDC_`, then you can search across the vCloud and find all OvDCs in one go.

A naming standard not only makes it easier to find objects but also helps understand what one is dealing with. When you deploy the vApp template `TvApp_Win2k8R2-Sp2_vanilla`, you know exactly what you are getting.

The last but most important point is that it helps you communicate with others in an easier way. Instead of telling your network team about Network Pool in vCloud, you can look at the naming standard and tell them that you are having problems with VLAN xxx.

Using service accounts in the vCloud environment

In this recipe, we will talk about how vCD connects to all the other parts of vSphere.

Getting ready

For this recipe, we only need a functioning vSphere **Single Sign On** (**SSO**) or **Active Directory** (**AD**). We also need the right to create users in either SSO or AD.

How to do it...

Now we will create service accounts. Either create them in AD or in SSO; there is no point doing it in both.

Creating a service account in AD

The following is a quick and easy way:

1. Open **Active Directory Users and Computers**.

2. Click on the OU **Users**.

3. Click on the icon for new user. You should see the following screen:

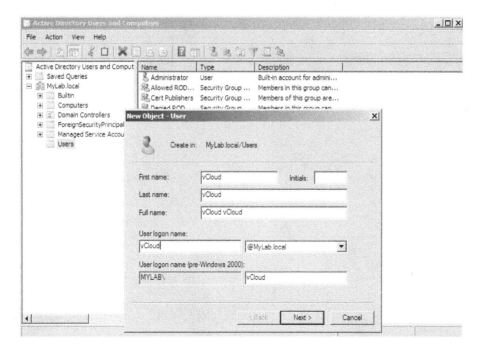

4. Enter the name of the service in **User logon name**.

5. Click on **Next** and assign a password. Disable **User must change password at next logon**, and enable **User cannot change password** and **Password never expires**.

6. Close the wizard.

If you have security concerns, you should assign the **Deny log on locally** AD Group Policy to this account. The policy is located in `Computer Configuration\Windows Settings\Security Settings\Local Policies\User Rights Assignment\Deny Logon locally`.

This will result in the user not being able to log in via the GUI. In addition to that, Windows 2008 R2 introduced the Managed Service Accounts; have a look at the link in the *See also* section.

Creating a service account in SSO

Perform the following steps to create a service account in SSO:

1. Connect to vCenter using the web client.

2. Log in with the user `admin@System-Domain`.

3. Navigate to **Administration | SSO Users and Groups**.

4. Click on the green icon (**+**). You should now get the following screen:

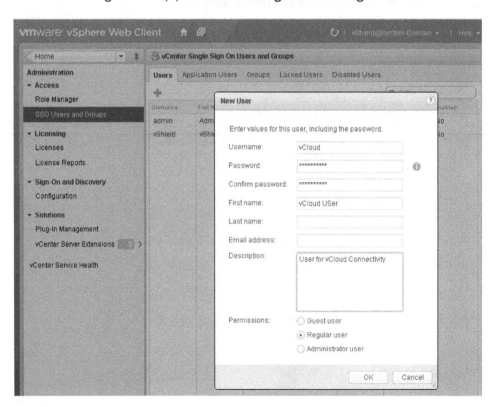

5. Enter a name for the service account as well as a password.

6. Assign it the permission **Regular User**.

7. Click on **OK** to add the user.

Assigning a service account in vCenter

This is a fast and dirty way. For a more secure environment, consider creating roles. Perform the following steps:

1. Log in to vCenter using the web client.

2. Click on **vCenter** and then on **vCenter Servers**.

3. Double-click on your vCenter Server.

4. Select **Manage** and then **Permissions**.

5. Click on the green icon (**+**) to add a new user.

6. Select the **Administrator** role and click on **Add**.

7. Select in **Domain** either the **AD domain** or **SYSTEM-DOMAIN** option.

8. Select the user you want to add and then click on **Add**. The user is now added to the list of users. You can add multiple users at the same time as shown in the following screenshot:

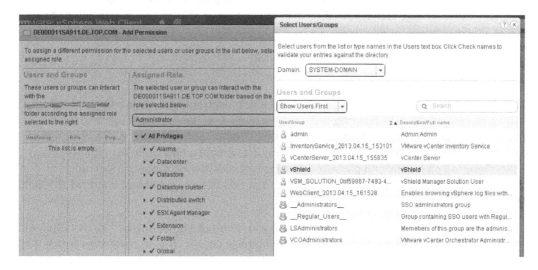

9. Click on **OK** and again on **OK**.

Adding a vCloud service account to vCNS

1. Log in to vCNS Web Manager.

2. Click on **Settings & Reports** and then on **Users**. You should see the following screen:

3. Click on **Add** to add a new user.

4. Select **Specify a vCenter user** and enter the name of the user from vCenter. This user can be from SSO or AD.

5. Give it the role **Enterprise Administrator**.

6. Don't limit its scope.

7. Finish the wizard.

How it works...

It is best practice to create a service account for every product that you connect with one another. The advantage is that you can see in the logfiles what each program is doing. A very important decision we have to make is whether to use Microsoft AD or vSphere SSO to create the service accounts in.

AD or SSO?

There are several advantages and disadvantages with each solution. Let's begin with AD. In AD, we can create service accounts, meaning accounts that have no login rights to the OS itself, but can be used for authentication between different servers and their services. While creating a service account in AD, the easiest way is to create a new OU in AD with the Group Policy **Deny log on locally** and password policies that allow for no password expiration or change. Have a look at the *See also* section for more details about the new Windows 2008 R2 Managed Service Accounts.

The advantage of an AD service account is that you can re-use it not only across the vSphere and vCloud environment but also for mail and database access. The disadvantage is that if AD is not available, the whole vSphere and vCloud structure grinds to a halt, making it necessary to restart all vSphere and vCloud services.

The alternative to using AD service accounts is to use user accounts in SSO. While using the SSO service, the disadvantage is that only vSphere, vCNS, and vCloud can access it, meaning that you still need to create AD accounts for e-mails and databases. The advantage is when AD is not available, the vSphere and vCloud infrastructure is still working. Please note that this would require a local database account for vSphere and vCloud, not an AD-based database account.

Understanding vCloud connections

vCloud primarily needs connections to vCenter, vCNS, ESXi, and the database. The following diagram shows all the connections and users. I prefaced all service accounts with `svc_`.

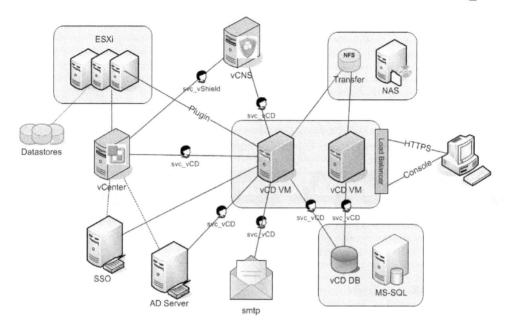

Use the vCNS service account to bind vCNS to vCenter. Use the vCloud service account to bind vCloud Director to vCenter, vCNS, mail, and database.

When you add LDAP services into vCloud, use the vCloud service account to authenticate to LDAP (AD). The connection between vCloud and ESXi Server is via a plugin and doesn't require an extra user, as it does the same functions as that of a vCenter and uses a dedicated internal user. For the initial installation, the root user of ESXi is sufficient.

The NFS connection normally doesn't require any special rights, but it may depend on your storage vendor or security settings.

There's more...

You should make sure that vCloud is connected not only to its dependent components using a service account but also to vCNS. The following steps show how to create and use a service account in vCNS:

1. Create a service account in AD or SSO for vCNS.
2. Add the vCNS service account to vCenter.

3. Log in to vCNS Web Manager.

4. Click on **Settings & Reports** and then on **Configuration**.

5. Click on the **edit** button next to **vCenter Server**.

6. Enter the vCNS user account and password, and make sure **Assign vShield "Enterprise Administrator" role to this user** is checked.

7. Click on **OK**.

See also

▸ Microsoft Windows 2008 Managed Service Accounts at `http://technet.microsoft.com/en-us/library/dd548356.aspx`

Setting up networks for the vCloud VM

We will have a look at how to set up the ESXi hosts and the vCloud Cell VM with an optimized network setup.

Getting ready

We need vSphere ESXi hosts that can be configured as well as the vCloud Director Cell VM, and root rights are needed for both of them.

How to do it...

We will first look at the ESXi network setup and then at the setup for the vCloud Cell.

Optimal ESXi network setup

This network setup is optimal for workload clusters. The following diagram shows that we are using the Distributed Switch to host the management and the vMotion VMKernel ports as well as all the VM networks. As vCloud creates the VM Network port groups itself, we don't have to worry about it too much.

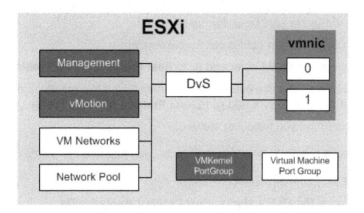

Perform the following steps for this network setup:

1. Make sure you have trunked all VLANs for Management, vMotion, and all the other networks you will be using for ESXi's network cards.

2. Base install the ESXi host as per normal instructions.

3. Add the ESXi host to your cluster.

4. Configure the ESXi host with all NTP, DNS, and routing settings. Add storage and configure the settings for it, especially the network settings for NFS and iSCSI. Consider using the storage APIs of your storage vendor.

5. Go to **Home | Inventory | Networking** and then right-click on your datacenter and select **New vSphere Distributed Switch**.

6. Create a new Distributed Switch (5.1) in vCenter without adding hosts or creating port groups. Choose the maximum amount of vmnics that are available to the ESXi host for the amount of uplinks.

7. Right-click on the newly created Distributed vSwitch and select **New Port Group**.

8. Create a new port group for vMotion and one for Management. Enter the VLAN ID of the new networks.

9. Right-click on the Distributed Switch and select **Add Host**.

10. Add the ESXi host to the Distributed Switch and assign the uplink ports.

11. Migrate the existing management port group that currently exists on a normal vSwitch to the Distributed Switch by selecting it in the **Network Connectivity** section of the wizard in the column **Destination port group** (see the *See also* section for help).

12. On the ESXi Server, go to **Configuration | Networking | vSphere Distributed Switch** and click on **Manage Virtual Adapter**.

13. Click on **Add** to **add** a new VMKernel adapter. Assonate it with the created distributed port group, select vMotion, and enter the IP information.

14. If you are using NFS, you need to repeat the previous steps (not using vMotion) to create a VMKernel port group for the NFS traffic.

15. The ESXi Server is now configured for networking.

16. Right-click on the ESXi Server and go to **Host Profile | Create Profile from Host**.

17. After the host profile has been created (it may take a few minutes), right-click on the cluster of the ESXi Server and go to **Host Profile | Manage Profile**.

18. Select the profile you have just created.

When you now add a new ESXi Server to this cluster, you just need to do the following:

1. Put the ESXi into maintenance mode.

2. Right-click on the ESXi and go to **Host Profile | Apply Profile**.

3. Answer all IP-related questions.

4. Wait until the ESXi Server has finished reconfiguring and then exit maintenance mode.

Optimal vCD Cell network setup

The following diagram shows the network setup of the vCloud Cell VM we will set up:

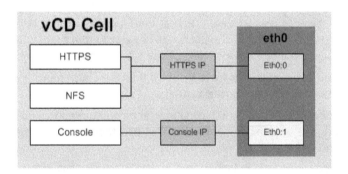

Perform the following steps for this network setup:

1. Log in to your new vCD Cell VM.

2. Gain root access, if you haven't already.

3. Run the following command:

```
cp /etc/sysconfig/network-scripts/ifcfg-eth0 /etc/sysconfig/
network-scripts/ifcfg-eth0:0
```

4. Then edit the new file with the following command:

```
vi /etc/sysconfig/network-scripts/ifcfg-eth0:0
```

5. Press *i* to start editing.

6. Change `DEVICE=eth0` to `DEVICE=eth0:0`.

7. Change the IP address.

8. The file should now look like:

   ```
   DEVICE="eth0:0"
   IPADDR=192.168.1.7
   NETMASK=255.255.255.0
   NETWORK=192.168.1.0
   ONBOOT=yes
   NAME="eth0:0"
   ```

9. Save and exit `vi` with `:wq`.

10. Edit the original `eth0` file with the following command:

    ```
    vi /etc/sysconfig/network-scripts/ifcfg-eth0
    ```

11. Remove the `GATEWAY` entry and exit `vi`.

12. Edit the network file with the following command:

    ```
    vi /etc/sysconfig/network
    ```

13. Enter here the `GATEWAY [gateway IP]` entry with the gateway IP and exit `vi`.

14. Run the command `ifup eth0:0` to activate the new card.

15. Run the command `service network restart` to restart the network devices.

16. The command `ifconfig` should now show the device `eth0` and `eth0:0`.

17. Do a `ping` test to verify if everything is working.

How it works...

Let's discuss the implications in setting up the networking for the workload and for the vCloud Cell as we did in the previous recipes.

ESXi setup

The optimal setup for an enterprise solution with vCloud is to use two clusters. One ESXi cluster is for Management and it contains the vSphere components, vCNS, and the vCloud Director Cell VMs. It may also contain the databases for vCenter, SSO, and vCloud.

This Management cluster should have HA and DRS enabled, configured, and optimized for HA. A lot of people still feel uncomfortable with the Distributed Switch in a DR situation or when vCenter is down. They use normal vSwitches in the ESXi host in the Management cluster, and that's okay. It's about how confident and experienced the admins who have to deal with an emergency situation are.

The workload cluster (or clusters) should be configured with HA if needed (see the *Using OvDCs for compute tiering* recipe in this chapter), but they need to be configured for DRS or else we cannot use resource pools. One of the best designs is to make the ESXi Servers for the workload cluster as generic as possible, as this makes them exchangeable. Imagine that you have a sudden need to increase the power in one cluster; if the ESXis are generic, you can shift them between clusters to allocate resources on demand.

This is where host profiles come in handy. We have created a very basic profile and we can use it to apply it to any new ESXi Server to make it similar to all the ESXi Servers that are already in the cluster.

vCloud Cell setup

While creating a vCloud Director Cell VM, we need two IPs: one for the HTTPS interface and one for the console traffic. The easiest way is to create two network cards and then configure them. However, there is a problem with that when one deploys the setup in a load-balanced setup: the routing issue. As both network cards are mostly in the same network range, the routing will occur via the first network card (eth0). What this means is that traffic will come in on the second network card (eth1), but leave the VM from eth0. Depending on your load balancing as well as on your network-security setting, this can lead to problems, as a device may believe it is witnessing a man-in-the-middle attack.

There are two solutions to this problem. The first one is the one we showed previously where we assign two IPs to the same network card (same MAC), and the second solution is where you define routing rules and force the traffic that comes in on eth1 to leave the VM from eth1 again. For simplicity and for ease of management, the first solution is more elegant and simple.

See also

> ▶ More details on Distributed Switches can be found at VMware KB 1010557 at `http://www.vmware.com/files/pdf/vsphere-vnetwork-ds-migration-configuration-wp.pdf`

> ▶ Create multiple IPs on the same NIC in RedHat at `https://access.redhat.com/site/documentation/en-US/Red_Hat_Enterprise_Linux/6/html/Deployment_Guide/s1-networkscripts-interfaces.html`

Working with vCloud roles

Let's talk about roles and what they can do for you.

Getting ready

You need a user or a group to which you want to give a different role. Roles can be assigned to users and groups.

How to do it...

Working with roles is split into two sections: creating the role and using it.

Creating a new role

Perform the following steps to create a new role:

1. Make a list of all the actions that the user should be able to do.
2. Make a list of all the actions that the user should not be able to do.
3. Log in to vCloud as `SysAdmin`.
4. Navigate to **System | Administration | Roles**.
5. Check if one of the preconfigured roles is satisfying the requirements.
6. If not, check what role is closed and copy this role by right-clicking on the role and choosing **Copy to**.
7. If no role fits, create a new one by clicking on the green icon (**+**).
8. While creating a new role or a copy of an existing one, it is important to give it a good name.
9. Check the rights you want to assign to that role, and uncheck options from the rights that you don't want.
10. Click on **OK** to finish editing of the new role.
11. Create a test user and assign him the role, and test if all your requirements are fulfilled. Modify the role as required.
12. When the role works, document the role in your design document with the reason for this role and who should use it.

Assigning a role to a user or a group

Perform the following steps to assign a user or a group to a role:

1. Log in as `SysAdmin` or `OrgAdmin`.
2. Navigate to your organization's **Administration** settings.
3. Click on **Users** or **Groups**, depending on what you would like to assign the role to.
4. Right-click on a user or group and select **Properties**.
5. Under **Role**, you can now assign the user or group a new role.

6. In an organization that is using LDAP and where users as well as groups are used, it is possible to assign a group member (one user) a different role than he would have through the group. Have a look at the button **Use group roles instead of user role** as well as the settings **User role** and **Group role**.

How it works...

Roles are really good tools to control your environment. Not everyone needs to be able to create VMs, deploy VMs from a public catalog, or use snapshots. Creating different roles for different purposes makes a lot of sense and helps you save resources.

A typical example is a developer group that needs to access vApps to create and change some coding. Such a developer actually only needs to use power operations, maybe snapshots, access the console, and add a vApp from a catalog. Assigning this user the role vApp User might give them too much control. Another typical one is that you want users to not be able to change the vCPU and Memory Allocation or change the disks. All this can be easily accomplished using roles.

In the following table, you will find all the preconfigured roles that exist in vCloud and their rights:

Rights		Catalog Author	Console Access Only	Organization Administrator	vApp Author	vApp User
All rights				X		
Catalog				X		
	Add a vApp from My Cloud	X		X	X	
	Change Owner			X		
	Create/Delete a new Catalog	X		X		
	Edit Catalog Properties	X		X		
	Share a Catalog	X		X		
	View Private and Shared Catalog	X		X	X	
	View Published Catalogs			X		
Catalog item				X		
	Add to My Cloud			X	X	X
	Copy/Move a vApp Template/Media			X	X	
	Create/Upload a vApp Template/Media			X		
	Enable vApp Template Download			X		
	Edit vApp Template/Media Properties			X		
	View vApp Template/Media			X	X	X
Disk		X		X	X	
	Change Owner	X		X	X	
	Create Disk	X		X	X	
	Delete Disk	X		X	X	
	Edit Disk Properties	X		X	X	
	View Disk Properties	X		X	X	X

Rights		Catalog Author	Console Access Only	Organization Administrator	vApp Author	vApp User
Gateway	Configure Services			X		
General				X		
	Administrator Control			X		
	Administrator View			X		
	Send Notification			X		
OvDC Network				X		
	Edit Properties			X		
	View Properties			X		
Organization				X		
	Edit Federation Settings			X		
	Edit Lease Policy			X		
	Edit Organization Network Properties			X		
	Edit Organization Properties			X		
	Edit Password Policy			X		
	Edit Quota Policy			X		
	Edit SMTP Settings			X		
	View Organization Networks			X		
	View Organizations			X		
OvDC				X		
	Set Default Storage Profile			X		
	View OvDC			X		
User	View Group/User			X		

Rights		Catalog Author	Console Access Only	Organization Administrator	vApp Author	vApp User
vApp				X		
	Access to VM Console	X	X	X	X	X
	Change Owner			X		
	Copy a vApp	X		X	X	X
	Create/Reconfigure a vApp	X		X	X	
	Create/Revert/Remove Snapshot(*)	X		X	X	X
	Delete a vApp	X		X	X	X
	Edit vApp Properties	X		X	X	X
	Edit VM CPU	X		X	X	
	Edit VM Hard Disk	X		X	X	
	Edit VM Memory	X		X	X	
	Edit VM Network	X		X	X	X
	Edit VM Properties	X		X	X	X
	Manage VM Password Settings	X		X	X	X
	Share a vApp	X		X	X	X
	Start/Stop/Suspend/Reset a vApp	X		X	X	X

* means new in vCloud 5.1.2.

Changes in vCloud 5.5

The changes in vCloud 5.5 only affect the catalogs as shown in the following table:

Rights		Catalog Author	Console Access Only	Organization Administrator	vApp Author	vApp User
Catalog				X		
	Add a vApp from My Cloud	X		X	X	
	Change Owner			X		
	Create/Delete a new Catalog	X		X		
	Edit Catalog Properties	X		X		
	Allow External Publishing/Subscription for the Catalogs	X		x		
	Share a Catalog to Users/Groups within current Organization	X		X		
	Share a Catalog to Other Organizations	X		X		
	View Private and Shared Catalogs within current Organization	x		X		x
	View Shared Catalogs from Other Organizations			X		

There's more...

The only special role that cannot be altered or created is the role of the system administrator (SysAdmin). The specialty of this role is that it allows you to log in to the System organization directly (https://[vcd-cell ip or name]/cloud). With all other users, you have to log in to an organization. Likewise, a SysAdmin role cannot log in to an organization directly; he can only log in to the System organization. However, he can open up all other organizations from there.

Keeping your templates under control

If you have the need to keep a very tight control over your templates, this recipe shows how you can easily achieve it.

Getting ready

To implement this recipe, we need to create a new organization, so we also need to create an OvDC. However, we don't really need any resources, so we could share the PvDC with some other organization.

I would recommend using a dedicated storage profile for this new organization (see the *How it works...* section).

How to do it...

We are now creating the ADMIN Organization with all the bits and pieces that we need. I personally always call it ADMIN (in caps) so it sticks out.

Creating the ADMIN Organization

Perform the following steps for creating the ADMIN Organization:

1. Log in to vCloud as SysAdmin.
2. Click on **Manage & Monitor** and then on **Organizations**.
3. Click on the green icon (**+**).
4. Give the organization a name that indicates that you are using it for templates only. I personally always use ADMIN.
5. Don't choose **LDAP**, as then this organization is only accessible by system administrators. If you want other users to log in to do work on the templates, choose **System LDAP**, or create a local user in the next step.
6. You normally should not need to create local users. See the last step.
7. We want to publish catalogs.

> See also the *Working with Catalogs in vCloud 5.5* recipe in this chapter for an advanced sharing option in vCloud 5.5.

8. As for SMTP and notifications, we are using the default settings.

9. The policy settings are important. We will set the **Maximum runtime lease** time to three days; the other leases are set to **Never Expires**. The rest of the settings we leave as default as shown in the following screenshot:

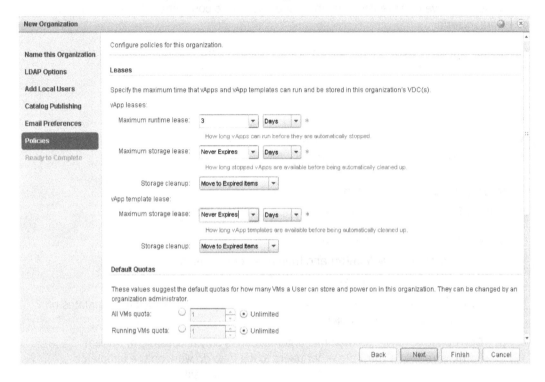

10. Finish the wizard.

Storage profile

Create and add a new storage profile to a PvDC that you would like to use. See also the *Adding a new storage profile to vCD* recipe in *Chapter 4, Datastores and Storage Profiles*.

Creating an OvDC

Perform the following steps for creating an OvDC:

1. Click on **Organization VDCs**.
2. Click on the green icon (**+**).
3. Select the organization you have just created.
4. Select the PvDC you want to use.
5. Select **Pay-As-You-Go** as the Allocation Model.

6. Set the **CPU quota** and **Memory quota** values to **Unlimited**. Set the **CPU resources guaranteed** and **Memory resources guaranteed** values to **0**. The **vCPU Speed** value can be set to **2** as shown in the following screenshot:

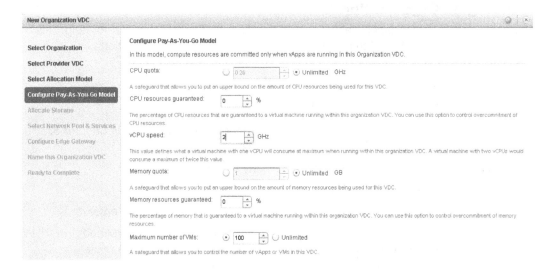

7. Select the storage profile you want to use for the ADMIN domain. Set the **Storage Limit** value to **Unlimited**. Enable **Thin Provisioning** and **Fast Provisioning**.

8. If your vApp templates have isolated vApp Networks, you want to attach a Network Pool to the OvDC, but you can limit the number of pools to 10 or less.

9. We don't need an Edge gateway.

10. Give the OvDC a good name and close the wizard.

Creating a published catalog

1. Click on **Organizations** and then double-click on the Organization you created.

2. Click on **Catalogs**.

3. Click on the green icon (**+**) to create a new catalog.

4. Give the catalog a name that makes it clear that it stores all templates for vCloud. Typically, something like General Templates will work.

5. In vCloud 5.5, we can now choose a storage profile on which all catalog items will be deployed.

6. Share your catalog with everyone in the organization with **Access level: Full Control** by clicking on **Add Members**.

7. Publish this catalog.

8. Close the wizard.

If you are running vCloud 5.5, also review the *Working with catalogs in vCloud 5.5* recipe in this chapter.

Creating an Organization Network

Create an isolated Organization Network. See *Chapter 1, Setting Up Networks*, for help. This network will be used with the templates, allowing for easier scripted automation.

The ADMIN Organization work cycle

Perform the following steps to add a catalog:

1. Either import a VM to the catalog (see *the Importing a VM into vCloud Chapter 3, Better vApps*) and perform the following steps:

    1. After the import, add the vApp to **My Cloud**.
    2. Delete the vApp template.
    3. Double-click on the vApp you have deployed in **My Cloud** to enter it.
    4. Repeat this step for all VMs in the vApp. Right-click on the VM and select **Consolidate**. This step might take a moment, but will make your VM a full clone.

2. Or create a new vApp in **My Cloud**.

3. You now have a new vApp in **My Cloud**. Now it's time to do some aftercare (see the *There's more...* section in the *Importing a vApp into vCloud* recipe in *Chapter 3, Better vApps*).

4. When you have cleaned up the vApp and are happy with the result, stop the vApp.

5. Now right-click on the vApp and choose **Add to Catalog**.

6. Give the vApp template a good name that makes clear what it contains.

7. Do not delete the vApp. Just leave it powered off where it is.

8. If you have to make any changes to the vApp template, do the following:

    1. Go back to the vApp in **My Cloud**.
    2. Make the changes.
    3. Delete the old vApp template and its shadow VMs.
    4. Add the new vApp to the catalog.

 If you are using vCloud 5.5, you can make the changes directly in the vApp template.

How it works...

The idea of an ADMIN Organization is to have one organization that is under the strict control of one team that is responsible for the base OS systems. Having one organization that publishes all templates has the advantage that you control the templates, thereby making sure that they are built to standard and have all the right tools installed. This also allows you to take control of which organization is able to access which templates.

Another advantage is that you can have an easier time scripting an automated solution. You may remember from *Chapter 5, Working with the vCloud API*, that in all languages, we had a problem where we had to find the vApp templates as well as the name of the network they were built with. Using these methods, we don't have to search for the names as we already know them, reducing the complexity of programming manifold. This is especially true when we have one standard Organization Network with which the templates are deployed.

Due to the fact that we are not deleting the vApps but are letting them stay in the **My Cloud** area, the separate storage profile makes sense. Not only is it letting us make sure that our template storage is isolated from the rest of the organizations, but it also makes sure that if linked clones are used, shadow VMs are created. This allows for a tied control of the shadow VMs as shown in the following diagram:

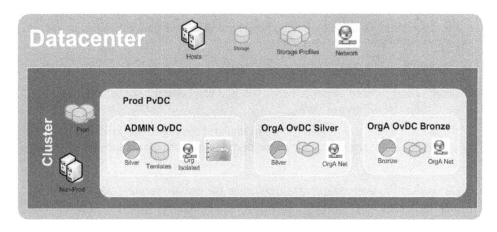

Let's talk about the organization and the OvDC and its setting. In the organization, we set the policies so that vApps do not run for longer than three days. The idea behind this is that this organization is a staging area where we run templates, clean them up, and then publish them. Normally, no VM should be running longer than is needed to clean them up. The policy makes sure that if an administrator forgets to shut down a vApp, it will do it for him.

The OvDC resource settings are set to reflect what I just said. As the VMs should not be running in general, we only need resources for the clean-up time. Therefore, minimal resources are needed.

Choosing the right Allocation Model

This section helps us determine which Allocation Model is needed to use with which OvDC.

Getting ready

We need an organization in which we can create OvDCs, and we need one or more PvDCs that we can take resources from.

How to do it...

Determining the right Allocation Model isn't easy, and it takes some thinking to find the right one. Therefore, this section will ask you the following questions to help you determine what Allocation Model you need:

- Do you need a fixed allocation of memory and CPU? Did the customer buy a dedicated cluster or resource allocation?

  Fixed allocations normally occur if customers buy clusters or a certain allocation they would like to use. The Allocation Model and the Reservation Pool would work here.

- Do you need to be flexible? Do you have an unknown amount of VMs you need to plan for? Will your VM count change a lot?

  This would call for the Pay-As-You-Go model.

- Do you need to have compute tiering? Would you benefit from using different allocations for different VMs?

  If this is the case, the Pay-As-You-Go model and the Allocation Model would work as they have the possibility to reserve certain amounts of resources, allowing for easy tiering.

- Do you want to overcommit resources because you are running, for example, a development cluster? The Pay-As-You-Go model and the Allocation Model let you overcommit resources.

  It is important to remember that you can have multiple OvDCs per organization, meaning you can have more than one Allocation Model assigned to the same organization, so that customers can choose which organization they deploy their VMs in.

▶ How will customers be charged for the usage of resources?

Most of the time, it comes down to the question of what customers pay for or what a corporation wants to spend on them with regards to resources. Even if companies don't have a charge model, there is only so much hardware that can be used, and someone has to pay for it. If your charge model should be easy, the Reservation Pool or Allocation Model is fine as you have a fixed amount of resources that the customer can use. If you have access to VMware Chargeback, things are a bit easier, and even OvDC that spans clusters can be calculated.

How it works...

Understanding the vCloud Allocation Model is not so hard when you understand the underlying principles, so let's have a look at them.

The three little Allocation Models

vCloud knows of three Allocation Models for itself:

▶ **Reservation Pool**: As shown in the following screenshot, it allocates a fixed amount of resources (in GHz and GB) from the PvDC to the OvDC. This model is good if the users want to define a per-VM resource allocation. This model only enables the **Resource Allocation** tab in VMs. You *cannot* overcommit resources with this model.

Configure Reservation Pool Model

In this model, you allocate resources to the organization VDC. All resources are guaranteed to the organization VDC, but users in the organization can control commitment on per-VM basis.

CPU allocation: 5.06 GHz (20% of available Provider vDC capacity of 25.29GHz)

The amount of CPU resources reserved for this organization VDC.

Memory allocation: 56.85 GB (20% of available Provider vDC capacity of 284.24GB)

The amount of memory resources reserved for this organization VDC.

Maximum number of VMs: ⦿ 100   ◯ Unlimited

A safeguard that allows you to control the maximum number of virtual machines in this organization VDC.

> ▶ **Pay-As-You-Go** (**PAYG**): It is similar to the allocation pool; however, resources are only consumed if vApps/VMs are running. All other models reserve resources even if the OvDC doesn't contain any running VMs. This model is useful if the number of resources is unknown or fluctuating. You can overcommit resources with this model. The following screenshot shows this model:

Configure Pay-As-You-Go Model

In this model, compute resources are committed only when vApps are running in this Organization VDC.

CPU quota: ○ 0.26 ⊙ Unlimited GHz

A safeguard that allows you to put an upper bound on the amount of CPU resources being used for this VDC.

CPU resources guaranteed: 20 %

The percentage of CPU resources that are guaranteed to a virtual machine running within this organization VDC. You can use this option to control overcommitment of CPU resources.

vCPU speed: 1 GHz

This value defines what a virtual machine with one vCPU will consume at maximum when running within this organization VDC. A virtual machine with two vCPUs would consume a maximum of twice this value.

Memory quota: ○ 1 ⊙ Unlimited GB

A safeguard that allows you to put an upper bound on the amount of memory resources being used for this VDC.

Memory resources guaranteed: 20 %

The percentage of memory that is guaranteed to a virtual machine running within this organization VDC. You can use this option to control overcommitment of memory resources.

Maximum number of VMs: ⊙ 100 ○ Unlimited

A safeguard that allows you to control the number of vApps or VMs in this VDC.

> ▶ **Allocation Pool**: It is similar to a Reservation Pool; however, you can also assign how many resources are guaranteed (reserved) for this OvDC. You can overcommit resources with this model. The following screenshot shows this model:

Configure Allocation Pool Model

In this model, you allocate resources to the organization VDC. You also control the percentage of resources guaranteed to the organization VDC. This packing factor provides a way to overcommit resources.

CPU allocation: 15.69 GHz

The maximum amount of CPU available to the virtual machines running within this organization VDC (taken from the supporting provider VDC, PvDC_DE-SSP-Ag).

CPU resources guaranteed: 50 % (7.85GHz, 10% of available Provider vDC capacity of 78.46GHz)

The percentage of the resources guaranteed to be available to virtual machines running within it.

Memory allocation: 74.12 GB

The maximum amount of memory available to the virtual machines running within this organization VDC (taken from the supporting provider VDC, PvDC_DE-SSP-Ag).

Memory resources guaranteed: 50 % (37.06GB, 10% of available Provider vDC capacity of 370.58GB)

The percentage of the resources guaranteed to be available to virtual machines running within it.

Maximum number of VMs: ⊙ 100 ○ Unlimited

A safeguard that allows you to control the maximum number of virtual machines in this organization VDC.

There are different settings that one can choose from for each model. The following table shows these settings:

Item	Allocation Pool	PAYG	Reservation Pool
CPU allocation (GHz)	Yes	Yes and unlimited	Yes
CPU resources guaranteed (percentage)	Yes	Yes	No
vCPU max Speed (GHz)	Yes	Yes	No
Memory allocation (GB)	Yes	Yes and unlimited	Yes
Memory resources guaranteed (percentage)	Yes	Yes	No
Maximum number of VMs (number or unlimited)	Yes	Yes	Yes
Allocate Storage	Yes	Yes and unlimited	Yes

When we look at the resource pools that vCloud creates for the OvDCs, we find the following for CPU and memory:

Item	Allocation Pool	PAYG	Reservation Pool
Reservation	% of Allocation	Variable	Allocation
Limit	Allocation	Variable	Allocation

Allocation is the amount we defined as the maximal allocation. Variable means that the Pay-As-You-Go model will recalculate and reset the limit and the reservation of a resource pool whenever a VM is powered on in this resource pool.

Overcommit, reservation, and limit

Overcommitting allows you to allocate more resources to OvDCs than there are physical resources. Overcommitment is explained easiest by looking at memory. Let's say an ESXi host has 128 GB of memory. Looking at a model without overcommit, you could only allocate 128 GB of memory to VMs. However, VMs seldom use all their allocated memory, meaning that a VM that has been configured for 8 GB of memory may not consume more than 2 GB on average.

Overcommitting means one can configure VMs with more memory than there is physically available. For instance, VMs that have a total of 192 GB of memory configured will overcommit memory on the example host by 150 percent. So far so good, but what happens now when the VMs, all of a sudden, demand all their configured memory? When a VM is powered on, a swap file (`.vswap`) of the same size as the configured memory is written to the Datastore where the VM is stored. If the VM needs more memory than what is physically available, the ESXi Server will start swapping the memory out to the `swap` file. This implication is important as we will trade memory against performance in the case of resource contention. If you know in advance that you will have memory contention, you may like to consider configuring the `.vswap` file that is stored on a different fast Datastore, thereby reducing the performance hit.

 Overcommitment will impact your performance when resource contentions exist.

Each VM and resource pool has two settings each for memory and CPU that are of importance for this discussion: reservation and limit.

Limit is the maximum amount of resources the VM or resource pool can get, and reservation is the amount of resources that it is guaranteed to have. Reservations will always guarantee the resources; this is especially the case if physical resources are spare. Limit corresponds to the allocation, and reservation corresponds to the guarantees in the Allocation Models.

vCPU speed

In the Pay-As-You-Go Allocation Model, you can set the maximum speed of the vCPU. It sets a limit on each of the VM's CPU resource allocation. For example, if the vCPU's maximum speed is set to 2 GHz and the VM has two vCPUs, vCloud will set a limit of 4 GHz on the CPU of this VM. Therefore, it is not a per-CPU setting as one may think; it's just a limit for the whole of the VM.

Setting the vCPU's max speed higher than the physical speed of the core of the ESXi doesn't make much sense. Finding the right setting is important not only for your performance but also for the amount of VMs you can deploy in that OvDC. For example, if you choose the maximum allocation as 10 GHz and you choose the vCPU speed as 2 GHz, you will only be able to deploy five VMs with one vCPU or two VMs with two vCPUs. If you choose 1 GHz as the vCPU speed, you could deploy 10 VMs with one vCPU or five VMs with two vCPUs. However, a vCPU with 1 GHz is mostly slower than the CPU in your phone.

There's more...

Starting with vCloud 5.1, the Allocation Model can be set to be elastic. What this means is that it recognizes that a PvDC may actually consist of multiple clusters or resource pools. When an Allocation Model is set to elastic, vCloud recalculates the limits and resources of a resource pool every time a VM is powered on.

See also

▸ More on resource usage and overcommitment can be found at
  `http://www.yellow-bricks.com/drs-deepdive`

▸ Refer to your vSphere documentation

Using OvDCs for compute tiering

We have already discussed storage tiering using storage profiles (see *Chapter 4, Datastores and Storage Profiles*); now we will talk about compute tiering and what one can do.

Getting ready

The requirements for this recipe vary wildly and depend on what you want to do and what you have.

The least demanding model requires one PvDC, and the more demanding ones require different clusters (PvDCs).

How to do it...

1. Define the kind of tiering you would want.

   Do you want to have different cluster settings (HA), or do you want to use different Allocation Model settings?

2. Create the different OvDCs. Depending on your requirements, you may need to create different PvDCs.

3. It is of the most importance to name the OvDCs so that customers can understand what they are getting. A very common method is to use the names Gold, Silver, and Bronze.

4. Publish the tiering and explain to the customers what they are getting with each tier and what it may cost them (or you). This will ensure that the customer is aware that a Gold OvDC is more expensive (someone has to pay for resources) than a Bronze one. Virtualization isn't free, as some users might still believe. Also, if you have **Service Level Agreements (SLAs)** with your customer, you will want to define the levels.

An example

We have only one PvDC (one cluster) to use, but we want different service settings. We want to use production and development VMs on the same cluster. This actually happens more often than one would think, as corporations want to save money and create a higher VM density. Even if you are not likely to use such a setup, it's a nice brain teaser.

Perform the following steps:

1. We create three organizations, `Prod`, `Dev`, and `ADMIN`, as we like to keep control of our VMs.

2. We create one PvDC as we only have one cluster.

3. We create the following OvDCs (CPU and memory will get the same allocation):

Name	Org	Model	Allocation	Guarantee
ADMIN	ADMIN	PAYG	Unlimited	0%
Gold	Prod	Allocation	50%	50%
Silver	Prod	Allocation	50%	25%
Dev	Dev	Allocation	50%	0%

You will notice that the percentages add up to 150 percent, meaning that we will overcommit the cluster at 150 percent. However, due to the guarantees that we give the production OvDCs, we can be sure that sufficient resources will be available to run the VMs. If VMs have to suffer from resource negligence, it will be the `Dev` ones. The `ADMIN` OvDC is set to `PAYG` as we don't want to impact `Prod` and `Dev` with resources used up by the power of VMs.

4. You may want to combine compute tiering with storage tiering and provide different storage profiles to the different OvDCs (see *Chapter 4, Datastores and Storage Profiles*).

How it works...

We discussed the allocation models in the *Choosing the right Allocation Model* recipe in this chapter and how it affects VMs. With tiering, you can create different levels of VM performance; it is done in vCloud by using different OvDCs with different settings. The easiest-to-understand example is the following:

You have two clusters, one is configured for HA and the other is not. You create two PvDCs, one for each cluster. Now you create two OvDCs, one for each PvDC, resulting in an OvDC that will protect your VMs with HA and one that will not. Not only do you have different protection levels but also the costs associated with the OvDCs will be different. An HA cluster will cost more as you cannot fully use all physical resources the cluster has. This is because you need to reserve capacity if an ESXi host dies. Whereas the cluster without an HA is cheaper as you can use all of its physical resources.

See also

▶ *Chapter 4, Datastores and Storage Profiles*

Understanding how the different vCloud types impact the design

There is a great deal of difference between a cloud you design purely for automation purposes and one that is a self-service one.

Getting ready

We need an empty vCloud.

How to do it...

Let's show the difference in creating the two different clouds. This is not intended to cover every use case, rather it will help in the understanding. There are basically two main types of clouds you can optimize a cloud design toward: Automation or Self-Service. The following table explains them:

Automation vCloud	Self-Service vCloud
▸ Organizations are environments. Organizations represent different environments such as `Prod` and `Dev` or `France` and `Germany`. ▸ All organizations will be created without LDAP and local users. Only human system administrators and script service accounts will log in. No special roles are needed. ▸ PvDCs are tiers. ▸ OvDCs are tiers. ▸ Network pools are not used. ▸ Mostly one vApp will have only one VM. ▸ Edges are seldom used, and if so, are heavily scripted via vCNS. ▸ vApp templates are shared. ▸ They use a simplified naming standard optimized for automation.	▸ Organizations are customers or projects. ▸ Customers log on roles and LDAP. ▸ PvDCs are shared hardware. ▸ OvDCs are defined allocations for customers. ▸ Networks pools are used. ▸ There are multiple VMs per vApp. ▸ Edges are used. ▸ vApp templates might not be shared. ▸ They use a user-understandable naming standard.

How it works...

In order to design a vCloud environment that is optimized for any environment, it is important to understand what kind of vCloud you want to build.

There's more...

Let's not forget about the very basic decision about what kind of cloud one is building; namely a **private cloud** or a **public cloud**. The main difference is the focus on where the users connect from. Will internal or external users use the cloud?

This decision will alter the way you need to apply SSL certificates, firewall rules on the vCloud Cell VMs, as well as firewalls between vCloud and the rest of the vSphere infrastructure.

Private vCloud

A private vCloud will have the following properties:

- **Attached to a local AD**: All organizations (as well as systems) are connected to a local AD
- **Relaxed security**: Users will be connecting to vCloud from the internal network; therefore, security could be relaxed
- **Internal billing or show back**: Users will utilize internal resources; billing is not needed in most cases; however, monitoring the usage and reporting it back can be a good idea

Public vCloud

A private vCloud will have the following properties:

- **Remote attached AD**: All organizations (but not systems) are connected to a remote AD via SLMA
- **Extended security**: Users will connect to the vCloud via the Internet or another public network; therefore, security should be an issue
- **Cost monitoring**: As external customers will be using the vCloud, monitoring the usage and establishing a billing method is important

Depending on if a public or private cloud is used, the firewalls and connections should be secured. The following diagram shows all the connections that a vCD Cell needs. It also contains a separation on how to separate the vCloud Cells using VLANs:

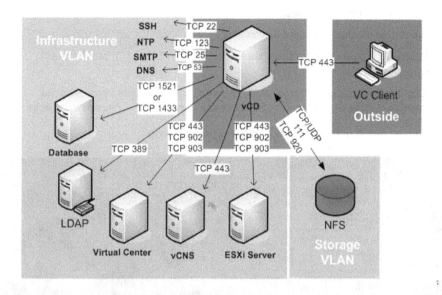

Retrofitting a shared directory into an existing vCD Cell

You need some more space in `. ./data/transfer` or you want to have more than one vCD Cell; this section shows how you do it.

Getting ready

We need a vCloud Director Cell VM with no shared directory. We need an NFS-shared directory we can use.

How to do it...

1. Log in to the vCloud Director Cell VM.

2. Gain root access, if you haven't already.

3. Shut down the cell (see the *A scripted cell shutdown* recipe in *Chapter 5, Working with the vCloud API*).

4. Run the following commands to copy the content of the `data/transfer` directory:

   ```
   cp -R /opt/vmware/vcloud-director/data/transfer /tmp/
   vcloudtreansfer
   ```

5. Add the NFS directory to the filesystem table by using the `vi` editor as follows:

   ```
   vi /etc/fstab
   ```

6. Scroll to the end of the list.

7. Press *o* to insert a new line at the end.

8. Enter the following text and replace the content of the [ ] brackets with your settings:

   `[ip or hostname of you NFS server]:[directory you share]    /opt/`
   `vmware/vcloud-director/data/transfer   nfs    rw,soft,_netdev  0   0`

   You will get something like the following screenshot:

9. Press *Esc* and then enter `:wq` to save an exit `vi`.

10. Mount the new directory with the command `mount -a`.

11. Copy the content of the directory back to the original with the following command:

    `cp -R /tmp/vcloudtreansfer opt/vmware/vcloud-director/data/`
    `transfer`

12. Set the ownership and permission on the new directory correctly by using the following commands:

    `cd /opt/vmware/vcloud-director/data`

    `chmod 750 transfer`

    `chown -R vcloud:vcloud transfer`

13. Start the vCloud Cell with `service vmware-vcd start`.

How it works...

The recipe consists mostly of common Linux operations. The only important part we have to remember here is that NFS stores the ownership of objects by the ID number of the user and the group, not the name. Therefore, we have to make sure that the ownership of the files and directory is set correctly after we have copied the content of the transferred directory back.

There's more...

Please check with your NFS storage vendor for optimized values for the /etc/fstab entry.

Connecting more than one vCloud Cell to the same infrastructure

There are situations where one will need two independent vClouds accessing the same vSphere infrastructure.

Getting ready

We just need an existing vCloud and the building blocks for a new one. These building blocks are:

- ▶ RedHat Linux VM (RHEL) 5 or 6 (6.3 is the highest version with vCD 5.1.2)
- ▶ Root credentials for RHEL VM
- ▶ vCloud Director Binary
- ▶ New NFS shared directory (optional)
- ▶ New database for vCloud
- ▶ New VMware vCloud Director licence

Or you can use the vCloud appliance.

How to do it...

1. Install RHEL on the VM.
2. Transfer the vCloud Director Binary to the new RHEL VM using SCP (with a program such as WinSCP), and put it in the /tmp directory.
3. Log in to the new RHEL.

4. Gain root access if you haven't logged in as `root`.

5. Assign the second IP to the interface `eth0:0` as shown in the *Setting up networks for the vCloud VM* recipe.

6. Configure the firewall to allow HTTPS (port 443) traffic.

7. Execute the vCloud Binary. You may have to change the permissions on the vCloud Binary with the command `chmod 777 [vcloud binary]`.

 Do not run the script at the end.

8. If there are any software dependencies, resolve them with `yum install [list of missing packages]`, then re-run the installer.

9. You may like to create the NFS mount (see the *Retrofitting a shared directory into an existing vCD Cell* recipe in this chapter).

10. Create the two self-signed SSL certificates with the following commands:

    `/opt/vmware/vcloud-director/jre/bin/keytool -keystore /opt/vmware/certificates.ks -storetype JCEKS -genkey -keyalg RSA -alias http`

    `/opt/vmware/vcloud-director/jre/bin/keytool -keystore /opt/vmware/certificates.ks -storetype JCEKS -genkey -keyalg RSA -alias consoleproxy`

11. Run the configuration script `/opt/vmware/vcloud-director/bin/configure`.

12. Make sure that you enter the settings for the new vCD database.

13. Start the new vCD service.

14. Open a web browser and navigate to the new vCloud instance.

15. The vCloud Setup wizard starts. Work through the wizard as normal; however, see the following important changes:

    1. Enter the new vCloud licence.

    2. In the section **System Settings**, make sure you enter different **System name** and **Installation ID** values:

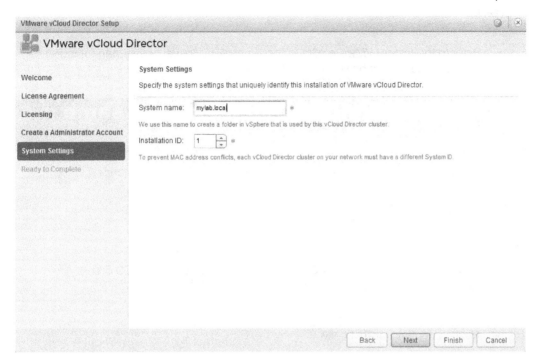

16. Finish the wizard.

17. Enter the new vCloud as `SysAdmin`.

18. Attach the already existing vCenter.

19. Start adding PvDCs, Organizations, and so on.

How it works...

Due to the difference in the system name and the installation ID, we can have two vCloud Director instances using the same vSphere infrastructure. A typical example for such a setup is when a vCloud production and a development environment are needed, but not enough vSphere resources are available to create two completely separate vCloud environments. Imagine the following: you need a full vCloud development environment; however, you only need the environment for a limited time frame. In addition to that, you need users that you don't trust to be `SysAdmin`. In these situations, a second vCD is a good and easy solution.

The separation of the vCloud elements is done via the **System ID** number. As each element has an HREF ID next to its name, a separation is guaranteed.

See also

▶ Refer to the *Instant VMware vCloud Starter* book by *Daniel Langenhan* for more detailed instructions on vCD Cell installation

Creating multiple vCD Cells for the same vCloud

In this section we will create a second vCD Cell without a need for load balancing.

Getting ready

We will need the following:

▶ RedHat Linux VM (RHEL) 5 or 6 (6.3 is the highest version with vCD 5.1.2)

▶ vCloud Director Binary

▶ vCD shared directory (NFS)

▶ Root credentials for RHEL VM

How to do it...

We will now configure a second cell without load balancing.

Preparation of the first cell

Perform the following steps as a preparation of the first cell:

1. Log in to the existing first cell.

2. Gain root access if you haven't already.

3. Run the following command to copy the `Config` files to the shared directory:

   ```
   cd /opt/vmware/vcloud-director
   cp etc/responses.properties data/transfer
   chown vcloud:vcloud data/transfer/responses.properties
   ```

4. Write down the IDs of the vCloud user and group (we will need that later on). Use the following commands:

   ```
   id -u vcloud
   id -g vcloud
   ```

Installing the second cell

Perform the following steps for installing the second cell:

1. Make sure the first cell is using the shared directory.

2. Install RHEL on the VM.

3. Assign the second IP to the interface `eth0:0` as explained in the *Setting up networks for the vCloud VM* recipe.

4. Configure the firewall to allow HTTPS (port 443) traffic.

5. Transfer the vCloud Director Binary to the new RHEL VM using SCP (with a program such as WinSCP) and put it in the `/tmp` directory.

6. Log in to the new RHEL.

7. Gain root access, if you haven't logged in as root.

8. Execute the vCloud Binary. You may have to change the permissions on the vCloud binary with the command `chmod 777 [vcloud binary]`.

 Do not run the script at the end.

9. If there are any software dependencies, resolve them with `yum install [list of missing packages]`, and then re-run the installer.

10. Check the IDs of the vCloud user and group (we need that later on). Use the commands with the `id` command as before. The IDs must be the same. If that is not the case, please see the *There's more...* section.

11. Add the NFS mount to the Linux filesystem as we did in the *Retrofitting a shared directory into an existing vCD Cell* recipe in this chapter.

12. Either create self-signed SSL certificates or import the certificates as shown in the *SSL certificates* section in the *Load balancing vCD* recipe in this chapter.

13. Run the `configure` script and use the response file we copied:

    `/opt/vmware/vcloud-director/bin/configure -r /opt/vmware/vcloud-director/data/transfer/responses.properties`

14. Define the interfaces for HTTP and console.

15. If you choose a different path for the certificate's keystore file, you are now asked to provide the correct one.

16. You will be asked for the password of the certificate's keystore.

17. There can be a substantial wait time until the system continues, so be patient. However, more than 15 minutes is too long; if this is the case, try to configure the system, not by using the response file but by manually adding the same database as the first cell to vCloud Director.

18. The database should now be configured automatically. If that's not the case, try to configure the system, not by using the response file but by manually adding the same database as the first cell to vCloud Director.

19. vCloud Director is now installed, and you can start the cell directly from the script or via `service vmware-vcd start`.

20. Log in to vCloud Director (use the IP or hostname of the new cell) as `SysAdmin`.

21. Navigate to **Manage & Monitor** | **Cloud Cells**; there should now be an entry for a second cell.

How it works...

We installed a second vCD Cell, but we are still using the same database and the same shared directory as well as the same vSphere infrastructure. Most people now finish up with a load balancer in front of both cells; however, it's not needed. This setup is good for situations where you need more and faster client connections to the consoles or for some network security considerations. You can publish one cell's URL to one pool of users and the other cell's URL to another, separating the number of people using a cell.

As both cells are still connected, the GUI and the REST API still share all resources and the configuration.

There's more...

If your Linux system is not attached to an LDAP (or AD) and doesn't share user and group IDs, the vCloud Director Binary will add the users to the local system.

If the IDs between the two installations are different, there are two solutions:

▶ Use a shared LDAP (AD) between the vCloud cells. See the *See more* sections for how to help.

▶ The other method is to change one of the IDs of the local user and group management. Please note that this is not for the Linux novice and can cause major problems. Perform the following steps to do so:

1. Log in to the first vCloud VM and gain root access.

2. Run the command `id` and note down the IDs for the vCloud user and group.

3. Log in to the second vCloud VM and gain root access.

4. Use `vi` to change the group ID of the vCloud group in the file `/etc/group` to the one from the first server.

5. Use `vi` to change the user ID and group ID in the file `/etc/passwd` to the ones from the first server.

6. Use `chown -R vcloud:vcloud /opt/vmware/vcloud-director` to reset all the ownerships.

If the user and group IDs on the second cell are already used, you might need to change them on both systems. Please note that this could cause a huge impact.

See also

▸ For help on vCloud Cell installation, refer to *Instant VMware vCloud Starter* by *Daniel Langenhan*.

▸ For adding Linux servers to AD, refer to the following link:

```
https://access.redhat.com/site/documentation/en-US/Red_Hat_
Enterprise_Linux/6/html/Deployment_Guide/ch-Configuring_
Authentication.html
```

Load balancing vCD

We will now add a second cell and load balance it.

Getting ready

We will need an existing cell that already uses the shared directory as well as the following items:

▸ RedHat Linux VM (RHEL) 5 or 6 (6.3 is the highest version with vCD 5.1.2)

▸ vCloud Director Binary

▸ vCD Shared directory (NFS)

▸ Root credentials for RHEL VM

We also need a load balancer and two new IPs for the load balanced interfaces with DNS entries.

How to do it...

We will now work through the steps to create a load-balanced vCD Cell.

Preparation

Please execute the *Creating multiple vCD Cells for the same vCloud* recipe in this chapter.

Configuring the load balancer

We need to configure the load balancer with two **Virtual IPs** (**VIP**); one for the HTTP and one for the console interface. Due to the fact that each brand of load balancer is differently configured, detailed instructions are not possible at this time; please see the *See also* section for links to detailed instructions.

However, the following generic steps should cover most points.

The HTTP interface

Perform the following steps to configure an HTTP interface:

- ▶ **Define the virtual servers**: These are the IPs of the HTTP interfaces of each cell.
- ▶ **Define the load-balanced port**: This is basically port TCP 443 (HTTPS).
- ▶ **Define the load-balanced servers**: This is the IP that the load balancer will respond to. The protocol should be HTTPS, port 443, and if possible, it should be using `SSL_Session_ID` as the persisted mode (stickiness).
- ▶ **The Health-Check options**: Set the **Health-Check** option to check for `https://[ip of the http interface of cell]/cloud/server_status`.

The console interface

Perform the following steps to configure a console interface:

- ▶ **Define the virtual servers**: These are the IPs of the console interfaces of each cell.
- ▶ **Define the load-balanced port**: This is basically port TCP 443 (TCP). It's important to use TCP here rather than HTTPS.
- ▶ **Define the load-balanced servers**: This is the IP that the load balancer will respond to. The protocol should be TCP, port 443.
- ▶ **The Health-Check options**: Set the Health-Check option to check for `https://[ip of the console interface of cell]/sdk/vimServiceVersion.xml`.

Configuring vCloud for load balancing

Perform the following steps for configuring vCloud for load balancing:

1. Log in to one of the vCloud Cells as `SysAdmin`.

2. Navigate to **Administration | Public Addresses**. You should now get the following screenshot:

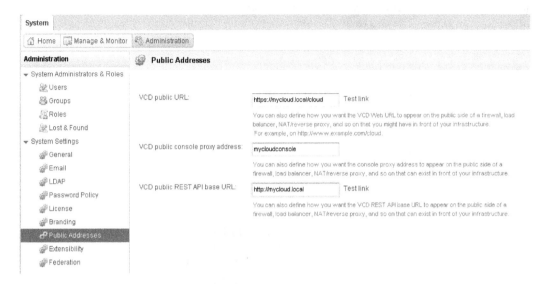

3. Enter in **VCD public URL** the URL of the HTTP VIP and add `/cloud`. For example, `http://mycloud.local/cloud`.

4. Enter in **VCD public console proxy address** the IP or hostname of the console VIP.

5. Enter in **VCD public REST API base URL** the URL of the HTTP VIP. For example, `http://mycloud.local`.

6. Click on **Apply**.

How it works...

Load balancing vCloud works by using two VIPs, one for the HTTP interface and one for the console proxy. Apart from the problem of getting the load balancer itself configured correctly, the setup is extremely simple and straightforward.

SSL certificates

Choosing the right SSL certificate type for the vCloud interfaces is an important topic. We basically have two choices: self-signed certificates or CA-issued certificates. CA-issued certificates are created by a **CA (Certificate Authority)**, whereas self-signed certificates can be created by anyone anywhere. The advantage of CA-issued certificates is that any browser in the network will accept them as valid and will not block the connection as untrusted. The advantage of self-signed certificates is that they don't require a CA and so don't cost any money; however, no browser will trust them, thereby requiring additional configuration.

vCloud Director needs two certificates: one for the HTTPS interface (first IP) and one for the console connection (second IP); both certificates are stored in a keystore file on the local system. vCloud Director uses the following aliases to identify the certificates, `HTTP`, and `consoleproxy`. The usage of aliases makes it a bit complicated with regards to load balancing, as we shall see a bit later.

Self-signed certificates can be created with the following command:

```
/opt/vmware/vcloud-director/jre/bin/keytool -keystore /opt/vmware/
certificates.ks -storetype JCEKS -genkey -keyalg RSA -alias [http |
consoleproxy]
```

To import a CA certificate, use the following command:

```
/opt/vmware/vcloud-director/jre/bin/keytool -import -file [certificate
file] -keystore  /opt/vmware/vcloud-director/certificates.ks -storetype
JCEKS -alias [http | consoleproxy]
```

While creating a new certificate, the most important question you will be asked is the question of the *first name*. The first name should be the FQDN name of the interface you create the certificate for. In the case of vCloud Director, you should have two DNS entries, one for the HTTP and one for the console IP; assign each to the first name of the certificate.

Load balancing modes and SSL certificates

The problem with the certificates comes from the abilities of the load balancer that is used. Some load balancers do not support all the SSL options or no SSL options at all, which leads automatically to different configurations. The two SSL options we are interested in are SSL offload and SSL pass through.

SSL offload means that the load balancer itself has an SSL certificate that is used to authenticate the connection. The load balancer will communicate to the servers by using their self-signed certificates.

SSL pass through means that the load balancer just redirects the traffic and will not take part in the authentication.

The reason we need both methods is that the console connection uses port 443, but it is not an HTTPS connection and doesn't use the HTTPS protocol. Therefore, we cannot use SSL offload for the console connection.

Depending on the SSL options supported, we end up with two cases:

  ▶   The load balancer doesn't support SSL or doesn't support both modes at the same time.

   If this is the case, we can only use certificates (CA or self-signed) that will use the VIP as the first name, meaning that we can use the same keystore for both cells as shown in the following diagram:

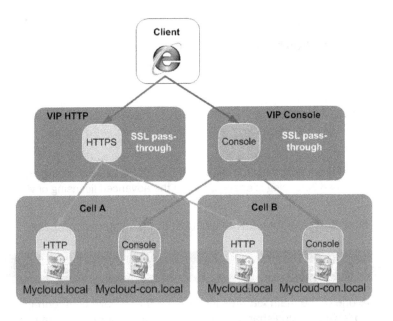

► The load balancer supports SSL offload and SSL pass through at the same time.

In this case, we should create certificates for the HTTP interface on the load balancer and use self-signed ones for the communication between the load balancer and the HTTP interface of the cells, as shown in the following diagram. However, we still need to use SSL pass through for the console, and we are required to make sure that the first name entry is the VIP of the console.

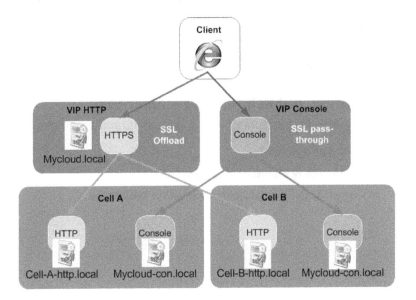

See also

▸ The *Using F5 for load balancing* article by *Duncan Epping* at `http://www.yellow-bricks.com/2012/02/16/using-f5-to-balance-load-between-your-vcloud-director-cells/`

▸ Using vCNS (vShield edge) for load balancing at `http://blogs.vmware.com/vcloud/2012/11/how-to-configure-a-load-balancer-using-vcloud-networking-and-security-edge-device-vshield.html`

 Please note that vCD comes with the vCNS basic licensing, but load balancing is enabled only in the advanced licensing of vCNS.

▸ Using Citrix Netscaler for load balancing at `http://anthonyspiteri.net/?p=70`

Working with catalogs in vCloud 5.5

The catalogs are one of the main features in vCloud 5.5 that have been enhanced. In this recipe, we will work with catalog sharing, publishing, and the subscribing features.

Getting ready

We need an organization where we can publish a catalog, as well as another organization that we can share the catalog with.

You will need vCloud 5.5 for this recipe; however, you do not need vSphere 5.5.

How to do it...

Let's have a look at the catalog improvements.

Configuring sharing, publishing, and subscribing

Perform the following steps for configuring sharing, publishing, and subscribing:

1. Log in to vCloud as `SysAdmin`.
2. Navigate to **Manage & Monitor | Organizations**.
3. Right-click on an existing organization and select **Properties**.

4. Click on **Catalog**. You should get the following screenshot:

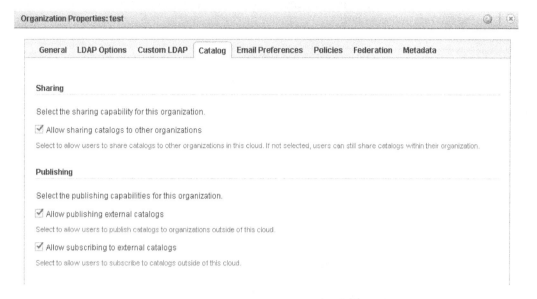

5. Enable sharing, publishing, and/or subscription by checking the checkboxes.

6. Click on **OK** to close the window.

Sharing an existing catalog

This requires the **Allow sharing catalogs to other organizations** setting in the organization. Now perform the following steps:

1. Navigate to the organization with the catalog you would like to share.

2. Click on **Catalogs**.

3. Right-click on the catalog and select **Share**.

4. Click on **Add Organizations**.

5. Either choose **All Organization** (the same setting as in the versions before vCloud 5.5) or select distinct organizations by clicking on **Add**. Notice the different icons in the following screenshot:

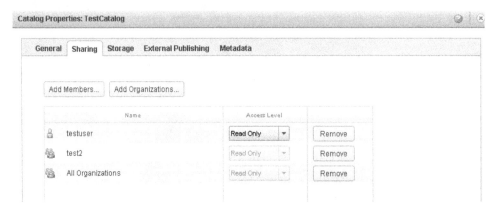

6. You can also add users from this organization. You cannot add users from other organizations.

7. Click on **OK** to close the window.

The shared catalog will appear as usual in the `Public Catalogs` folder in the organization you shared it with.

Publishing an existing catalog

This requires the **Allow publishing external catalogs** setting in the organization. Perform the following steps:

1. Navigate to the organization with the catalog you would like to publish.

2. Click on **Catalogs**.

3. Right-click on the catalog and select **Publish/Subscribe Settings...**. You should get the following screen:

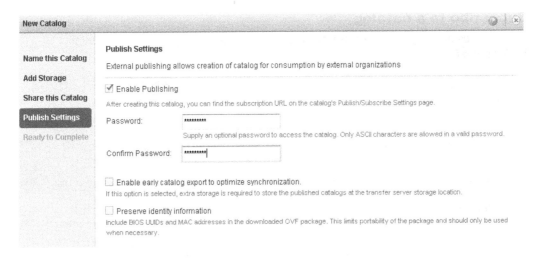

4. Check **Enable Publishing**.

5. Enter a password for the sharing.

6. Choose if you would like to create pre-copies into the transfer storage of the vCD cell (the `/data/transfer` directory).

7. Choose if you would like to preserve UUIDs and MACs of the VM.

8. Click on **OK** to close the window.

9. Right-click on the catalog again and select **Publish/Subscribe Settings....** You should see the following screen:

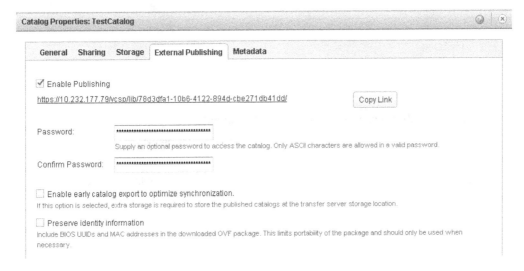

10. Copy the link and use it later to enable other organizations to subscribe to this catalog.

Subscribe to a catalog

This requires the **Allow subscription to external catalogs** setting in the organization. Perform the following steps:

1. Navigate to the organization that should receive a published catalog.

2. Click on **Catalogs**.

3. Click on the green icon (**+**).

4. Give the catalog a name, as shown in the following screenshot:

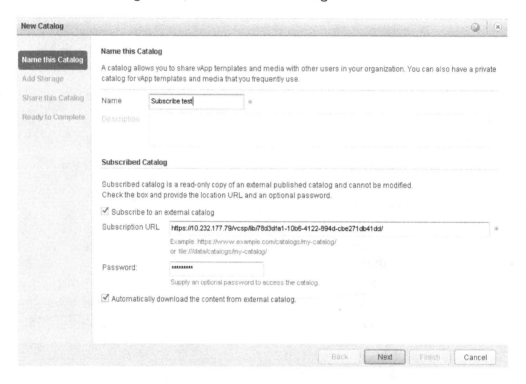

5. Check the checkbox **Subscribe to an external catalog**.

6. Paste the URL for the published catalog into the field **Subscription URL** and enter the password.

7. Select if you would like to copy all catalog items from the published catalog to the local storage by checking the checkbox **Automatically download the content from the external catalog**.

8. Verify the SSL thumbprint to establish a secure connection.

9. Select either a storage profile to store the catalog items on, or **select Use any storage available in the organization**.

10. You are now able to define sharing for this catalog.

11. Click on **OK** to finish the wizard.

12. The catalog items from the published catalog are now synced to the local storage.

How it works...

The new catalog features in vCloud 5.5 allow a lot more control over catalogs than before. Before vCloud 5.5, you were only able to share catalogs with everyone; now you can select who you are sharing with.

One of the major changes you need to be aware of is the definition of the word *published* in vCloud. Before 5.5, it meant that you shared the catalog with all organizations; now it means that you allow an export to other organizations and other vClouds.

One thing that has been removed in vCloud 5.5 is that when you add a catalog item, you cannot choose the storage profile or the OvCD anymore. The storage profile is now managed centrally for the whole catalog. vApp templates appear to be stored (in vSphere) in the first OvDC resource pool that was created. As vApp templates are powered off, they will not take up any of the OvDC resources.

Sharing

The difference between sharing and publishing is that sharing only works in the same vCloud. It uses the same method as it did before 5.5, but now you can select what organizations can use the catalog.

Publishing/subscription

The publishing feature is a completely new feature of vCloud. It uses an OVA export/import mechanism to move catalog items from one organization to another. As you can see in the following diagram, the idea is that you can use this publishing feature to share catalog items between vClouds:

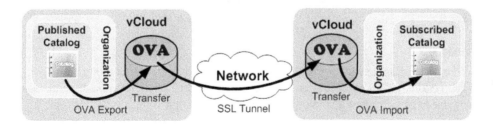

There's more...

The following sections provide some more topics worth looking at.

Synchronizing published/subscribed catalogs

When you activate the settings **Enable early catalog export to optimize synchronization**, all the current catalog items will be exported as OVA to the `data/transfer` directory on the vCloud Cell. This will make synchronization faster as the first step is already done, leaving only the copy and the import to be done. However, this also requires a lot of extra storage.

When you activate the setting **Automatically download the content from the external catalog**, all catalog items that are currently in the published catalog will be imported as soon as the new catalog has been created.

You can manually synchronize catalog items from the published catalog to the subscriber catalog by right-clicking on any catalog item and selecting **Sync**.

Media & Other

One of the long-awaited features in vCloud is the ability to share media files. Before vCloud 5.5, this wasn't possible. This will improve vCloud design monumentally. You can now create a catalog that contains only the base Windows and Linux images that you share with everyone as well as a catalog that contains specialized ISOs, and share them with selected organizations.

Another thing that is now possible is to import *any* file. So you can also upload, for example, a text file that contains licensing information or a Word document that describes what the templates or ISOs contain. The following screenshot shows the **Media & Other** tab:

Versioning

Also new in vCloud 5.5 is versioning. Each time you upload a new version of a catalog item, the version counter is increased. This helps you to keep track of your templates and ISOs, reducing the need to amend a versioning number to the naming standard.

If you want to upload a new version of a media file (or any other file), follow the ensuing instructions:

1. Right-click on the file in the catalog you would like to update and select **Update**.

2. Follow the normal import process to upload a file.

3. After the import, the version number will be increased.

If you would like to upload a new version of a vApp to the catalog as a vApp template, follow the ensuing instructions:

1. Navigate to **My Cloud**.

2. Right-click on the vApp you would like to upgrade and select **Add to catalog**. You should now see the following screen:

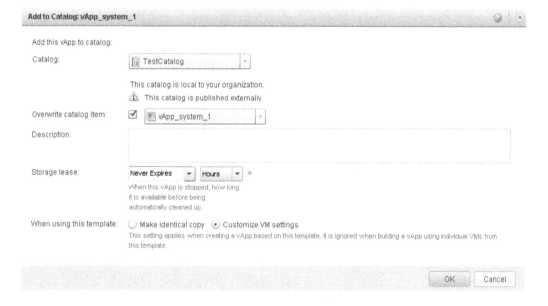

3. Select **Overwrite catalog item**.

4. Select from the drop-down menu the vApp template you would like to overwrite.

5. Follow the normal process for adding a vApp to the catalog.

6. After the item has been added to the catalog, navigate to the catalog and see that the version number has been increased.

7
Operational Challenges

This chapter is dedicated to all the little problems that come along with an operational vCloud. We will be looking into these problems covered in the following recipes:

- Loading Windows Sysprep packages in vCloud
- Exchanging SSL certificates
- Bypassing SSO login into vCloud
- Backing up vCloud
- Recovering the vCloud system
- Changing the name of an organization
- Shutting down and starting up the vCloud environment
- Using metadata to improve provisioning
- Using vSphere Host Profiles with vCloud
- Using vCloud with vCenter Auto Deploy
- Defining a vCloud development cycle
- Making the VM BIOS ID (UUID) unique
- Importing from Lab Manager into vCloud
- Using branding to make vCloud look different
- Putting an ESXi host into maintenance
- Updating vCloud Cells without interruption
- Updating a vCloud with only one cell
- Updating a vCenter in vCloud
- Updating vCNS
- Expanding vCD resources

> ▸ Resizing a VM hard disk
> ▸ Cloning a running vApp
> ▸ Removing infrastructure from vCloud

Loading Windows Sysprep packages in vCloud

If you are using Windows XP or Windows 2003, you need to include the Sysprep packages in the vCloud VM.

Getting ready

Download the latest Sysprep packages from `www.microsoft.com`.

You only need to download the Sysprep files for any systems older than Vista and Windows 2008, because in these versions the Sysprep tools are stored locally on the OS. Check the *VMware KB 1005593* for locations and direct links to the Sysprep packages. However, ignore the directory names the KB gives, as vCloud uses different ones from vSphere.

Don't forget that XP and Win2003 come in 32 bits and 64 bits respectively, and the Sysprep packages are different, so you may need to download both. We also need a means to transfer the packages to the Linux OS of the vCD VM; therefore, an SCP program such as WinSCP would be useful.

How to do it...

We will now work through the integration of the Sysprep packages in vCloud.

Downloading and preparing the Sysprep files

On your Windows desktop, prepare the Sysprep files you need using the following steps:

1. Create the following sub-directories in a directory you call `Sysprep`:

    ❑ `win2000`

    ❑ `winxp`

    ❑ `win2000`

    ❑ `winxp_64`

    ❑ `win2k3`

    ❑ `win2k3_64`

2. Download all the Sysprep files from Microsoft.

3. Unpack the files by executing the `.exe` files with the `/x` option.

4. Find the `deploy.cab` file.

5. Extract the `deploy.cab` file's content into the directories you have created. You can do that by simply double-clicking on them. This is the only content we need from the Sysprep packages.

Uploading and integrating the Sysprep files

Perform the following steps for uploading and integrating the Sysprep files:

1. Use an SCP program (such as WinSCP) to upload the `Sysprep` folder to `/tmp` of your vCD VM.

2. Log in to your vCD VM.

3. Gain root access if you haven't already.

4. Run the following small script to create the packages:

```
cd /tmp

chown -R root:root Sysprep

/opt/vmware/vcloud-director/deploymentPackageCreator/
createSysprepPackage.sh /tmp/SysPrep/
```

5. The package should have been created now; if you are getting error messages for Sysprep packages that you haven't downloaded, you can ignore them.

6. The package is copied to `/opt/vmware/vcloud-director/ guestcustomization` with the name `windows_deployment_package_ sysprep.cab`. Make sure that the permissions are set correctly to:

```
- rw - r - - r - -   vcloud:vcloud
```

Use the following commands to do so:

```
chmod 644 windows_deployment_package_sysprep.cab

chown vcloud:vcloud windows_deployment_package_sysprep.cab
```

7. If you have multiple cells, the best idea is to copy the package to the `../data/ transfer` directory, so you can insert it into the other cells. There is no need to repeat the process; just copy the file to the same directory.

8. The last step you have to do is restart the vCD Cell.

See the *A scripted cell shutdown* recipe in *Chapter 5, Working with the vCloud API*.

How it works...

vCloud uses Sysprep for Windows and a shell script for Linux to customize the operating system. In Windows, things are more difficult than in Linux, as different versions of Windows require different Windows Sysprep `deploy.cab` files. From Windows 2008 and Vista onwards, you don't need the extra Sysprep files anymore as they are contained within the OS.

When you add the Sysprep files to vCloud, and you are only using vCloud to provision VMs, you don't have to add them to vSphere too. As already mentioned in *Chapter 3, Better vApps*, vCloud doesn't use vSphere to run Guest Customization, but uses its own ESXi plugin to do it.

See also

- ► The *Using Guest Customization with pre and post deploy* recipe in *Chapter 3, Better vApps*
- ► The *Using PowerShell or Perl to perform Guest Customization tasks* recipe in *Chapter 3, Better vApps*
- ► The *Joining VMs automatically to domains* recipe in *Chapter 3, Better vApps*

Exchanging SSL certificates

Use this recipe if your SSL certificate has expired or if you want to exchange self-signed certificates for CA certificates.

Getting ready

We need a working vCD Cell. If you have CA certificates, that's great, otherwise, we will create self-signed ones.

How to do it...

We will now exchange the existing SSL certificates.

Preparation

Perform the following steps as preparation:

1. Log in to the vCD Cell.
2. Gain root access, if you haven't already.
3. Shut down the cell. See the *A scripted cell shutdown* recipe in *Chapter 5, Working with the vCloud API*.

4. Navigate to the vCloud directory with the following command:

```
cd /opt/vmware/vcloud-director
```

5. Make a backup of the certification keystore with the following command (you need to use the path and filename that you gave the file):

```
cp certificates.ks certificates.ks.bak
```

Deleting an old certificate

Perform the following steps to delete old certificates:

1. Use the following command to list the contents of the certificate keystore:

```
Jre/bin/keytool -keystore certificates.ks -list
```

2. Use the following command to delete a certificate using its alias:

```
Jre/bin/keytool -keystore certificates.ks -delete -alias [http |
consoleproxy]
```

3. List the content again and verify that the certificate has been deleted.

Creating a certificate request and importing it

If you want to use self-signed certificates, skip this step. Perform the following steps to create a certificate request and import the CA-signed certificate:

1. Generate a new certificate request with the following command:

```
Jre/bin/keytool -keystore certificates.ks -storetype JCEKS -
certreq -alias alias [http | consoleproxy] -file [certificate
file]
```

2. Transfer the file and have it signed by your CA.

3. Import the CA's root certificate into the keystore using the following command:

```
jre/bin/keytool -storetype JCEKS -keystore certificates.ks -import
-alias root -file root.cer
```

4. Import the CA's intermediate certificates into the keystore:

```
jre/bin/keytool -storetype JCEKS -keystore certificates.ks -import
-alias intermediate -file intermediate.cer
```

5. Import the CA-signed certificate into the keystore:

```
jre/bin/keytool -import -file [certificate file] -keystore
certificates.ks -storetype JCEKS -alias [http | consoleproxy]
```

Creating a new self-signed certificate

If you are using CA-signed certificates, skip this step, else perform the following step:

1. Create a self-signed certificate:

   ```
   jre/bin/keytool -keystore certificates.ks -storetype JCEKS -genkey
   -keyalg RSA -alias [http | consoleproxy]
   ```

Finishing touches

Perform the following steps to provide the finishing touches to our recipe:

1. Import the new certificates into the vCloud Director Cell by running the following command (if you are using a second cell, your `response.properties` file could be in the `data/transfer` directory):

   ```
   bin/configure -r etc/responses.properties
   ```

2. Start the vCloud cell with the following command:

   ```
   service vmware-vcd start
   ```

3. Check the logs for errors with the following command:

   ```
   tail -f log/cell.log
   ```

How it works...

The `keytool` command is a common Java tool that ships with all Java versions. As vCloud Director uses Java, the tool comes with it in the `/opt/vmware/vcloud-director/jre` directory. There is a great deal of configuration that can be done with the tool; however, the only commands we need are the `create`, `import`, and `delete` commands.

Self-signed certificates with longer duration

The default duration for a self-signed certificate is 90 days. In most cases, that is not enough, and depending on the security settings, connections to vCloud may be refused. To change the default time, just add the following option to your self-signed certificate request:

```
-validity [amount of days]
```

This will set the time for which the certificate will be valid.

Exporting and importing self-signed certificates

If you have problems with load balancing, you may need to export and import certificates.

Use the following command to export a self-signed certificate:

```
jre/bin/keytool -keystore certificates.ks -storetype JCEKS -export -alias
[http | consoleproxy] -file [certificate file]
```

Use the following command to import a self-signed certificate:

```
jre/bin/keytool -keystore certificates.ks -storetype JCEKS -import -alias
[http | consoleproxy] -file [certificate file]
```

See also

▸ To find out how to import self-signed certificates in to Internet Explorer, refer to `https://www.poweradmin.com/help/sslhints/ie.aspx`

▸ To find out how to create a CA Server and how to issue certificates with Active Directory, refer to `http://technet.microsoft.com/en-us/library/cc772393%28v=ws.10%29.aspx`

Bypassing SSO login into vCloud

You have configured vCloud to use SSO and now you can't login anymore. This section explains how to get around this.

Getting ready

You need a vCloud that is configured to use SSO.

To configure vCloud for SSO, follow the ensuing steps:

1. Log in to vCloud as `SysAdmin`.

2. Navigate to **Administration | Federation**.

3. Click on **Register**. You should now see the following screen:

4. Enter the lookup service URL as `https://[sso server]:7444/lookupserice/sdk`.

5. Enter a username and password of an SSO administrative user.

6. Enter the vCloud URL as `https://[vcloud server]/vcloud`. If you are using load balancing, the URL you enter is that of the VIP.

7. Check the checkbox **Use vSphere Single Sign-On**.

In order to test this recipe, make sure you enter the vCloud URL incorrectly.

How to do it...

1. Open a web browser.

2. Enter the URL of your vCloud.

3. Add `/login.jsp` to the end of the URL, for example, `https://[vcloud server]/vcloud/login.jsp`.

4. Press *Enter*.

5. The normal vCloud login page should now load.

6. Log in as `SysAdmin`.

7. Navigate to **Administration | Federation**.

8. Uncheck the box **Use vSphere Single Sign-On**.

How it works...

vCloud can use LDAP or SSO for authentication.

There's more...

You can also switch off the authentication directly using the vCloud database. You can use the following code to alter an MSSQL DB:

```
UPDATE [vcloud].[dbo].[identity_provider]
SET [is_enabled] = '0'
WHERE provider_type = 'SAML'
GO
```

Backing up vCloud

We have already discussed the backup of vApps in vCloud, but what about the vCloud system itself?

Getting ready

We need a functioning vCloud environment containing SSO, vCenter, vCNS, and vCloud. Therefore, we should also have a backup method.

How to do it...

You can either back up the VMs of all the management systems (including the database) or you can follow the approach described in this section.

SSO backup

SSO backup is done by backing up the SSO database. See your database vendor for best practices.

vCenter backup

vCenter backup is done by backing up the vCenter database. See your database vendor for best practices.

vCNS backup

vCloud Network and Security (vCNS) is easy to back up. Perform the following steps to do so:

1. Log in to vCNS web service.

2. Navigate to **Settings & Reports | Configuration | Backups**. You should see the following screen:

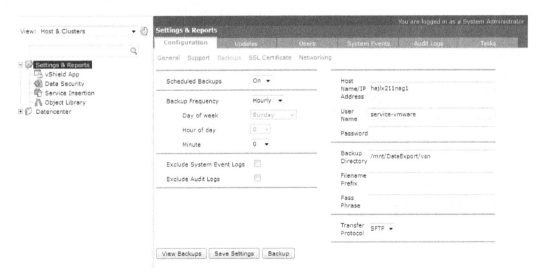

3. Set **Scheduled Backups** to **On**.

4. Select a **Backup Frequency** value. Think how often the vCNS configuration will change, meaning how often vApp Networks or Edges are deployed.

5. Select the host and the host credentials that should be used for backup.

6. Select the **Transfer Protocol** option. Your choices are **FTP** or **SFTP**.

7. Click on **Save Settings**.

8. Re-enter the password and click on **Backup** to back up the vCNS now and to essentially test your settings.

9. You will now see the new backup listed underneath.

10. Log in to the backup host and check the backup file.

vCloud backup

vCloud backup is mainly done by backing up the vCloud database.

A one-off backup of the following items should be considered:

- ▶ `/opt/vmware/vcloud-director/data/transfer/*`
- ▶ `/opt/vmware/vcloud-director/etc/response.properties`
- ▶ `/opt/vmware/vcloud-director/guestcustomization/ windows_ deployment_package_sysprep.cab`
- ▶ `/opt/vmware/vcloud-director/certificates.ks` (or the location you specified)

You should consider a backup of the `certificates.ks` file whenever you change certificates.

How it works...

There are basically two methods to back up vCloud. You can either back up all the Management VMs including the database or you can back up the systems separately.

What is important to understand about the backup is how the vCloud system and the vCenter system hang together. Have a look at the explanation in the *The problems associated with the backup and restore of vCloud* recipe in *Chapter 4, Datastores and Storage Profiles*. Because of the connections between the MoRef and the Href, the backup of the vCloud environment isn't trivial.

Which backup method is best for your environment depends solely on your **Recovery Time Objectives (RTO)** and **Recovery Point Objectives (RPO)**.

Backing up all the Management VMs will work; however, if storage is lost, and with it the VMs too, this backup won't help. It will only protect against failure or loss of a part of the Management structure. This backup will take a bit of time and will require a lot of backup space, as we back up not only the important core elements but also the OS systems around them. The advantage is that a restore in the case of a full outage is fast, as we just need to restore the VMs.

Using the previous approach will reduce the volume of backup, as we back up only the essential core elements; however, a restore will take longer as we will still need to rebuild the shells (the Management VMs). The advantage in this method is that we can also restore the systems separately. We can restore only vCloud by restoring the database and then restarting the existing vCloud VM.

There's more...

Let's look at setting up an MSSQL automated backup.

It is better to use professional integrated backup tools to back up an SQL DB, but the following is a fast and easy way:

1. Connect to your MSSQL server using Microsoft SQL Server Management.
2. Log in as an administrator.
3. Click on **Management**.
4. Right-click on **Maintenance Plans** and select **New Maintenance Plan**.
5. Drag-and-drop the item **Back Up Database Task** in to the empty space.

6. Right-click on the **Back Up Database** task and select **Edit**. You should now see the following screen:

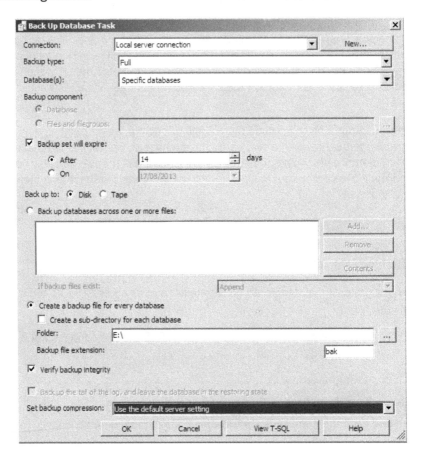

7. Click on **Database(s)**. In this window, select the databases you would like to back up.

8. Select where you would like to back up the database(s).

9. Check **Verify backup integrity**.

10. Click on **OK**.

11. Click on the calendar icon (**Subplan schedule**).

12. Select the time of the backup.

13. Click on **OK**.

14. Click on the **X** icon in the upper-right corner of **Maintenance Plan**.

15. Allow the saving of **Maintenance Plan**.

See also

▶ Backup of Oracle Database at `http://www.orafaq.com/wiki/Oracle_database_Backup_and_Recovery_FAQ`

Recovering the vCloud system

So how do we restore a vCloud environment?

Getting ready

Depending on the point of loss from which you have to recover, different items are needed:

▶ For total loss, the following items are needed:
   ❑ Backup
   ❑ Documentation
   ❑ Windows and Redhat VMs
   ❑ vSphere installation disk
   ❑ vCloud Director Binary
   ❑ vCNS OVA

▶ For loss of the vSphere system, the following items are needed:
   ❑ Backup
   ❑ Documentation
   ❑ Windows and RHEL VMs
   ❑ vSphere installation disk

▶ For loss of vCNS, the following items are needed:
   ❑ Backup
   ❑ Documentation
   ❑ vCNS OVA

▶ For loss of the vCloud DB, the following item is needed:
   ❑ Backup

▶ For loss of one vCloud Cell (in a multicell setup), the following items are needed:

  ❑ Backup

  ❑ RHEL VM

  ❑ Documentation

  ❑ vCloud Director Binary

How to do it...

Let's look at the various scenarios.

Restore vSphere from scratch

Perform the following steps to restore vSphere from scratch:

1. Restore the databases.
2. Install the vSphere environment using the restored databases.
3. Continue with restoring vCNS.
4. Continue with restoring vCloud.

Restore the vSphere environment from DB

Perform the following steps to restore the vSphere environment from DB:

1. If the vCenter and SSO VMs are still working, stop all VMware services on them.
2. Restore the databases.
3. Start the VMware services as described in the *Shutting down and starting up the vCloud environment* recipe in this chapter.
4. Continue with restoring vCNS.
5. Continue with restoring vCloud.

Restore vCNS

Perform the following steps to restore vCNS:

1. Deploy the vCNS OVF template.
2. Power on the vCNS VM.
3. Open a vCenter remote console on the vCNS.
4. Log in with the username `admin` and the password `default`.
5. Type `enable` and then re-enter the previous password.
6. Type `setup`.

7. Configure the IP settings of the vCNS VM (see your documentation).

8. Exit and wait until the system is ready.

9. Connect to the HTTPS GUI of vCNS with a browser by browsing to `https://[vCNS ip]`.

10. Log in with the username `admin` and the password `default`.

11. Navigate to **Settings & Reports** | **Configuration** | **Backups**.

12. Enter all the settings to connect to the host where you placed your backup on (see the *Backing up vCloud* recipe in this chapter), as shown in the following screenshot:

13. Click on **View Backups**.

14. Select the backup you want to restore by checking the checkbox in front of it.

15. Click on **Restore**.

16. Select what you want to restore.

17. Wait until the restore has finished, then log in again.

Restore vCloud

Perform the following steps to restore vCloud:

1. Install the RHEL system.

2. Follow the *Connecting more than one vCloud Cell to the same infrastructure* recipe in Chapter 6, *Improving the vCloud Design*.

3. Transfer the vCloud Director Binary to the new RHEL VM using SCP (with a program such as WinSCP) and place it in the `/tmp` directory.

4. Log in to the new RHEL.

5. Gain root access if you haven't logged in as `root`.

6. Assign the second IP to the interface `eth0:0` as shown in the *Setting up networks for the vCloud VM* recipe in *Chapter 6, Improving the vCloud Design*.

7. Configure the firewall to allow HTTPS (port 443) traffic.

8. Execute the vCloud Binary. You may have to change the permissions on the vCloud Binary with the command `chmod 777 [vcloud binary]`.

 Do not run the script.

9. If there are any software dependencies, resolve them with `yum install [list of missing packages]`, then rerun the installer.

10. Create the NFS mount (see the *Retrofitting a shared directory into an existing vCD Cell* recipe in *Chapter 6, Improving the vCloud Design*).

11. Restore the files to the shared directories:

    `/opt/vmware/vcloud-director/data/transfer/*`

    `/opt/vmware/vcloud-director/etc/response.properties`

    `/opt/vmware/vcloud-director/guestcustomization/ windows_deployment_package_sysprep.cab`

    `/opt/vmware/vcloud-director/certifcates.ks`

    (or the location you specified)

12. Run the configuration script `/opt/vmware/vcloud-director/bin/configure`.

13. Select the restored certificates' file.

14. Use the old database connection.

15. Start one cell with the command `service vmware-vcd start`.

16. Monitor closely the logfiles with the following command:

    `tail -f /opt/vmware/vcloud-director/log/vcloud-debug.`

Restore vCloud DB

To restore vCloud using a DB perform the following steps:

1. If the vCloud Cells are still up, shut them all down with `service vmware-vcd stop`. Do not use the cell management tool.

2. Follow best practices of the database vendor to restore a database backup.

3. If the login credentials to the database have been changed, you will need to rerun the `/opt/vmware/vcloud-director/bin/configure` script.

4. Start one cell with the command `service vmware-vcd start`.

5. Monitor the logfiles closely with the following command:

   tail -f /opt/vmware/vcloud-director/log/vcloud-debug.

Restore one vCloud Cell (in a multicell environment)

Follow the *Creating multiple vCD Cells for the same vCloud* recipe in *Chapter 6, Improving the vCloud Design*.

How it works...

Restoring is the key to a working backup. Without knowing how to restore, any backup is useless. Therefore, it is of the highest priority to design, document, and test the restore process. Previously, we had several scenarios and each had a slightly different approach; however, they all come into play if total loss takes place.

I cannot stress the value of a restore test. There is a high economical risk involved for any business that is not testing the restore of its backup. The important points to think about here are:

  ▸ How to do the recovery, step-by-step?

  ▸ What recovery scenarios are likely and what is the worst-case scenario?

  ▸ How long does each recovery scenario take?

  ▸ What is the loss? There is always loss as there is always some change between backups.

  ▸ Who is required to restore and what is needed, with regards to additional material, passwords, access, and so on, to perform the recovery?

The backup process will improve based on the experience of testing the restore process.

Changing the name of an organization

In this recipe, we will change the name of an organization and you will gain a better understanding about vCloud objects.

Getting ready

We need an existing organization.

How to do it...

1. Log in to vCloud as `SysAdmin`.
2. Navigate to **Manage & Monitor | Organizations**.
3. Right-click on the organization and select **Disable**.
4. Right-click on the organization again and select **Properties**.
5. Rename the organization. You will see that the organization's URL will be updated too.
6. Click on **OK**.
7. Right-click on the renamed organization and select **Enable**.
8. Check the URL of the new organization.

How it works...

A lot of elements in vCloud can only be renamed when they are disabled. **Disabled** indicates that no one can actively use the object in any way.

Most objects in vCloud have to be disabled before they can be effectively renamed or deleted.

In addition to that, you cannot delete objects that have child objects. For instance, if you want to delete an organization, you have to first delete the OvDC; to delete the OvDC, you have to delete all vApps, templates, and media as well as networks and Edges.

Shutting down and starting up the vCloud environment

In this recipe, we will discuss the proper start-up and shut-down order for the vCloud environment.

Getting ready

We need a complete vSphere and a vCloud environment.

How to do it...

Let's have a closer look at the starting and stopping of the vCloud environment.

Start-up sequence

Start up the following items in the following order:

1. SSO database
2. SSO service

3. Configuration service
4. vCenter database
5. vCenter service
6. Web client service
7. vCNS
8. Shared directory
9. vCloud database
10. vCloud Director's first cell
11. vCloud Director's other cells

Shut-down sequence

Shut down the items in the following order:

1. All vCloud Director cells except one
2. vCloud Director last cell
3. vCloud database
4. Shared directory
5. vCNS
6. Web client service
7. vCenter service
8. vCenter database
9. Configuration service
10. SSO
11. SSO database

How it works...

The start-up and shut-down sequence of vCloud is important as vCloud will not start up correctly, or worse, it will start up in an inconsistent state if the underlying infrastructure is not available. The most important components to start up vCloud are the database and the shared directory (if used). vCloud will come up and work without the vCNS and vSphere infrastructure; however, it will not be able to interact with any infrastructure, and it is highly recommended to try to do anything that involves vSphere or vCNS.

To make sure that nobody can work with vCloud while you shut down the system, it is a good idea to disable all organizations before shutting down vCloud. Enable the organizations when you are sure that everything is back to normal. For testing purposes, I normally use the Admin organization that was introduced to you in the *Keeping your templates under control* recipe in *Chapter 6, Improving the vCloud Design*. Disabling and enabling all organizations is also a very good idea for scripting.

If the vCloud environment started before the vSphere environment was ready, or if you lost your vSphere environment for some time, follow the ensuing steps:

1. Log in to vCloud as `SysAdmin`.

2. Navigate to **Manage & Monitor | vCenter**.

3. Right-click on the vCenter that just came back to life and select **Reconnect** as shown in the following screenshot:

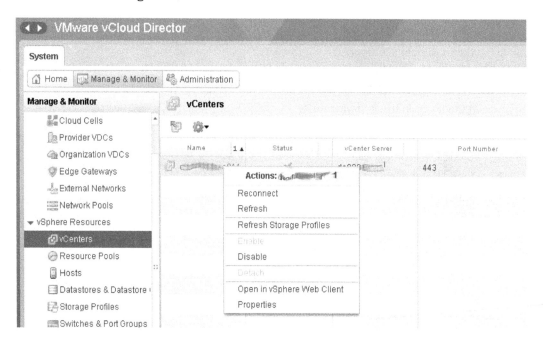

4. Wait until the task has finished successfully.

There's more...

We can create a vCenter vApp to automate the correct start-up and shutdown using the following steps:

1. Log in to vCenter using the web client.

2. Navigate to **vCenter | Hosts and Clusters**.

3. Select the cluster that contains your vSphere infrastructure and vCloud Cells.

4. Right-click on that cluster and select **New vApp**.

5. Select **Create a new vApp**.

6. Enter a new name for the vApp and select a folder (you may like to create a separate one for the infrastructure).

7. Enter the values for the CPU and memory resources. It is a good idea to enter the minimum MHz and MB that the combined infrastructure needs to function.

8. Close the wizard.

For every infrastructure VM, do the following:

1. Right-click on the VM and select **Move To**.

2. Select the vApp you have created.

3. After you have moved all the VMs to the vApp, right-click on the vApp and select **Edit Settings**. You should now see the following screen:

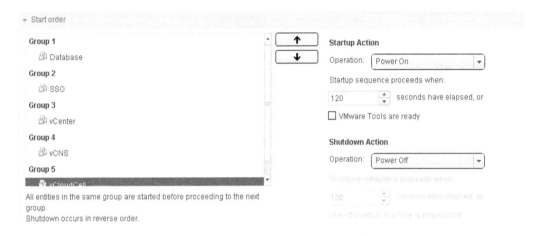

4. Arrange the infrastructure VMs as follows:

VM	Group	Startup		Shutdown	
		Operation	Time [s]	Operation	Time [s]
Database	1	PowerOn	180	Guest Shutdown	180
SSO	2	PowerOn	120	Guest Shutdown	120
vCenter	3	PowerOn	120	Guest Shutdown	120
vCNS	4	PowerOn	60	Power Off	60
vCloud Cell	5	PowerOn	0	Guest Shutdown	60

5. Click on **OK**.

Use the **PowerOn** and **Shutdown** operations of the vApp to make sure that the VMs are shut down or started in the correct order. The values stated in the **Time [s]** in the previous table may need to be adjusted depending on your own infrastructure.

Using metadata to improve provisioning

In this recipe, we use metadata to improve general provisioning of VMs and vApps.

Getting ready

We need a VM and a vApp and some space to deploy and clone them. For a full test, have two user logins handy.

How to do it...

We will now create metadata and then use it.

Creating metadata

Perform the following steps to create metadata:

1. Log in to your organization.
2. Create a new vApp or use an existing vApp.
3. Right-click on the vApp and select **Properties**.
4. Click on **Metadata**.
5. Enter the metadata in the fields as shown in the following screenshot:

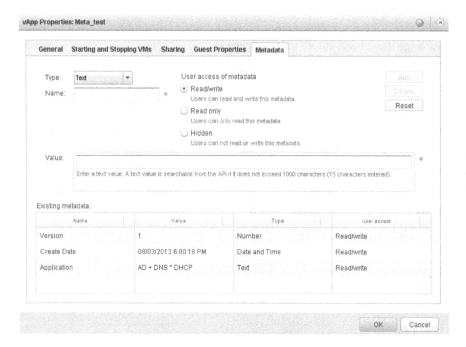

6. Click on **OK**.

7. Create a template from the vApp.

Using metadata

Perform the following steps to use metadata:

1. Log in with a different user.

2. Deploy the template.

3. Right-click on the vApp and select **Properties**.

4. Click on **Metadata**.

5. You can now see all the data you entered.

How it works...

Metadata is not only restricted to vApps and VMs but also to most other vCloud objects. Metadata comes in handy to keep things such as version numbers, ownership, and installed applications of VMs or vApps organized. When a vApp or VM is created, you can record all of the information that other users may require, and when you create a template from it, all copies of this template will inherit the metadata.

There are three different access levels to metadata that the owner can choose:

▸ **Read/Write**: Users can edit this setting.

▸ **Read Only**: Users can only read the settings.

▸ **Hidden**: The user cannot see this setting, only the owner can, thereby making this a good choice for tracking the usage of an object or for scripting purposes.

For a user to be able to change metadata, he/she at least needs read/write sharing rights. Hidden data cannot be seen even if the user has full-access sharing rights.

There's more...

You can read metadata by using the API.

The following is an example on how to access the metadata via PowerShell:

```
$test = get-civapp -name "your vapp"
$test.ExtensionData.GetMetadata().MetadataEntry
```

See also

▸ Have a look at the following link or some really good PowerShell scripts that will help in dealing with metadata:

```
http://blogs.vmware.com/vipowershell/2012/03/working-with-
vcloud-metadata-in-powercli.html
```

Using vSphere Host Profiles with vCloud

In this recipe, we will learn how Host Profiles are affected due to vCloud.

Getting ready

You will need access to vCenter as an administrator as well as some ESXi hosts to use.

How to do it...

1. Log in to your vCenter web client.
2. Create a base cluster with connections to a Distributed Switch.
3. Create a base ESXi host connected to networks.
4. If you are using NFS or iSCSI, make sure you have all the required settings configured.
5. Modify the Host Profile to include a default password.
6. Create a Host Profile of this base server and name it so that its association with the cluster is clear.
7. Apply the new profile to a second ESXi and test the Host Profile.
8. If the Host Profile is good, use it from now on, otherwise start over at step 3.

How it works...

Host Profiles store all the configuration of an ESXi Server for a given cluster. They can be used to configure new ESXi hosts that join a cluster, or they can be used for validation of ESXi hosts. Validation means that the vCenter checks the current configuration against the one that is stored in the Host Profile.

The problem while using vCloud Director is that vCloud Director makes a lot of changes to a cluster; it changes the amount of resource pools (OvDCs) and the port groups on a Distributed Switch (vApp Networks, Edges, Network pools, and so on). So, creating a Host Profile doesn't seem to be a very good idea due to the high amount of change. However, as I have already shown in the *Setting up networks for the vCloud VM* recipe in *Chapter 6, Improving the vCloud Design*, you can use the Host Profile of a basic ESXi host with only the basic Distributed Switch and storage. Using such a basic Host Profile allows us to redistribute ESXi Servers between clusters to become a cloud. This is especially handy if you are using a blade infrastructure where basic hardware profiles are used (for example, HP c7000 and Cisco UCS). This allows (with a touch of automation and auto VMware deployment) that you can add capacity to a cluster by just pushing a new blade into a predefined slot. The *Using vCloud with vCenter Auto Deploy* recipe in this chapter will show how this is done.

But let us get back to the Host Profiles. The usage of Host Profiles with vCloud is extremely powerful, however, only for deployment. Using Host Profiles for checking the ESXi configuration's consistency doesn't work due to the high amount of change that vCloud introduces to the cluster.

Using vCloud with vCenter Auto Deploy

In this recipe, we will explore the possibilities that the integration of vCloud with other VMware products can accomplish. This recipe isn't easy, but will teach you a lot.

Getting ready

We need the following:

- ▶ vCenter
- ▶ PowerCLI
- ▶ Auto Deploy
- ▶ A dedicated user for Auto Deploy
- ▶ A TFTP server (either a Linux setup or something similar to `http://tftpd32.jounin.net/`)
- ▶ A DHCP server (either a Linux or a Windows one)

Depending on the size of your installation, a separate Windows host for the deployment is a good idea; however, it can also work directly on the vCenter's VM.

How to do it...

This is not a step-by-step explanation as you are used to, as this recipe alone would fill 20 pages; however, I have laid out the most important steps one after another.

Preparing the infrastructure

Perform the following steps to prepare the infrastructure:

1. Install vSphere Auto Deploy on a separate server or on the vCenter Server.

2. Install VMware PowerCLI and VMware PowerCLI for Auto Deploy on the vCenter Server; we need that for automated scripting later.

3. Add a dedicated user for scripting to vCenter with administrator rights.

4. You may like to install a PowerShell editing tool such as PowerGUI (see the *Using PowerShell with vCloud Director* recipe in *Chapter 5, Working with the vCloud API*, for details).

5. Install and configure a DHCP server.

    A Linux DHCP server should have the following entries:

    ```
    # TFTP SERVER ADDRESS
    next-server [TFTP Server];
    # BOOTFILE NAME
    if ((exists user-class) and (option user-class = "gPXE")){
    # STAGE 2 GPXE BOOTFILE
            filename = "https:// [TFTP Server]:6501/vmw/rbd/
    tramp";
            }
    else {
    # STAGE 1 PXE PRE-BOOT
            filename = "/undionly.kpxe.vmw-hardwired";
            }
    ```

    A Windows DHCP server should be configured with the following options:

    ❑   Option 66 TFTP IP

    ❑   Option 67 Boot, filename `undionly.kpxe.vmw-hardwired`

6. Install and configure a TFTP Server.

    If you would like to use a Windows-based TFTP, you can refer to `http://tftpd32.jounin.net/`.

    A Linux TFTP server will need the following settings:

    ```
    #/etc/xinetd.d/tftp
    service tftp
    ```

```
{
        protocol        = udp
        port            = 69
        socket_type     = dgram
        wait            = yes
        user            = nobody
        server          = /usr/sbin/in.tftpd
        server_args     = /tftpboot
        disable         = no
}
```

7. Download the first-boot file from vCenter as shown in the following screenshot:

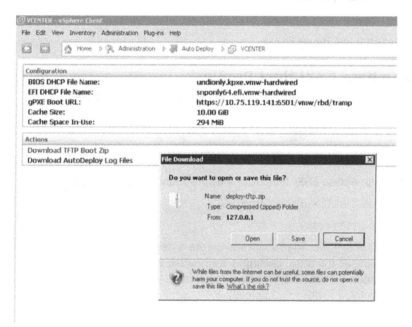

8. Unzip the files and place in the TFTP download directory.

9. To set up bulk licensing in vCenter, use the following PowerShell code:

```
Connect-VIServer [vcenter]
$licenseDataManager = Get-LicenseDataManager
$hostContainer = Get-Datacenter
$licenseData = New-Object VMware.VimAutomation.License.Types.
LicenseData
$licenseKeyEntry = New-Object Vmware.VimAutomation.License.Types.
LicenseKeyEntry
```

```
$licenseKeyEntry.TypeId = "vmware-vsphere"
$licenseKeyEntry.LicenseKey = "[esxi licensing code]"
$licenseData.LicenseKeys += $licenseKeyEntry
$licenseDataManager.UpdateAssociatedLicenseData($hostContainer.
Uid, $licenseData)
$licenseDataManager.QueryAssociatedLicenseData($hostContainer.Uid)
```

Preparing Blade Center

This is only needed if you have a Blade Center. If you don't, just prepare your hardware to be ready for deployment using PXE boot. Perform the following steps to prepare a Blade Center:

1. Prepare Blade profiles.
2. Assign base profiles to Blade slots.
3. Power on a test Blade Profile.

Creating a base ESXi Host Profile

Follow the *Using vSphere Host Profiles with vCloud* recipe in this chapter.

Preparing a base image for Auto Deploy

Perform the following steps for preparing a base image for Auto Deploy:

1. Download a base ESXi files from VMware (they come as `.zip`).
2. Download the vCloud agent from vCD.
3. Create a base image.

   The following PowerShell script will create a new base image for Auto Deploy and will include all the basic packages we need. It will also reset the existing Auto Deploy rules, making it possible to rerun the script as you need it (please replace the content between the [] with your choices):

```
#Log into VCenter
$vCenter=commect-viserver [vcenter server]
#Create New Image
$NewImage="esx5.1.1-"+(Get-Date -Format yyyyMMdd)
#download from vmware.com ESXI Download
Add-EsxSoftwareDepot d:\Autodeploy\depot\ESXi\[VMware-ESXi…zip
image]
$esximg=Get-EsxImageProfile|where {$_.name -like "*standard"}
New-EsxImageProfile -CloneProfile $esximg -Name $NewImage -Vendor
$esximg.vendor
# from vCD install /opt/vmware/vcloud-director/agent/vcloudagent-
esx51-….zip
Add-EsxSoftwareDepot d:\Autodeploy\depot\vCD\vcloudagent-
esx51-5.1.0-799577.zip
```

```
Add-EsxSoftwarePackage -ImageProfile $NewImage -SoftwarePackage
vcloud-agent
add-EsxSoftwareDepot http://10.75.119.139/vSphere-HA-depot
Add-EsxSoftwarePackage -ImageProfile $NewImage -SoftwarePackage
vmware-fdm
#export Image for later usage
Export-EsxImageProfile -ImageProfile $NewImage -ExportToBundle
("d:\Autodeploy\depot\"+$NewImage+".zip")
#reset all existing Rules
Get-DeployRule|Remove-DeployRule -Delete
#Create New Rules
new-DeployRule -Name ([profile name]) -Item ($NewImage)," [profile
name]"
Add-DeployRule ("[profile name]")
#reset existing Deployrules and Image associations for Clusters
$esxis = Get-Cluster -Name "[Cluster name]" |Get-VMHost
foreach ($esxi in $esxis) {
Test-DeployRuleSetCompliance  $esxi|Repair-DeployRuleSetCompliance
}
Disconnect-VIServer $vcentersession -Confirm:$false
```

4. Create an alarm script for preparing the ESXi Servers for vCloud.

   The alarm script is needed to make sure that any new ESXi host that is added to vCloud will be prepared. The following is our alarm script:

```
$targetHostIP = $args[0]
Connect-ciserver [vcloud server]
  $targetHost = Get-VMHost $targetHostIP;
  $ESXuser = "root"
  $ESXpass = [root password]
  Write-Host "Preparing Host: $targetHostIP"
    $Search = Search-cloud -QueryType Host -Name $targetHostIP
    $HostView = Get-CIView -SearchResult $Search
  if ($HostView.Ready -eq $false) {
  Write-Host "Preparing Host: $targetHostIP"
    $HostView.Prepare($ESXuser, $ESXpass)
  }
```

   This script must be stored on the vCenter server (for example, D:\AutoDeployScripts\preparevCDESxi.ps), but in order to run it, we need a wrapper around it. We will create the following DOS script that we name preparevCDESxi.bat:

```
start /wait C:\Windows\System32\WindowsPowerShell\v1.0\powershell.
exe -File D:\AutoDeployScripts\preparevCDESxi.ps1 %1
exit %ERRORLEVEL%
```

Finally, we need to create an alarm in vCenter that will call this script. The following are the parameters for the alarm:

Name	`Script Trigger: Prepare vCD Esxi`
Description	This script is used to set a host VM Swap location Datastore. Currently, it cannot be done through Host Profile configuration.
Monitor	Host, events
Trigger	Host configuration changes applied to host, unset, no advanced
Action	Run a command.
	`D:\AutoDeployScripts\preparevCDESxi.bat {targetName}`
	Once, once, once, once

Testing Deploy

Perform the following steps to test Deploy:

1. Power on the new ESXi.

2. Wait until it joins the cluster and is active in vCloud.

How it works...

The previous recipe is long and not easy; however, with a bit of trial and error, you will be able to replicate the setup. Using Blade Centers such as Cisco UCS and HP c7000, Auto Deploy and vCloud will create a system that is truly a cloud. Your ESXi Servers are basically only resource delivery, but do not contain any functional information. All this information is centralized in vCenter using Host Profiles. If you are automating your Blade Centers, you can, for example, predefine slots for certain clusters so that you just need to physically plug an ESXi Blade into a slot to add capacity to a given cluster, adding the new resources to PvDCs and organizations automatically. Or you can use automation inside the Blade Center to assign a new server profile to an existing ESXi. Reboot the blade and switch the physical capacity that way.

Auto Deploy functions as follows:

▸   Blade Center assigns an automated network and a disk profile to ESXi

▸   ESXi Server boots

▸   DHCP gives ESXi an IP as well as the instructions to get the tramp file for initial boot from the TFTP server

▸   The ESXi Server loads the first-boot file from the TFTP server and then executes it

- The first-boot file contains instructions to download the packages that we have created with PowerShell from the vCenter Server.

- After the ESXi base files are downloaded, they are executed, and the ESXi system starts up

- The ESXi Server will now follow the rules we defined and join the cluster we defined in these rules

- While joining the cluster, the ESXi host will execute the Host Profile associated with the cluster

- The Host Profile will configure the ESXi with networking and storage

- When the Host Profile configuration is finished, the alarm we created will go off and will execute the script

- The script will connect to vCloud and prepare the ESXi Server for vCloud.

- The new server is ready to take load

Personally, I have deployed such systems, and the devil is truly hidden in the detail, and it can take quite a lot of time to design and engineer it properly. So don't be disheartened if your first attempt is unsuccessful; keep on trying.

See also

- Find out more about understanding Auto Deploy looking at VMware KB 2005131

- Find out more about Auto Deploy's best practices at `http://pubs.vmware.com/vsphere-50/index.jsp#com.vmware.vsphere.install.doc_50/GUID-5E99987C-9083-47E8-9282-08CD1C8830C8.html`

Defining a vCloud development cycle

This section provides an example of a development cycle using vCloud as a development tool.

Getting ready

We need an application that we can import (a vApp) as well as three organizations. The organizations will be used for administration, development, and **User Acceptance Testing** (**UAT**). If the need for additional training environment exists, just create an additional organization.

How to do it...

Using the following diagram we will work through a typical development cycle:

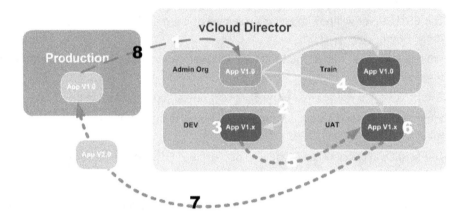

Perform the following steps to work through a typical development cycle:

1. Import your application into vCloud. Apply the proper aftercare to it and create a template out of it. Publish the template.

2. Developers will now deploy a copy of the application from the Admin organization into the Dev organization, and start developing the next version (or fix the old one).

3. After the development has reached a point where the code can be tested, the developers will create documentation that describes how to update the existing application to the developed version. They will try out their instructions by deploying a new copy of the application to the Dev organization and applying the instructions. If this works out, they will proceed to the next step.

4. When the time has come for testing, the UAT people will deploy a new copy of the base image from the Admin organization to the UAT organization.

5. The patch and/or instruction that have been developed in the Dev organization will be applied to the UAT image.

6. The instructions and/or patches will be tested in UAT. The test will determine if the instructions work and if they are non-destructive. If the test fails, the development cycle will be turned back to step 2.

7. After a successful test, the patch and/or instructions will be rolled out to the production environment.

8. The new version will be imported into vCloud and the development cycle will start over.

How it works...

The software development cycle that I have just described is just an example; however, it actually works really well. The secret of success in this case lies in the air gaps between the organizations. You may have noticed that we will not copy VMs from `Dev` into UAT and then in to `Prod`, and there are three very good reasons for this. Firstly, while moving a VM around, we move not only the VM but also all the unnecessary leftovers that have been accumulated during the development phase, so we are actually never 100 percent sure what the VM contains. These extras could be leftover code, developer backdoors, or undocumented installed software or configurations. This leads us directly to the second reason. If we move the VM around, we cannot verify that the install instructions are correct and that the application will actually work as intended. This again leads us to the third reason following the change process. Using the air gaps, we make sure that after the development process, the developers need to prove that the documentation they have provided actually works, and that if the software is installed during production, it will not impair production.

Following a proper development cycle improves the quality and resistance of development.

Development can be further improved by using automation tools such as Puppet or Microsoft SCCM. These tools allow to roll out VMs with the same configuration. The tricky part is integrating them into vCloud.

There's more...

There are several other thoughts that play into this as well as recipes we have already had a look at.

While creating the copy of the `Prod` environment, you can use an Isolated Network to copy the IP range of the production. Using the recipes in *Chapter 2, vCloud Networks*, you can make sure you can access it. Also, in the same chapter, we had a look at the "hole-in-the-fence" method, which can be used to connect the isolated development environment to something such as an application that controls code, for example, MS Team Foundation Server.

We already used the `Admin` organization that I introduced in *Chapter 4, Datastores and Storage Profiles*, in this recipe. Its purpose is to make sure that the imported production copy stays pristine, and to make sure that when a deployment to UAT of this environment is done, it actually represents production.

A typical example of aftercare of a VM is the fact that an imported production AD contains a lot of users that are not needed and can be cleaned out of the system. Another example is the database server or an application that contains sensible data that has to be cleaned up (or scrambled) before developers can work on it.

For new developments, it is not a bad idea to create play copies of the main production infrastructure to deploy from the administration domain or as a shared access via an Organization Network. These play copies contain the same configuration, but a simplified set of data that is used only for development.

With vCloud 5.5, we now also have the ability to clone running vApps. Have a look at the *Cloning a running vApp* recipe in this chapter.

See also

- Puppet at `http://puppetlabs.com/`
- Microsoft SCCM at `http://www.microsoft.com/en-us/server-cloud/system-center/configuration-manager-2012.aspx`

Making the VM BIOS ID (UUID) unique

The UUID of VMs in vCloud is not unique. In this recipe we will see how to change this.

Getting ready

We need a vCloud environment where we have the need for a unique UUID (see the *How it works...* section).

How to do it...

1. Shut down your vCloud environment (all cells).
2. Log in to your database.
3. Create a backup of the database.
4. Run the following SQL statement:

   ```
   update config set value = '0' where cat='vcloud' and
   name='backend.cloneBiosUuidOnVmCopy';
   ```
5. Start your vCloud environment.

How it works...

When you deploy a vApp from a vApp template, the VMs will have the same UUID. The UUID of a VM is stored in the `.vmx` file of the VM. When vCloud creates a copy of the VM, it will keep the UUID. This is normally not a problem. However, some backup and DR software, such as Comvault, keeps track of the VMs by using the UUID. If you have VMs with the same UUID, this will lead to the problem of backups not working correctly, and restores will be a major nightmare. There are probably other systems out there that have similar problems, so be aware.

Importing from Lab Manager into vCloud

Lab Manager is not supported anymore, so it's high time to get your stuff from LM to vCD.

Getting ready

We need a Lab Manager environment as well as a vCloud environment.

We also need a way to transfer a lot of data across. As Lab Manager can only work on vSphere 4.1, and vCloud should be installed on vSphere 5.1, we are probably looking at a minimum of two vCenters but probably more like two environments. The best way to solve this is to either have a VMFS Version 3 formatted LUN attached to both environments or you can provide an NFS or iSCSI mount. Alternatively, you can export the VMs/vApps as OVFs and import them again.

How to do it...

The transfer of Lab Manager objects falls into several separate tasks.

Transferring networks

The External Networks in vCloud do not support DHCP as the Physical Networks in Lab Manager did, so, you need to either switch to an IP Pool, or you can use DHCP on the VM level. To do that, you enter just one IP in the IP range of the External Network and then use DHCP to connect the VMs of a vApp to the Direct Organization Network of the External Network, as shown in the following steps:

1. Log in to the Lab Manager as `SysAdmin`.
2. Use the global organization.
3. Navigate to **Resources | Physical Networks**.

4. Hold the mouse on one of the Physical Networks and select **Properties**. You should now see the following page:

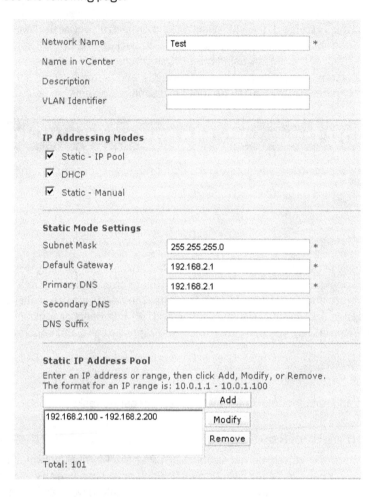

5. Write down the settings.

6. Make sure you have trunked the VLAN of the Physical Network to your new infrastructure.

7. Create a port group in vSphere with the correct settings.

8. Log in to vCloud as SysAdmin.

9. Create a new External Network (see the *Setting up an External Network* recipe in *Chapter 1, Setting Up Networks*).

Transferring organizations and their resources

If you have a design of your Lab Manager environment, the transfer is rather easy as you could implement the items directly. If you don't have one, the following steps show how to do a 1:1 transfer of an organization and its resources:

1. Log in to the Lab Manager as `SysAdmin`.
2. Make sure you are using the organization you want to transfer.
3. Navigate to **System | Organizations**.
4. Hold the mouse on the organization you would like to transfer and then select **Properties.**
5. Write down the following item values; we will need them:
   - **User and Groups**
   - **Resource Pools**
   - **Datastores**
   - **Physical Networks**
   - **Stored VM Template**
   - **Deployed VM Template Quota**
6. Close the window. Click on **VM Templates**.
7. Check all your VM templates if they are shared. Hold the mouse on one VM template and then select **Sharing**. Note down if they are shared.
8. Navigate to **System | Settings**.
9. Click on **Resource Cleanup**.
10. Write down the workspace and the VM template lease's settings.
11. Log in to vCloud as `SysAdmin`.
12. Navigate to **Manage & Monitor | Organization**.
13. Click on the green icon (**+**).
14. Enter the name of the organization.
15. Select LDAP and enter the base LDAP OU.
16. If you had any local users, create them now. If your users and groups were AD based, then go to the next step.
17. If you share your templates then select **Publishing**.
18. Select the default for all e-mail settings.

19. Select the lease times and add the quotas.

20. Finish the organization creation.

21. The resource pools you have used for your Lab Manager are either your new PvDC or represent your OvDCs. Add a PvDC and OvDCs according to your resource pool settings, as shown in the *Choosing the right Allocation Model* recipe in Chapter 6, *Improving the vCloud Design*.

22. Add the storage back to your organization as shown in the *Adding a new storage profile to vCD* recipe in Chapter 4, *Datastores and Storage Profiles*.

23. Double-click on the new organization, so it opens up as a new tab.

24. Click on **Administration** and then add your users and groups from AD.

25. Double-click on one of the OvDCs so that it opens up.

26. Click on **Org vDC Networks** and then on the green icon (**+**).

27. Add a direct-connected Organization Network to the External Network.

Transferring library or VM template elements

We first need to export from Lab Manager and then perform the following steps:

1. Log in to the Lab Manager as `SysAdmin`.

2. Make sure you are using the organization you want to transfer.

3. Click on **VM Templates** or **Library**.

4. Hold the mouse on the VM template or the library element you want to export and then select **Export**. You should now see the following screen:

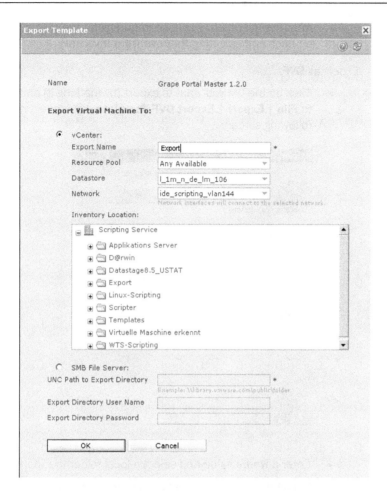

5. Give the export a name; select the Datastore you want to export it to as well as the External Network you have created.

6. Click on **OK** to start the export.

7. Wait until the export has finished. Depending on the size of the VM template, this could take some time.

8. Log in to vCenter 4 where you exported the VMs to.

9. Depending on your storage, you can now perform one of the following:

   ❑ Move to shared storage:

      ▸ If you have not already exported to the shared storage, then you should move it now to it by right-clicking on the export and selecting **Migrate**.

> ▶ After the migration, you have to unregister the VMs by right-clicking on each and selecting **Remove from Inventory**.

- ❑ Export as OVF:

    > ▶ Click on the VM you want to export (by marking it) and then navigate to **File | Export | Export OVF Template**. You should now get the following screen:

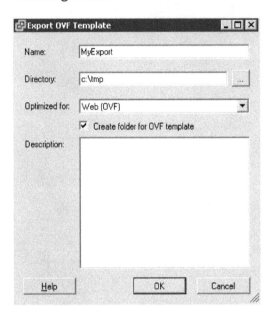

    > ▶ Enter a **Name** value and select a local folder to export it to.

    > ▶ Select the checkbox **Create folder for OVF template**.

    > ▶ Click on **OK** and then wait until the export has finished.

    > ▶ After the export, you can delete the exports by right-clicking on the VMs and selecting **Delete from Disk**.

    > ▶ We are now importing into vCloud:

1. Log in to vCenter 5.1 web client.
2. If you have chosen to use shared storage, proceed here, or else skip ahead to step 8.
3. Navigate to **vCenter | Storage**.
4. Click on the shared Datastore and then go to **Manage | Files**.
5. Enter the directory of the exported VM and find the .vmx file.
6. Right-click on the .vmx file and select **Register VM...** as shown in the following screenshot:

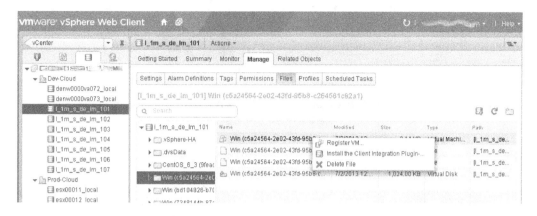

7. Select a name, folder, and cluster to store the VM.

8. Log in to vCloud as `SysAdmin`.

9. Import the VM as described in the *Importing a vApp into vCloud* recipe in *Chapter 3, Better vApps*, either from vCenter or from OVF.

After the import, the following instructions are a good idea:

1. Deploy the imported vApp.

2. Delete the template in the catalog.

3. Clean up the VMs by installing a new version of VMware tools, thereby upgrading the virtual hardware.

4. Add the vApp back to the catalog.

The rest

If you were using vApp Networks and host spanning networks in Lab Manager, you will need to create a network pool as shown in the *Creating 1.000 isolated networks without VXLANs* recipe in *Chapter 1, Setting Up Networks*.

How it works...

As vCloud Director is the product that replaces Lab Manager, it should be rather easy to transfer workload; however, it's not that straightforward as we have seen previously. This is mostly down to the way that Lab Manager stores VMs.

The best advice I give to my customers is to rebuild from scratch. It helps to know how to transfer some of the most-needed Lab Manager VMs to vCloud, but in general, the upgrade should be seen as an opportunity to implement lessons learned from Lab Manager. The basic principles of Lab Manager with regards to resource design and workflow are the same; however, due to extended capabilities of vCloud, you can expand your existing designs and workflows.

Exporting every configuration from Lab Manager to vCloud Director makes no economic sense in most situations. Normally it should be enough to transfer your library elements.

There's more...

The following table gives an overview of the differences between Lab Manager and vCloud Director. It provides a translation table between concepts and terms:

Lab Manager	vCloud Director
Global Organization | Resources	Provider vCD
Organization | Resources	Org vCD
Global Organization | Physical networks	External Networks
Organization	Organization
Global Org | Host Spanning Networks	Network Pool
Library	Catalog
Configuration	vApp
Linked clones	Fast deployment (needs vSphere5)
Network templates	Organization Networks
Fenced networks	Fenced vApps
Media stores	Catalogs can use Datastores and a storage profile can be assigned to a catalog
Workspace	No equivalent, but it can be done with sharing
History	No equivalent, but metadata can be used
LiveLink	Cone running VMs (vCloud 5.5)

Using branding to make vCloud look different

Let's make vCloud look the way we want it to.

Getting ready

We need a vCloud environment.

We need to download the `.css` templates from the following VMware KB 1026050. This KB contains three `.css` files:

- `cloud-director-template.css`
- `cloud-director-51-template.css`
- `cloud-director-51-login-template.css`

In addition to this, we need Adobe Flex SDK that you can download from `http://www.adobe.com/devnet/flex/flex-sdk-download.html`.

How to do it...

We will now work through the possible changes that can be applied to vCloud.

Changes to vCloud

For all the following actions, we start at the same spot:

1. Log in to vCloud as `SysAdmin`.
2. Navigate to **Administration | Branding**. You should now see the following screen:

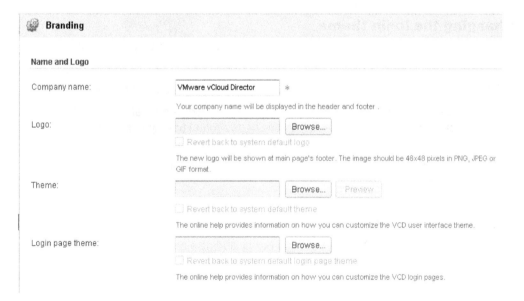

Changing the company name

Changing the company name will change the name in the upper-left corner, the lower-middle as well as on the login screen. In this example, we have changed the company name to `My vCloud`:

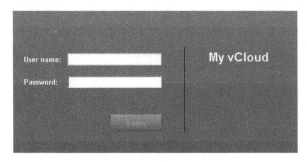
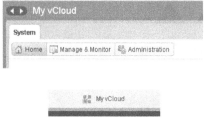

Changing the logo

We can upload any PNG, JPEG, or GIF; however, the size cannot exceed 48 x 48 pixels. The logo we can upload is more an icon than a full logo and will only appear in the lower-middle next to the company logo.

Changing the login theme

Let's change the login page of vCloud. This is rather straightforward if you know a bit about CSS:

1. Open `cloud-director-51-login-template.css` using Notepad.

2. Change the background color by changing the color schema after the HTML background tag from `#3A86C5` and `#1D4362` (blue) to maybe `#808080` and `#c0c0c0` (gray).

3. Move the credential login screen by changing the bottom and left tag under `#credentials`:

   ```
   bottom: 100px;
   left: 400px;
   ```

4. Add a background color to the login box by adding a background color and making the box a bit rounder:

   ```
   background: #c0c0ff;
   border-radius: 50px;
   ```

5. Add an image to your login screen by editing the `.title` tag. Add the following lines:

```
background:url("http:// [image location]") no-repeat top
transparent;
height: 200px;
width: 200px;
color: black;
```

The image location can be a local file, but for the sake of making it easy, use an HTTP source. The tags `height` and `width` are the dimensions of your image, and `color` is the color of your text.

6. Save the changes to a file with a new name.

7. Log in to vCloud Director as `SysAdmin`.

8. Navigate to **Administration | Branding**.

9. Click on **Browse** next to the login page theme.

10. Select the .css file you have been editing and click on **OK**.

11. Click on **Apply**.

12. Close the browser and reopen the vCloud page; the new design should be online now:

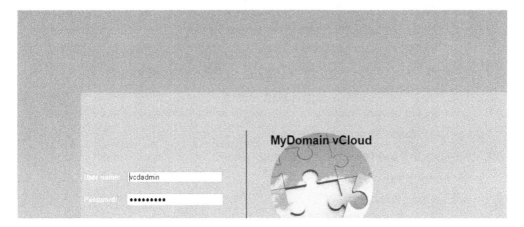

13. Navigate to **Administration | Branding**.

14. If you don't like it, you can always go back to the original design by going back to the **Branding** page, selecting **Revert back to system default login page theme**, and clicking on **Apply**. After are start of the browser, the old style will be reinstated.

Changing the theme

Now things will get a bit more complicated, as this part uses Adobe Flex. Installing Adobe Flex under Windows can be a bit difficult as there are quite some prerequisites; that's why I choose the Linux method for this example as shown in the following steps; however, you are welcome to use Windows:

1. Download Adobe Flex SDK as a `.zip` file.

2. Copy the `.zip` file to your vCloud Cell (using SCP).

3. Run the following command:

   ```
   mkdir /opt/flex

   unzip flex_sdk_4.6.zip -d /tmp/

   export PATH=/opt/flex/bin:$PATH

   export PATH=/opt/vmware/vcloud-director/jre/bin/:$PATH
   ```

4. If you now run the command `mxmlc –help` and you get a help text displayed, you have installed Flex.

5. The downloaded `.css` file `cloud-director-51-template.css` contains several `.png` references that are not part of the download. You can either create images with that name or you can delete the references from the `.css` file.

6. You can edit the `.css` file as normal.

7. Copy the edited `.css` file to the vCloud.

8. Compile the file with the command `mxmlc [.css file name]`.

9. The result will be a `.swf` file with the same name.

10. Copy the file back to the system that you are using to browse vCloud.

11. Log in to vCloud Director as `SysAdmin`.

12. Navigate to **Administration | Branding**.

13. Click on **Browse** next to **Theme**.

14. Upload the `.swf` file.

15. You will now see a preview of your theme; if you don't like it or there's a problem, just don't click on **Apply**.

16. If you don't like it, you can always go back the original theme by going back to the **Branding** page, selecting **Revert back to system default theme**, and clicking on **Apply**. After are start of the browser, the old style will be reinstated.

How it works...

Branding in vCloud uses two methods. First there is the **CSS (Cascading Style Sheets)** method that can be directly used with the login screen as shown previously. This method is straightforward and not very confusing. vCloud only knows of the stylesheets that are defined in the `.css` file you have downloaded. In the following screenshot, I have mapped the different stylesheets to areas in the login screen:

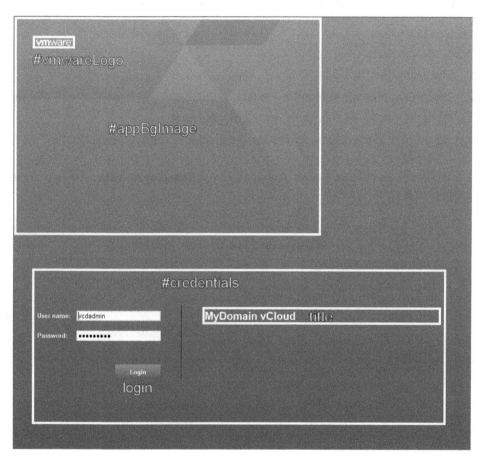

See also

▸ Learn about CSS from `http://www.w3schools.com/css/`

Putting an ESXi host into maintenance

This recipe describes what to do if one of your ESXi Servers needs maintenance.

Getting ready

We need a vCloud environment with deployed VMs as well as access to vCenter.

How to do it...

1. Log in to vCloud as `SysAdmin`.
2. Navigate to **Manage & Monitor | Hosts**.
3. Right-click on the ESXi host and select **Disable Host**.
4. Have a look at the column **Total VMs**. If the value is zero, you can skip the next step.
5. Right-click on the ESXi Server again and select **Redeploy All VMs** as shown in the following screenshot:

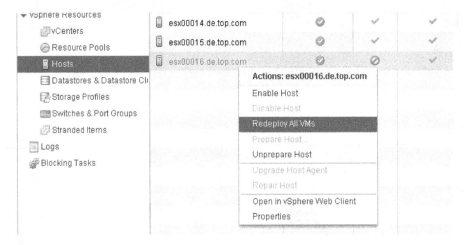

6. Accept the warning.
7. Using vMotion, vCloud will now move the VMs from this ESXi to other ESXis in the cluster.
8. Log in to vCenter using the web client.
9. Navigate to **vCenter | Hosts as Clusters**.
10. Expand the cluster and click on the ESXi you want to put into maintenance.
11. Right-click on the ESXi and select **Enter Maintenance Mode**.

12. Make sure that in the pop-up window, the option **Move powered-off and suspended VMs to other hosts in the cluster** is checked. Click on **Yes**.

13. If DRS is not configured as fully automated (which is the recommended setting), you will need to manually migrate the VMs.

14. Wait until the ESXi has entered maintenance mode. You can also see in vCloud that the host is now in maintenance.

15. Now it is the time to make changes to the ESXi Server.

16. Go back into vCenter.

17. Right-click on the ESXi Server and select **Exit Maintenance Mode**.

18. Wait until the ESXi Server is ready.

19. Go back into vCloud.

20. Right-click on the ESXi host and select **Enable Host**.

21. The ESXi host is now ready again to take load.

How it works...

It is important to make sure that before you patch an ESXi host, you use vMotion to first move all its deployed VMs off the host.

If you don't put the ESXi host into maintenance mode, or at least move the VMs off, major problems can arise. The less severe case would be that VMs are not running anymore to the more severe cases where the vCNS Edge VMs are down.

If the ESXi host was lost, have a look at the *Recovering from an outage* recipe in *Chapter 8, Troubleshooting vCloud*.

See also

▶ The *Working with vCloud logfiles* recipe in *Chapter 8, Troubleshooting vCloud*

Updating vCloud Cells without interruption

When you need to patch one of your vCloud Cells and you can't afford to bring the vCloud system down, this is how it works.

Getting ready

You need a vCloud with more than one cell.

How to do it...

1. Log in to vCloud as `SysAdmin`.

2. Navigate to **Manage & Monitor | Cloud Cells**. You should now see the following screen:

3. Check if the cell has the vCenter Proxy running on it (the green tick).

4. If the vCenter Proxy had been running on the cell you want to shut down, proceed, otherwise skip ahead to step 8.

5. Click on **vCenters**.

6. Right-click on your vCenter and select **Reconnect**.

7. Go back to **Cloud Cells** and check that the vCenter Proxy has now moved to the other cell.

8. Shut down the cell gracefully. See the *A scripted cell shutdown* recipe in *Chapter 5, Working with the vCloud API*.

9. Do your maintenance on the vCloud Cell.

10. Start the cell with `service vmware-vcd start`.

11. Go back to **Cloud Cells** and check that the cell's status is enabled (green tick).

How it works...

The vCenter Proxy service is responsible for listening to vCenter. When vCloud gives vCenter a command, it will wait for a given time until vCenter responds that the task has been done. This is due to the fact that vCenter uses SOAP and not REST, and task scheduling is different in SOAP and REST. If the vCenter Proxy is not running, the vCloud will give commands to vCenter, but you will receive an error at the end.

Losing the vCenter Proxy is not really desired. If this happens, please follow the *Recovering from an outage* recipe in *Chapter 8, Troubleshooting vCloud*.

See also

▸ The *Working with vCloud log files* recipe in *Chapter 8, Troubleshooting vCloud*

Updating a vCloud with only one cell

In this recipe, we will learn how to update a vCloud that has only one cell.

Getting ready

We need a vCloud with only one cell and downtime to bring it down. Make sure you have e-mails configured in vCloud.

How to do it...

1. Log in to vCloud as `SysAdmin`.
2. Navigate to **Manage & Monitor | Provider VDCs**.
3. Right-click on each PvDC and select **Notify...** as shown in the following screenshot:

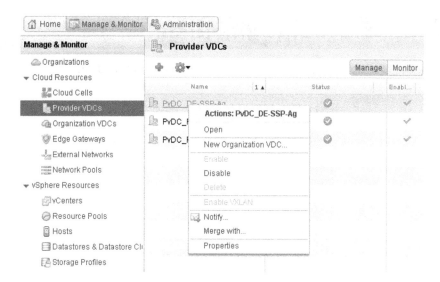

4. Enter a title for the notification e-mail into **Subject**.

5. Enter a text that describes to the users in easy terms why, when, and how long you plan to shut down the cells. Also, it always helps to put a sentence in about how this downtime helps them.

6. Shut down the cell. See the *A scripted cell shutdown* recipe in *Chapter 5, Working with the vCloud API*.

7. Do your maintenance on the vCloud Cell.

8. Start the cell with `service vmware-vcd start`.

9. Wait until vCloud is fully up.

10. Go back to the PvDCs and send out another notification that vCloud is accessible again.

How it works...

If you have only one cell, there is not much you can do; you have to bring it down. However, don't forget that your VMs are still running in vCenter. So, as long as the users connect to the VMs using RDP or SSH, they can still work and are not impacted.

What will not be working from a user's perspective is the provisioning of new vApps/VMs using the remote console and changing of vApp and VM properties.

If you have any automation running on your vCloud, it is a good idea to pause the scripts.

Updating a vCenter in vCloud

When you have to update vCenter, the following recipe shows how to do it.

Getting ready

We need a vCloud environment and a vCenter that can be taken down.

How to do it...

1. Log in to vCloud as `SysAdmin`.

2. Navigate to **Manage & Monitor | vCenter**.

3. Right-click on the vCenter Server and select **Disable**.

4. vCenter is now disabled, and no further vCloud-vCenter interaction will be performed.

5. Do your vCenter updates.

6. Go back to your vCenter in vCloud.

7. Right-click on the vCenter Server and select **Enable**.

8. Verify that vCenter is ok by right-clicking on it again and selecting **Reconnect**.

How it works...

When we update vCenter, we have to make sure that vCloud knows about it, so that it can stop giving commands to vCenter.

Updating vCenter is not as scary as it sounds; while we take vCenter down, the VMs are still running on the ESXi Servers. While vCenter is down, we are not able to provision new vApps, VMs, or Edges. However, we can actually use the vCloud VM remote console as the remote console establishes a direct connection between vCloud and ESXi.

See also

▶ Methods of upgrading to vCenter 5.1 can be found in VMware KB 2021188

Updating vCNS

This is how you update vCNS.

Getting ready

We need a vCloud environment and a vCNS Manager.

We also need the update file. With each release of vCNS, there is an OVF file for a full redeploy as well as a `tar.gz` file that contains the updates.

 You should always read the **Release Notes** section, as there may be a special update path that has to be taken.

How to do it...

1. Log in to vCNS with an Enterprise Admin role.

2. Navigate to **Settings & Reports | Updates**. You should now see the following screen:

3. Click on **Upload Upgrade Bundle**.

4. Browse to the `tar.gz` update file and click on **Upload**.

5. Wait until the file has been uploaded.

6. Check that the version is the correct one and click on **Install** as shown in the following screenshot:

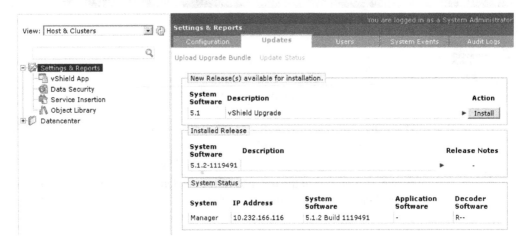

7. Wait until the update is finished and the vCNS reboots.

8. Log back in.

9. Navigate to **Settings & Reports | Updates**.

10. Check the update status.

How it works...

Updating vCNS is like updating a core infrastructure element. While vCNS is down, we cannot deploy any Edge devices or change any Edge settings. However, all deployed Edges, VMs, and vApps will continue running.

Depending on the vCNS update, you may need to redeploy the Edge devices so that these are updated.

Updating an Edge

Perform the following steps to update an Edge:

1. Log in to vCloud as `SysAdmin`.
2. Navigate to **Manage & Monitor | Edge Gateways**.
3. Right-click on an Edge you want to upgrade and select **Re-Deploy**.
4. Wait until the Edge has been redeployed.

Updating a vApp Network

As we know from *Chapter 1, Setting Up Networks*, a vApp network is actually an Edge, so we need to redeploy it. You will only need to update vApp networks that are currently deployed. Undeployed vApps will create a new Edge when they are deployed. Perform the following steps to update a vApp Network:

1. Log in to vCloud as `SysAdmin` or as `OrgAdmin` directly into the organization.
2. Enter the vApp with the vApp network that needs upgrading.
3. Click on **Networking**.
4. Right-click on the vApp network and select **Reset Network**.
5. Wait until the vApp network (Edge) has been redeployed.

Expanding vCD resources

So you have run out of resources? The following recipe shows how to fix that.

Getting ready

You need a vCloud environment and new resources.

How to do it...

We will work through the different areas to which we can add resources.

An OvDC storage profile needs more space

Perform the following steps if an OvDC storage profile needs more space:

1. Log in to vCloud as `SysAdmin`.
2. Navigate to **Manage & Monitor | Organization VDCs**.
3. Double-click on the OvDC for whose storage profile you want more space.
4. Click on **Storage Profiles**.
5. Have a look at how much storage is left.
6. Right-click on the storage profile and select **Properties**.
7. Set the storage limit to a higher level.

A storage profile needs more space

Perform the following if a storage profile needs more space:

1. Log in to vCenter using the web client.
2. Click on **vCenter** and then on **Datastores**.
3. Select the first Datastore that should be part of the new storage profile.
4. Select **Manage** in the tabs and select **Profiles**.
5. Now we will add a user-defined storage capability to a Datastore by clicking on the **Assign Storage Capability** button.
6. Now you can select from an existing user-defined storage capability.
7. Click on **OK** and again on **OK**. Now the Datastore should show the name you entered under **User-Defined Storage Capability**.
8. Log in to vCloud as `SysAdmin`.
9. Click on **Manage & Monitor** and then on **vCenter**.
10. Right-click on the vCenter you have added the storage profile to, and select **Refresh Storage Profiles**.
11. Wait until the task has finished.
12. Your existing storage profile should now have more space.

An Organization needs more resources

Perform the following steps if an organization needs more resources:

1. Log in to vCloud as `SysAdmin`.
2. Determine if the organization needs a new OvDC or if an existing OvDC needs more resources.
3. If the organization needs another OvDC, continue here.
4. Navigate to **Manage & Monitor | Organization VDCs**.
5. Click on the green icon (**+**).
6. Select the PvDC that should contain the new OvDC.
7. Select the appropriate Allocation Model.
8. Set the CPU and memory quota.
9. Set **Thin Provisioning** and **Fast Provisioning** as needed.
10. Choose a network pool (if you need it).
11. Give the OvDC a name and finish the creation.

An OvDC needs more resources

Perform the following steps if an OvDC needs more resources:

1. Log in to vCloud as `SysAdmin`.
2. Navigate to **Manage & Monitor | Organization VDCs**.
3. Right-click on the OvDC you want to add resources to.
4. Click on **Allocation**.
5. Assign more resources, **CPU Allocation** and **Memory Allocation**, to this OvDC.
6. Click on **OK**.

A PvDC needs more resources

Perform the following steps if a PvDC needs more resources:

1. Log in to vCloud as `SysAdmin`.
2. Navigate to **Manage & Monitor | Provider VDCs**.
3. Double-click on the PvDC you would like to add resources to.
4. Click on **Resource Pools**.
5. Click on the green (**+**) icon.
6. Select the resource pool (a cluster is a resource pool) that you want to add.

7. Click on **OK**.

8. If you get the message that there is no resource pool available to join this PvDC, you need to add ESXi hosts and clusters to vSphere.

9. You should now redistribute some extra resources to the OvDCs of this PvDC.

How it works...

As you saw, adding resources is rather easy; the hard part is to figure out in advance when you need to do it.

There are several tools on the market that can do this; there is also **VMware Operations Manager (vCOPS**—but it is pronounced VC-OPS). vCOPS is a very nice tool for managing any virtual environment as it also contains a planning component that was formally known as **VMware CAPIQ**. If you are running an enterprise environment, this is a really good tool.

If you have to watch your budget, there are always the monitor buttons that exist in PvDCs, OvDCs, and under **Storage**. At least they give you an idea of where you are at the moment.

Resizing a VM hard disk

This recipe shows you how to resize a hard disk of a VM in vCloud.

Getting ready

We need a VM that we can resize.

How to do it...

Depending on the way the VM has been provisioned, the resizing is different.

Not fast-provisioned VMs

If your VM has to be provisioned on an OvDC that is not enabled for fast provisioning, the following recipe works with a powered on VM:

1. Log in to your organization.

2. Click on **My Cloud** and then double-click on the vApp that contains the VM you want to resize.

3. Right-click on the VM whose hard disk you want to resize and select **Properties**.

4. Click on **Hardware**, and you should see the following screenshot:

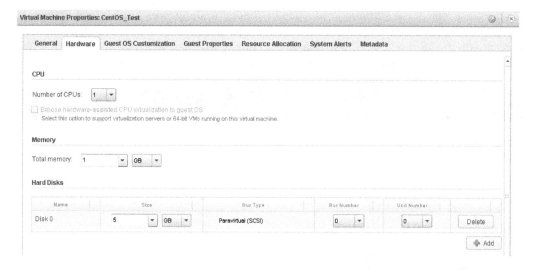

5. Enter a new size that is larger than the original one (you cannot make the hard disk smaller).

6. Click on **OK**.

7. Wait until the task has finished.

8. Now you just need to change the size of the partitions in the operating system.

Fast-provisioned VMs

VMs that have been provisioned in an OvDC configured with fast provisioning are not able to be resized. Even in vSphere, the HD settings are greyed out. We need to do a little trick as shown in the following steps:

1. Navigate to the vApp that contains the VM you want to resize the hard disk.

2. Right-click on the VM and select **Consolidate**.

3. Wait until the task has finished.

4. Execute the steps from the *Not fast-provisioned VMs* section (the previous section).

How it works...

Resizing a hard disk of a VM is not such a hard task; however, linked clones make it harder.

Making hard disks smaller is possible using vSphere; however, doing so to linked cloned VMs is fatal and should not be done. If you have to do it, consolidate the VMs first.

Have a quick look at the *Introduction* section in *Chapter 4, Datastores and Storage Profiles*, to review linked clones. Resizing a hard disk of a linked cloned VM is not possible as we are not dealing with the `vmdks` files but with snapshots of the `vmdk` files. When we consolidate a VM, we reduce the chain length to 1, and we have a VM that uses a `vmdk` file, not a snapshot.

Cloning a running vApp

Using vCloud 5.5, you are now able to clone running vApps. This comes in very handy for debugging.

Getting ready

You will need a vApp that is running.

You also need to have the vApp you want to clone on a vSphere 5.5 environment, as this function only works with vSphere 5.5.

How to do it...

We have three possibilities where we can clone the vApp to.

Clone to a catalog

Perform the following steps to clone to a catalog:

1. Navigate to the vApp that is running.
2. Right-click on the vApp and select **Add to Catalog**.
3. Select the catalog and give the vApp template a name. Make sure that the name reflects the state of the vApp.
4. Select **Make identical copy**.
5. Click on **OK** and wait until the clone has finished.

Deploy a cloned VM from a catalog

Perform the following steps to deploy a cloned VM from a catalog:

1. Navigate to **My Cloud**.
2. Click on **Add vApp from Catalog** (the green (**+**) icon).
3. Select the live-cloned vApp. There is no way one can distinguish between the vApp stages in this window.
4. Select a new name of the vApp and select an OvDC.

5. Wait until the vApp has been cloned.

6. Power on the vApp.

Clone to My Cloud

Perform the following steps to clone to **My Cloud**:

1. Navigate to the vApp that is running.

2. Right-click on the vApp and select **Copy to**.

3. Give the clone a new name, select the OvDC as well as the storage profile for each VM.

4. Click on **OK** and wait until the clone has finished.

5. Power on the vApp.

How it works...

The ability to clone a vApp in its current running stage is extremely handy when one is developing or debugging software. A similar feature existed in Lab Manager and was called LiveLink.

Imagine the following scenario: A tester has found a bug in the software (vApp) he was testing. He now creates a catalog item of it and shares it with the software developer. The software developer can now deploy the vApp in the state that the bug occurs in and sees it first hand.

What happens is that the vApp will be suspended and made transportable this way. Putting a VM into suspension means that it is instantly frozen and its memory stage is copied completely into a `vswap` file. In addition to that, the VM is marked in the `vmx` file as suspended. While you are redeploying the vApp, the process is reversed.

Cloning a running vApp combined with the new sharing and publishing features becomes very powerful. You now can deploy and configure vApps in one organization (or even vCloud) and can transfer them, suspended to a different organization.

There's more...

There is also a new additional option when right-clicking on each vApp and VM called **Discard Suspended Stage**.

If you have a live-cloned vApp, you may wish to get rid of the current stage of the VM and prefer to have it boot normally again. Discarding the suspended state does exactly that; it deletes the `vswap` file from the VM and deletes the suspension flag. When you then power on the VMs, they will behave as if a **Force shut down** operation has happened.

Removing infrastructure from vCloud

In this recipe, we will see how we can remove ESXi hosts, clusters, vCenters, and cells from vCloud.

Getting ready

We need a vCloud where you can remove resources.

How to do it...

We will now work through the individual resources that we can remove.

Removing an ESXi Host from vCloud

If you want move the ESXi Server out of this cluster (and out of vCloud), you should do the following:

1. Log in to vCloud as SysAdmin.
2. Navigate to **Manage & Monitor | Hosts**.
3. Right-click on the ESXi host and select **Disable Host**.
4. Right-click on the ESXi Server again and select **Redeploy All VMs**.
5. Accept the warning.
6. Wait until the VMs have vMotioned the ESXi Hosts.
7. Right-click on the ESXi Server and select **Unprepare Host**.
8. Log in to vCenter using the web client.
9. Navigate to the ESXi Server you want to remove.
10. Right-click on the ESXi host and select **Disconnect**.
11. Right-click on the ESXi host again and select **Remove**.

Removing a cluster

Removing a cluster is not very easy as we will need to remove all its children.

A cluster is typically associated with a PvDC. The PvDC has OvDCs. The OvDCs have vApps, vApp Networks, Edges, and vApp templates and media files.

All these objects have to be removed before we can remove the cluster as shown in the following steps:

1. Log in to vCloud as SysAdmin.
2. Navigate to **Manage & Monitor | Provider VDCs**.

3. Right-click on the PvDC you would like to remove and select **Disable**.

4. Remove all child elements of this PvDC.

5. Right-click on the PvDC again and select **Delete**.

Removing a cell from vCloud

If you want to remove a cell from vCloud, follow the ensuing procedure:

1. Log in to vCloud as `SysAdmin`.

2. Navigate to **Manage & Monitor | Cloud Cells**.

3. Check if the cell has the vCenter Proxy running on it.

4. If the vCenter Proxy is running on the cell, just shut down to proceed, otherwise, skip ahead to step 8.

5. Click on **vCenters**.

6. Right-click on your vCenter and select **Reconnect**.

7. Go back to **Cloud Cells** and verify that the vCenter Proxy has now moved to the other cell.

8. Shut down the cell. See the *A scripted cell shutdown* recipe in *Chapter 5, Working with the vCloud API*.

9. Go back to **Cloud Cells**.

10. Right-click on the cell you have shut down and select **Delete**.

The cell is now removed from vCloud. To add it back in, you have to run the configuration script on the cell.

Removing a vCenter from vCloud

This is a task that requires a lot of work. As we have seen with the cluster, we have to remove all its child objects. Be aware that this not only indicates vCenter child elements but also the child elements from the vCNS that are associated with this vCenter. For a vCenter that would be PvDCs, External Networks, and network pools, perform the following steps:

1. Log in to vCloud as `SysAdmin`.

2. Navigate to **Manage & Monitor | vCenters**.

3. Right-click on the vCenter you would like to remove and select **Disable**.

4. Remove all vCenter and vCNS child elements.

5. Right-click on the vCenter again and select **Detach**.

The vCenter and vCNS are now removed.

How it works...

Removing the infrastructure from vCloud is a task that is not done that often, but you should still know how to do it and what is involved.

Before removing the infrastructure from vCloud, make sure that you transfer the resources that you would like to keep to an other infrastructure.

8
Troubleshooting vCloud

In this chapter we will look closely at how to troubleshoot vCloud. We will cover the following recipes:

- ▶ Looking for errors in the vCloud GUI
- ▶ Working with vCloud logfiles
- ▶ Creating and uploading VMware support files
- ▶ Setting up and using vSphere Syslog Collector
- ▶ Troubleshooting vCloud Router traffic
- ▶ Troubleshooting the Java client
- ▶ Recovering from an outage

Introduction

When something doesn't work as it should, things can become stressful very fast. This is why you should be mindful of all the trouble spots beforehand.

Knowing where to look, what it should normally look like, and what an actual error looks like, helps determine the severity and accelerate the repair.

Where to look for help

Most problems can be solved by searching on Google. A useful Google search is:

```
(vCD OR vCloud director) [Search words] or for vCNS (vCNS OR
vShield) [Search words].
```

Please note that the OR has to be capitalized when you search on Google.

Other really good resources are the VMware Communities. I would encourage you to sign up (its free), and then you can search for answers or post your questions, and you are likely get help from them. VMware Communities can be accessed at `Communities.vmware.com`.

As you purchased vCloud Director, you have their support. Call VMware support for any help you require or go to `www.vmware.com/support/`.

If everything else fails, remember the most important message from the *Hitchhikers Guide to the Galaxy* book by *Douglas Adams*:

"Don't Panic"

Looking for errors in the vCloud GUI

In this recipe we will explore the location where the errors in vCloud GUI are shown.

Getting ready

We just need an organization where we can create a minor error.

How to do it...

You can do this recipe as `SysAdmin` or as `OrgAdmin`.

Creating an error

We will now create an error on purpose, so we can then go and look for it. Create the error by performing the following steps:

1. Log in to vCloud into your organization as `SysAdmin` or as `OrgAdmin`.
2. Build a new vApp (not by clicking on the green +).
3. Create a VM with 64 vCPUs and 255 GB of hard disk space(if that's not enough, use several TBs of hard disk).
4. Watch it fail when it tries to create the vApp.

Fail log

We will now check the fail log by performing the following steps:

1. Click on the failed log in the lower left corner.

You will now see all the existing errors at this time.

2. Double-click on your error.

3. A detailed error message will appear as shown in the following screenshot:

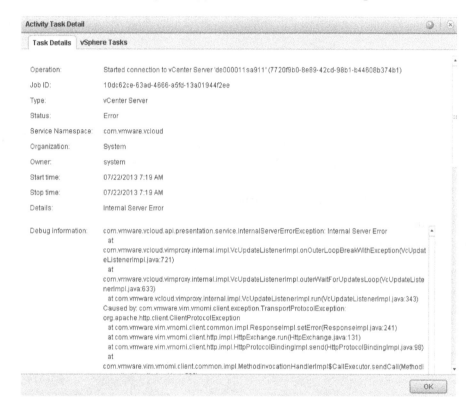

Direct error messages

1. Underneath the object that has an error, a red **X** appears with a short error message:

2. Click on the short error message.

3. The same detailed error message as shown in the previous screenshot will appear.

Organization of error logs

1. Click on **My Cloud**.

2. Click on **Logs**.

3. You will now see a list of all tasks as shown in the following screenshot:

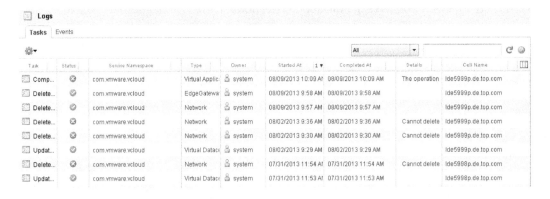

4. Click on any log entry to see more details.

5. Exit the details window.

6. Click on **Events**:

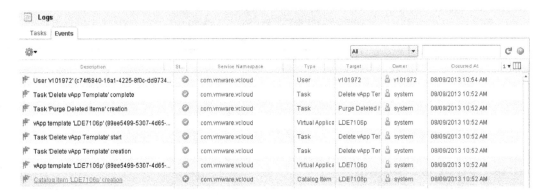

7. You will now see a list of all events; you can click on one to see more details about it.

System logs

1. Log in to vCloud as `SysAdmin`.

2. Navigate to **Manage & Monitor | Logs**.

3. You will now see all the system tasks.

4. Click on **Events** to see all the system events.

How it works...

There are two types of logs that can be accessed via the vCloud GUI, the Tasks and the Events.

The Tasks log contains long running operations, such as VM or vApp creation. The Events log contains one-time occurrences, such as user logins and object creation, or deletion.

The logs are different for the organization and for the system. System logs contain all events that are related to the system, such as purges and changes to OvDCs, PvDCs, and so on. Organizational logs contain events and tasks that are related to the organization only.

Filtering the events

You can filter events and tasks by selecting from these categories:

Tasks	Events
All	All
Task	Description
Status	Status
Service Namespace	Service Namespace
Type	Type
Owner	Target
Started At	Owner
Completed At	Occurred At
Details	
Cell Name	

A typical filter is Status, which comes in three states: Running, Successful, or Error. Another useful filter in a multi-cell environment is a cell name.

There's more

You can set the amount of time you would like to keep the logs, as well as the amount of days shown in the logs by navigating to **System | Administration | General | Activity Log**:

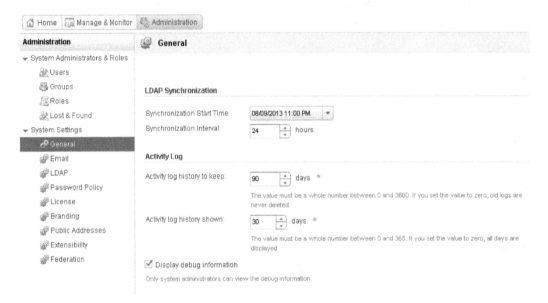

There is also the **Display debug information** checkbox that allows you to display the debug info of failed tasks, which is useful as it will provide you with more details.

Working with vCloud logfiles

In this recipe we will see how to access the logfiles and make sense of its contents.

Getting ready

We just need a working vCloud environment.

How to do it...

We will first see how to access a logfile and then we will go into the specifics of the two most important files, followed by a look at the vCNS logfiles.

Working with a vCD cell logfile

1. Log in to the vCloud Cell.

2. Gain root access, if you haven't already.

3. Run the following command:

```
less /opt/vmware/cloud-director/logs/[logfile]
```

4. Use the cursor to move around or refer to the *There's more* section for more detailed instructions on how to work with `less`.

5. Exit the program by pressing *q* (lower case).

Cell log

The cell log shows the boot status of a cell. The file is located at `/opt/vmware/cloud-director/logs/cell.log`.

It contains the percentage of the cell boot. If you restart a cell after a crash or an update, this is the place to monitor (using `tail -f`; refer to the *There's more* section), as it will tell you what fails. Typical problems occur at the following places:

▶ If the database of vCD is not available, the log will show this in the marked section in the following code (line 4 of the log):

```
Application startup begins: 8/18/13 3:36 AM

Successfully bound network port: 80 on host address: 192.168.10.10

Successfully bound network port: 443 on host address:
192.168.10.10

Successfully connected to database: jdbc:jtds:sqlserver://
mySqlserver:2053/vCloudDirector;socketTimeout=90;instance=ISQL53

Current locale "en" verified successfully
```

▶ If the vCD web server isn't able to start or bind to SSL, the log will note this at 11 percent:

```
Application Initialization: 11% complete. Subsystem 'com.vmware.
vcloud.api-framework' started

Successfully bound network port: 443 on host address:
192.168.10.10
```

▶ If the data/transfer director is not available, the log will show this at 64 percent:

```
Application Initialization: 64% complete. Subsystem 'com.vmware.
vcloud.fabric.net' started

Successfully verified transfer spooling area: /opt/vmware/vcloud-
director/data/transfer
```

▶ If the cell was successfully booted, the last line in the log will read:

```
Successfully started remote JMX connector on port 8999
```

Debug log

The debug log contains detailed information about any error that has occurred. This includes logging information of the cell as well as actions that have been run on the cell. The log can be found at `/opt/vmware/cloud-director/logs/vcloud-container-debug.log`.

▶ As debug logs can be rather long, it's important to know how an error looks visually. In the next screenshot you can see how the error sticks out visually, it starts after the red line:

```
2013-09-12 09:33:28,613 | DEBUG    | pool-jetty-59          | UriUtils                    | Unable to read property restapi.baseUri from the configuration file.
Using primary cell IP. |
2013-09-12 09:33:28,614 | DEBUG    | pool-jetty-59          | JaxRsDispatcherServlet      | Successfully completed request |
2013-09-12 09:33:28,615 | DEBUG    | pool-jetty-59          | ConversationTransactionManager | Creating new transaction with name
[com.vmware.vcloud.api.framework.manage.impl.ExtensibilityManagerImpl.getEnabledServicesForContentType]: PROPAGATION_REQUIRED,ISOLATION_DEFAULT; '' |
2013-09-12 09:33:28,615 | DEBUG    | pool-jetty-59          | ConversationTransactionManager | Initiating transaction commit |
2013-09-12 09:33:28,616 | DEBUG    | pool-jetty-67          | UriUtils                    | Unable to read property restapi.baseUri from the configuration file.
Using primary cell IP. |
2013-09-12 09:33:28,617 | DEBUG    | pool-jetty-67          | JaxRsDispatcherServlet      | Successfully completed request |
2013-09-12 09:33:28,617 | DEBUG    | pool-jetty-67          | ConversationTransactionManager | Creating new transaction with name
[com.vmware.vcloud.api.framework.manage.impl.ExtensibilityManagerImpl.getEnabledServicesForContentType]: PROPAGATION_REQUIRED,ISOLATION_DEFAULT; '' |
2013-09-12 09:33:28,617 | DEBUG    | pool-jetty-67          | ConversationTransactionManager | Initiating transaction commit |
2013-09-12 09:33:28,631 | DEBUG    | pool-jetty-59          | ConversationTransactionManager | Creating new transaction with name
[com.vmware.vcloud.api.framework.manage.impl.ExtensibilityManagerImpl.getEnabledServicesForUri]: PROPAGATION_REQUIRED,ISOLATION_DEFAULT; '' |
2013-09-12 09:33:28,631 | DEBUG    | pool-jetty-59          | ConversationTransactionManager | Initiating transaction commit |
2013-09-12 09:33:28,632 | DEBUG    | pool-jetty-67          | ConversationTransactionManager | Creating new transaction with name
[com.vmware.vcloud.api.framework.manage.impl.ExtensibilityManagerImpl.getEnabledServicesForUri]: PROPAGATION_REQUIRED,ISOLATION_DEFAULT; '' |
2013-09-12 09:33:28,632 | DEBUG    | pool-jetty-67          | ConversationTransactionManager | Initiating transaction commit |
2013-09-12 09:33:28,633 | DEBUG    | pool-jetty-53          | ConversationTransactionManager | Creating new transaction with name
[com.vmware.vcloud.api.framework.manage.impl.ExtensibilityManagerImpl.getEnabledServicesForUri]: PROPAGATION_REQUIRED,ISOLATION_DEFAULT; '' |
2013-09-12 09:33:28,633 | DEBUG    | pool-jetty-53          | ConversationTransactionManager | Initiating transaction commit |
2013-09-12 09:33:28,633 | DEBUG    | pool-jetty-70          | ConversationTransactionManager | Creating new transaction with name
[com.vmware.vcloud.api.framework.manage.impl.ExtensibilityManagerImpl.getEnabledServicesForUri]: PROPAGATION_REQUIRED,ISOLATION_DEFAULT; '' |
2013-09-12 09:33:28,633 | DEBUG    | pool-jetty-70          | ConversationTransactionManager | Initiating transaction commit |
2013-09-12 09:33:28,639 | DEBUG    | pool-jetty-67          | CustomExceptionMapper       | REST API CustomExceptionMapper caught following exception |
com.vmware.vcloud.api.presentation.service.ReferenceNotFoundException: The VCD entity (com.vmware.vcloud.entity.vapp:3d04afc9-362c-468f-a1ed-f05902010979) does not
exist.
    at com.vmware.ssdc.backend.services.impl.VappManagerImpl.getVappModel(VappManagerImpl.java:481)
    at sun.reflect.GeneratedMethodAccessor3648.invoke(Unknown Source)
    at sun.reflect.DelegatingMethodAccessorImpl.invoke(Unknown Source)
    at java.lang.reflect.Method.invoke(Unknown Source)
    at org.springframework.aop.support.AopUtils.invokeJoinpointUsingReflection(AopUtils.java:309)
    at org.springframework.aop.framework.ReflectiveMethodInvocation.invokeJoinpoint(ReflectiveMethodInvocation.java:183)
    at org.springframework.aop.framework.ReflectiveMethodInvocation.proceed(ReflectiveMethodInvocation.java:150)
    at org.springframework.aop.aspectj.MethodInvocationProceedingJoinPoint.proceed(MethodInvocationProceedingJoinPoint.java:80)
    at com.vmware.vcloud.common.diagnostics.GenericMethodDiagnosticsInterceptor.aroundMethod(GenericMethodDiagnosticsInterceptor.java:39)
    at sun.reflect.GeneratedMethodAccessor1115.invoke(Unknown Source)
    at sun.reflect.DelegatingMethodAccessorImpl.invoke(Unknown Source)
    at java.lang.reflect.Method.invoke(Unknown Source)
    at org.springframework.aop.aspectj.AbstractAspectJAdvice.invokeAdviceMethodWithGivenArgs(AbstractAspectJAdvice.java:621)
    at org.springframework.aop.aspectj.AbstractAspectJAdvice.invokeAdviceMethod(AbstractAspectJAdvice.java:610)
    at org.springframework.aop.aspectj.AspectJAroundAdvice.invoke(AspectJAroundAdvice.java:65)
    at org.springframework.aop.framework.ReflectiveMethodInvocation.proceed(ReflectiveMethodInvocation.java:161)
    at org.springframework.aop.interceptor.ExposeInvocationInterceptor.invoke(ExposeInvocationInterceptor.java:89)
    at org.springframework.aop.framework.ReflectiveMethodInvocation.proceed(ReflectiveMethodInvocation.java:172)
    at org.springframework.aop.framework.JdkDynamicAopProxy.invoke(JdkDynamicAopProxy.java:202)
    at $Proxy425.getVappModel(Unknown Source)
    at com.vmware.ssdc.backend.annotation.OrgSwitchInterceptor.getOrgIdFromEntityRef(OrgSwitchInterceptor.java:336)
    at com.vmware.ssdc.backend.annotation.OrgSwitchInterceptor.performOrganizationSwitch(OrgSwitchInterceptor.java:233)
    at com.vmware.ssdc.backend.annotation.OrgSwitchInterceptor.beforeSecurePresentationLayerMethod(OrgSwitchInterceptor.java:213)
    at sun.reflect.GeneratedMethodAccessor1738.invoke(Unknown Source)
```
Error

 If you would like to search for such an error, it's best to search for `at java` as this line will be in every such error.

▶ Looking at the previous error in more detail, we get this:

```
2013-09-12 09:33:28,639 | DEBUG    | pool-jetty-67          |
CustomExceptionMapper      | REST API CustomExceptionMapper
caught following exception |
```

```
com.vmware.vcloud.api.presentation.service.
ReferenceNotFoundException: The VCD entity (com.vmware.vcloud.
entity.vapp:3d04afc9-362c-468f-a1ed-f05902010979) does not exist.
```

The error message already tells us that a vApp was not found and that the vApp had the Href `3d04afc9-362c-468f-a1ed-f05902010979`. This only helps us if we would go to the REST API and look for that Href (refer to the *Accessing REST with Firefox* recipe in *Chapter 5, How to Work with the vCloud API*); however, it is often possible to work out from the context what went wrong.

▸ You can also search for the keyword "error" to find errors such as the following:

```
2013-09-13 08:26:34,101 | ERROR     | pool-jetty-53              |
NetworkServiceImpl             | Could not find Vim Network Info
for network e9c729f4-9c0d-48d7-ae3b-84e80807abea
```

 If you feel overwhelmed by the amount of data in the debug log, you can have a look at `vcloud-container-info.log` as it only contains content for the log level info.

Refer to the *There's more* section for additional information on how to make looking for things easier.

vCNS logs

The logfiles of vCNS are located in the GUI, and for the VM vCNS is running on, it is located in the console.

To access the VM system logs, perform the following steps:

1. Log in to vCNS console by using the VMware console.
2. Log in with `admin` as the username and your password (the initial password is `default`).
3. Type `enable` and then type the password again.
4. Type `ssh start`.
5. The SSH server now starts and you can connect via SSH to vCNS allowing more space to see the logs. If you want SSH to be always on (not recommended), you can type `copy running -config startup-config` to save the altered configuration.
6. Type `exit` and then type `exit` again.
7. Use SSH to connect to vCNS and log in with the admin user.
8. Type `show log`.
9. You can now browse the log with the cursor keys. You can use the same keys that you used with `less` (refer to the *There's more* section).
10. You stop SSH again by entering the command `ssh stop`.

The vCNS GUI logs come in three versions: System, Audit, and Tasks. You can access them by logging in to the GUI with a system administrator role or higher.

The system vCNS GUI log can be accessed by navigating to **Settings & Reports | System Events**.

This log shows all events the system has encountered, as shown in the following screenshot:

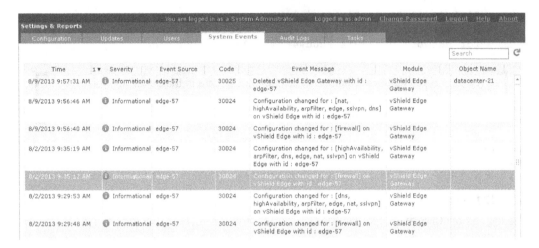

The Audit vCNS GUI log can be accessed by navigating to **Settings & Reports | Audit Logs**.

This log shows all the tasks that users have started and when they were started, as shown in the following screenshot:

The Tasks vCNS GUI log can be accessed by navigating to **Settings & Reports | Tasks**.

This log contains all the tasks that have been completed, as shown in the following screenshot:

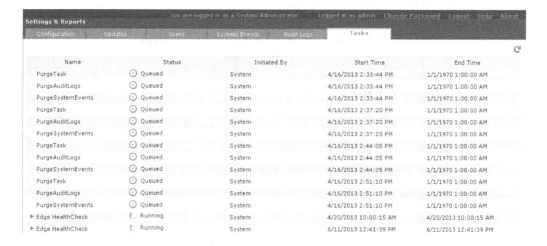

How it works...

Knowing the location of important logfiles lets you access them more easily. Becoming familiar with the way a logfile looks helps you determine if something is wrong so that you can find the errors faster.

Other logfiles

- `yyyy-mm-dd.request.log`: This shows you all the requests that have been issued via the API or the HTTPS interface.

- `vcloud-container-info.log`: This is the same as `vcloud-container-debug.logfile`; however, it logs only up to the info level, making it shorter and easier to read.

- `upgrade-yyyy-mm-dd-hh-mm-ss.log`: This contains the log of a vCloud update.

- `jmx.log`: This is a Java management extension log. Here, the java engine maintains the logs of its objects, such as `MBeans`.

- `cell-management-tool.log`: This log contains all information that is logged when the `bin/cell-management-tool` is used. Refer to the *See also* section in the *A scripted cell Shutdown* recipe in *Chapter 5, How to Work with the vCloud API*.

- `vmware-vcd-log-collection-agent.log`: This logfile keeps all information that is logged when using the VMware support log collector. Refer to the *Creating and uploading VMware support files* recipe in this chapter.

> ► `vmware-vcd-watchdog.log`: This log shows the start of the cell, and if the cell was found dead and has been restarted.

> ► `diagnostics.log`: This logfile is disabled by default. If switched on, it will keep a very detailed log (TRACE) level. You can switch it on in the `log4j.properties` file. Refer to the *Log rotate* subsection in this recipe.

Important logfile locations

Server	Logs	Location
vCD	vCD events	`/opt/vmware/cloud-director/logs/cell.log`
		`vcloud-container-debug.log`
		`vcloud-container-info.log diagnostic.log`
	OS System	`/var/log/messages`
		`/var/log/secure`
	API Web Access	`/opt/vmware/cloud-director/logs/*.request.log`
vCNS	System Events	`Settings & Reports	System Events`
	Audit logs	`Settings & Reports	Audit Logs`
	Tasks	`Settings & Reports	Tasks`
	VM System	`Type show log on console`

Cell.log

The cell log contains sections from the main log, and is good for a quick look when you bring up a cell to check if everything is fine. If the cell isn't starting, you can find out here when (at what percent level) the error occurred.

It is not a bad idea to write a mini script that starts the cell and then tails the cell log.

Debug log

The debug log contains all the debug level information. Because of this, it gets very large and complex. However, it is the best source of information for any vCloud-related issue.

The best way to get accustomed with it is to look at it regularly, especially when errors happen. In the beginning, the Java error may not be easy to read, but after a while, one gets used to it. The best way to find answers is to search for the main Java error message on Google (first line of the message).

Log rotate

The vCD logs rotation is defined in the file: `/opt/vmware/cloud-director/etc/log4j.properties`. The following logfiles can be configured here:

- `vcloud-container-debug.log`
- `vcloud-container-info.log`
- `diagnostics.log`
- `jmx.log`

The properties file contains a lot of configuration; however, only the following lines should be changed for each logfile:

`log4j.appender.vcloud.system.debug.MaxFileSize=10240KB`

`log4j.appender.vcloud.system.debug.MaxBackupIndex=9`

Changing any additional lines may result in loss (or at least a very slow response time) of VMware support, as other lines alter the way the logfiles are stored or formatted, which means VMware would have problems phrasing them.

The previous settings mean that a logfile can grow to the maximum size of 10 MB before a new file is created. A maximum of nine old logfiles will be kept. This means that you will have the current logfile (`.log`) plus 9 old logfiles (`.log.1` to `.log.9`). This results in maximum of 100 MB of logfiles for this specific log.

You can consider reducing the amount of logging by changing the line `log4j.appender.vcloud.system.debug.threshold=DEBUG`.

Setting the threshold to `info` will reduce the amount of lines written to the logfiles; however, in the case of a problem, you will also have reduced information. The following log levels exist and are listed in decreasing detail levels, beginning with TRACE as the most detailed, and OFF being the least and not logging any information at all:

- TRACE, DEBUG, INFO, WARN, ERROR, FATAL, OFF

Changes to the `log4j.properties` file become active after a restart of the cell. Please refer to the section *How it works* in the *A scripted cell shutdown* recipe in *Chapter 5, How to Work with the vCloud API*.

The following logfiles do not have a log rotate, but will always keep the last logfile (`.log.last`).

- `cell.log`
- `vmware-vcd-watchdog.log`

There's more

There are several good and easy Linux commands that come in handy if one is trolling the logs.

- `tail -f [file]`: Tail shows you the last 10 lines of a given file; however, with the –f option in it, it updates the display when a new line is added to the log. This makes it a good choice to watch a logfile live. This is especially effective if you have more than one monitor.

- `less [file]`: "Less is more than more" (Linux joke). What this means is that the command `more` shows you a logfile and then pauses until you press *Enter* or *Space* to continue with the next page or line. `Less` can do more than that. Here are some of the keys you can use while using `less`:

Cursor keys	Scroll through the file
G	Jumps to the end of the file
g	Jumps to the start of the file
PgUp	One page up
PgDn	One page down
/word	Searches downward for "word"
?word	Searches upwards for "word"
n	Jumps to the next search result
N	Jumps to the previous search result
:10	Jumps to line number 10 in the file
q	Exit less
h	Displays help page

- `grep [search string] [filename]`: With the command `grep` and some pipe commands, one can easily extract information from large logfiles. The following line will extract all lines from the logfile `file.log` that contain the word "error" and will save them in the file `/tmp/error.log.grep "error" file.log > /tmp/error.log`.

The following options exist:

-i	Ignores word case (upper/lower case). It searches for test, Test, TEST, and so on.
-w	Searches for whole words. It would find "test" but not "testing".
-n	Shows the line number the search string was found in. This is a very useful option as it lets you use `less` and directly jump to the line number and have a look around.

You can then use `less` to view the file.

Creating and uploading VMware support files

When you open up a case with VMware for support, one of the first things they will ask for are the support files. In the following sections, we will see how to create and upload them:

Getting ready

You need an SCP tool to transfer the files from vCloud onto your desktop, and you need an FTP connection to upload the files to VMware. If your vCloud Cell has a connection to the Internet, you may upload the files directly to VMware.

You will also need the support request number you have been given by VMware.

How to do it...

The process of creating and uploading support files is split into three tasks, obtaining the vCloud and vCNS support files, and uploading them.

Create vCloud support files

To obtain the vCloud support files, you normally have to execute the following steps on one individual vCloud Cell:

1. Log in to a vCloud Cell.
2. Gain root access, if you haven't gained already.
3. Run the command `/opt/vmware/vcloud-director/bin/vmware-vcd-support` if you have multiple cells, then attach `-all -multicell` at the end of the command.

 The support files can be rather large, so make sure you have enough disk space to store them. Check the disk space with the Linux command `df -h`.

4. A collector will now run and collect all the necessary files, including a database dump, and will store it as `vmware-vcd-support-[hostname]-[date].tgz` in the current directory.
5. From your desktop, use an SCP program (for example, winSCP) to transfer the file from the vCloud Cell to your desktop.

Create vCNS support files

1. Log in to vCNS as an `Admin`.

2. Navigate to **Settings & Reports | Configuration | Support**.

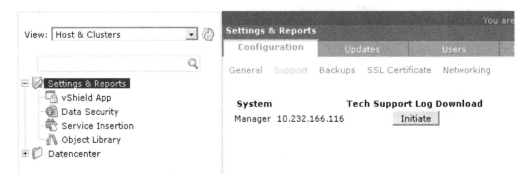

3. Click on **Initiate**.

4. Wait until the logfile has been generated.

5. Download the logfiles by clicking on **Download**.

Upload to VMware

You basically have two methods via which to upload support files. You can upload via the web browser (HTTPS, TCP port 443) or via FTP (TCP port 22).

Support files can be uploaded via the web browser by performing the following steps:

1. Open a web browser and browse to `https://ftpsite.vmware.com`:

VMWARE FTP SERVER

Enter username and password and click Login.

Username: *   inbound

Password: *   •••••••

User Interface: ◉ HTML   ○ Java Applet

[🌐 Login]

Lost password

2. Log in with username `inbound` and password `inbound`.

3. Make sure you select **HTML**:

4. Click on **New Directory** and put in your support request number (just the number, not the SR before it) as the new name.

5. Click on **Change Directory** and change to the directory you have just created.

6. Click on **Add** to add files to the upload directory (max 2 GB).

7. When you have added all files, click on **Upload**.

Support files can be uploaded via FTP by performing the following steps:

1. In Windows, click on **Start** and type `cmd` and press *Enter*. In Linux, just log in. If your vCloud is connected directly to the Internet, you can run the commands directly from the vCloud Cell.

2. Change to the directory where the support file is located (with the command `cd`).

3. Run the command `ftp ftpsite.vmware.com`.

4. Log in with username `inbound` and password `inbound`.

5. Run the following two commands to enable binary transport and enable hash markers to show the progress of the upload:

   ❑ `bin`

   ❑ `hash`

6. In Windows, you will have to activate the passive mode by running the command `QUOTE PASV`.

7. Create the directory for your support files and then enter the support request number (just the number, not the SR before it). Run the following commands:

   ❑ `mkdir [SUPPORT REQUEST NUMBER]`

   ❑ `cd [SUPPORT REQUEST NUMBER]`

8. Upload the files with the command `put [support file]`

After you have finished uploading, you may like to notify VMware support by sending an e-mail with the subject line `VMware Support Request SR# [SUPPORT REQUEST NUMBER]`.

How it works...

If you are really in trouble and you want help fast, the first thing, even before you lift up the phone to call VMware support, is to run the logfile creation. The reason is simple; while you are dealing with the preliminaries to raise the support call with VMware to get a support request number, the logfiles will be generated in the background. Now that you have the support request number, you can go straight to uploading the support files.

Uploading the support files can take quite some time, as you are uploading to a location in USA. So factor this in. In addition to that, support files can grow large over time, and the ones with more than 1 GB grow frequently.

Another problem I constantly face on client sites is that, sometimes one is not able to use FTP (TCP port 22) or HTTPS (TCP port 443) for security reasons. It is extremely important to provision at least one terminal that can upload large files via FTP to the VMware site. The reason for this is that the HTTPS upload only accepts files up to 2 GB, and sometimes, if a proxy is configured, the session can time out or is interrupted.

There's more

The FTP commands for MAC are slightly different; use the previous recipe, but alter steps 1 and 6 as follows:

1. Open the command line by navigating to **Applications | Utilities | Terminal**.
6. In MAC, you have to disable the passive mode with the `epsv` command.

Setting up and using vSphere Syslog Collector

A Syslog server centralizes logging and can be used for further analysis.

Getting ready

You need the vSphere install DVD and a Windows VM to install it on.

How to do it...

We will now install and use the vSphere Syslog Collector.

Installing VMware Syslog server

To install the VMware Syslog server, perform the following steps:

1. Insert the vSphere 5.1 installation DVD.
2. Click on **VMware vSphere Syslog Collector**.

3. Follow the installation instructions and choose the path where the Syslog data will be stored:

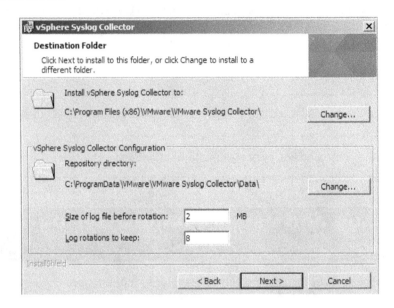

4. Select **VMware vCenter Server Installation** if you want the Syslog server to be integrated in the vSphere Client.

5. Finish the installation.

6. Make sure the TCP port 514 is open.

Integrating vCloud into Syslog

To integrate the vCloud into Syslog, perform the following steps:

1. Log in to vCloud as `SysAdmin`.

2. Navigate to **Administration | General**.

3. Enter the IP of the Syslog server:

4. Click on **Apply**.

5. Log in to vCloud Cell via SSH.

6. Edit the `global.properties` file found at `/opt/vmware/vcloud-director/etc/`.

7. Add your Syslog host to the `audit.syslog.host` = line.

8. Restart the vCloud Cell.

Working with Syslog

To locate and work with Syslog, perform the following steps:

1. The data files for Syslog are stored by default in `ProgramData\VMware\VMware Syslog Collector\Data\[ip or hostname of Server]\syslog.log` or the path you chose during installation.

2. Open the `syslog.log` file as shown in the following screenshot:

How it works...

It is a good idea to also enter the Syslog in the `responses.properties` file, so that if you are creating a new cell from the `response` files, the Syslog is already part of the installation.

If you like to watch the Syslog file, you can use `tail -f` in Linux, and `Get-Content myTestLog.log -Wait` in Windows.

A very useful tool for Windows is BareTail (`http://www.baremetalsoft.com/baretail/`) it lets you monitor log files and has also an extremely good search engine.

See also

Other Syslog servers you could use instead of the VMware ones are:

- ► `http://www.kiwisyslog.com/`
- ► `http://www.splunk.com`
- ► `http://www.balabit.com/network-security/syslog-ng`

All Linux servers come with a Syslog service installed and can be used as well; however, they do not have a comfortable web or GUI frontend.

Troubleshooting vCloud Router traffic

Syslog comes in very handy when one wants to log what is happening on vApp Network Edges.

Getting ready

We need a vApp Router or an Edge with firewall and/or NAT rules. You can use one of the recipes from *Chapter 2, vCloud Networks* for this.

We also need a configured Sysprep server.

How to do it...

1. Log in to vCloud as `SysAdmin` or into your Organization as `OrgAdmin` or `vAppauthor`.
2. Navigate to vApp.
3. Click on **Networking**.
4. Right-click on the network and select **Configure Services**.
5. Select either **Firewall** or **NAT**.

6. While you are configuring firewall rules, check **Log network traffic for firewall rule**, as shown in the following screenshot:

7. Create some traffic that flows through the rule that is being logged.

8. Check out the logfiles in the Syslog server.

How it works....

All firewall and NAT rules can be activated for logging. This means that every package will be logged. With this information, it is easy to figure out why a given firewall or NAT rule isn't working as expected.

Troubleshooting the Java client

As vCloud uses Java, there could be problems with the connection. We will now see how to activate logging and the Java Console.

Getting ready

You need to have Java installed on your desktop where you can connect to vCloud.

How to do it...

1. Use your Desktop client.

2. In Windows 7, navigate to **Start | Control Panel | Programs | Java**, and in MAC, navigate to **Apple | System Preferences | Java**.

3. Click on **Advanced**:

4. Check **Enable logging** and **Show console**.

5. Click on **OK**.

How it works...

For example, when you start uploading Media from vCloud, you will see the console and you can find the logging files in the user's home directory. You can configure the location of the logfiles at `Program Files\Java\jre7\lib\logging.properties`.

The Java Console gives you an overview of what is currently happening, and the logfiles will tell you what has happened previously:

See also

▸ *The Java tutorials* at `http://docs.oracle.com/javase/tutorial/`

Recovering from an outage

The following sections explains the things to look at after your vCloud infrastructure has experienced an outage:

Getting ready

This recipe will prove to be useful in the case of a vCloud environment that is currently down.

How to do it...

1. Make sure the vCloud service has stopped.

2. Check the vSphere infrastructure and make sure that all the ESXi servers are running and that the datastores are accessible. If this is not the case, work on these issues first.

3. Start the vCloud service in only one cell.

4. Monitor the cell's start-up (`tail -f /opt/vmware/cloud-director/logs/ vcloud-container-debug.log`).

5. Check if there are any errors while the vCloud Cell starts. If there are errors and the vCloud service isn't starting, fix these issues.

6. When the vCloud service has started, check if the connection to vCenter is working correctly. Do this by forcing a sync of the vCenter services. Navigating to **Manage & Monitor| vCenters**. Right-click on your vCenter and then select **Reconnect**. If the task finishes with an error, use VMware KB 1035506 to fix this issue.

7. If the task works, right-click on the vCenter again and click on **Refresh**.

8. These two options will make sure vCloud syncs with vCenter.

9. There can still be dead objects in vCloud, such as vApps that haven't fully deployed or VMs or Edges. Delete these objects in vCloud first, before deleting any leftovers in vSphere.

10. Start vCloud service in the rest of the cells.

How it works...

After vCloud has lost the underlying vSphere infrastructure, or if the sync between vCenter and vCloud is lost, it is very important to recreate this sync as soon as possible.

The vCenter proxy (listener) that we have already discussed in *Chapter 7, Operational Challenges*, will store commands, and the more it stores, the more corrupted it becomes. The mechanics behind this are that vCloud uses `QRTZ` tables to store the commands. VMware KB 1035506 explains how to purge these tables.

Appendix

This appendix contains a list of all the abbreviations that are mentioned across all the chapters in this book. The abbreviations along with their full forms are given as follows:

AD	Microsoft Active Directory
ARP	Address Resolution Protocol
CA	Certificate Authority
Dev	Development environment
DHCP	Dynamic Host Configuration Protocol
DNS	Domain Name System
DRS	VMware vSphere Distributed Resources Scheduler
ESXi	VMware ESXi Host
GUI	Graphical User Interface
HBA	Host Bus Adapter (basically a fiber channel card)
HREF	Unique identifier for vCloud objects
IP	Internet Protocol (however, IP refers to the address itself)
IPSec	Internet Protocol Security
LACP	Link Aggregation Control Protocol
LDAP	Lightweight Directory Access Protocol
MAC	Media Access Control
MoRef	Managed object reference (unique identifier in vCenter)
MTU	Maximum Transmission Unit
NAT	Network Address Translation (also D-NAT (Destination NAT) and S-NAT (Source NAT))

NFS	Network File System
NIC	Network Interface Controller
Org	Organization
OrgAdmin	vCloud Organizational Administrator role
OS	Operating System
OvDC	Organizational Virtual Data Center
OVF	Open Virtualization Format
Prod	Production environment
PvDC	Provider Virtual Data Center
REST	Representational state transfer
RHEL	Red Hat Enterprise Linux
RPO	Recovery Point Objective
RTO	Recovery Time Objective
SLA	Service Level Agreements
SOAP	Simple Object Access Protocol
SSL	Secure Sockets Layer
SSO	VMware Single Sign On
SysAdmin	vCloud System Administrator role
UAT	User Acceptance Testing
URI	Uniform Resource Identifier
UUID	Universally Unique Identifier, unique identifier in ESXi
VAAI	vStorage APIs for Array Integration
vCD	VMware vCloud Director
vCNS	VMware vCloud Network and Security (formally know as vShield)
VEM	Cisco Virtual Ethernet Module (Cisco 1000v)
VIP	Virtual IP
VLAN	Virtual Local Area Network
VM	Virtual Machine
vmknic	VMware Kernel NIC
vNDS	VMware vCenter Network Distributed Switch (also called DvS or Distributed Switch)
VPN	Virtual Private Network
VSM	Cisco Virtual Supervisor Module (Cisco 1000v)
VXLAN	Virtual Extensible LAN
WebClient	vSphere Web Client

Index

Thank you for buying
VMware vCloud Director Cookbook

About Packt Publishing

Packt, pronounced 'packed', published its first book *"Mastering phpMyAdmin for Effective MySQL Management"* in April 2004 and subsequently continued to specialize in publishing highly focused books on specific technologies and solutions.

Our books and publications share the experiences of your fellow IT professionals in adapting and customizing today's systems, applications, and frameworks. Our solution-based books give you the knowledge and power to customize the software and technologies you're using to get the job done. Packt books are more specific and less general than the IT books you have seen in the past. Our unique business model allows us to bring you more focused information, giving you more of what you need to know, and less of what you don't.

Packt is a modern, yet unique publishing company, which focuses on producing quality, cutting-edge books for communities of developers, administrators, and newbies alike. For more information, please visit our website: www.PacktPub.com.

About Packt Enterprise

In 2010, Packt launched two new brands, Packt Enterprise and Packt Open Source, in order to continue its focus on specialization. This book is part of the Packt Enterprise brand, home to books published on enterprise software – software created by major vendors, including (but not limited to) IBM, Microsoft and Oracle, often for use in other corporations. Its titles will offer information relevant to a range of users of this software, including administrators, developers, architects, and end users.

Writing for Packt

We welcome all inquiries from people who are interested in authoring. Book proposals should be sent to author@packtpub.com. If your book idea is still at an early stage and you would like to discuss it first before writing a formal book proposal, contact us; one of our commissioning editors will get in touch with you.

We're not just looking for published authors; if you have strong technical skills but no writing experience, our experienced editors can help you develop a writing career, or simply get some additional reward for your expertise.

Implementing VMware
Horizon View 5.2

ISBN: 978-1-84968-796-6   Paperback: 390 pages

A practical guide to designing, implementing, and administrating an optimized Virtual Desktop solution with VMware Horizon View

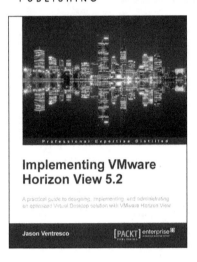

1. Detailed description of the deployment and administration of the VMware Horizon View suite

2. Learn how to determine the resources your virtual desktops will require

3. Design your desktop solution to avoid potential problems, and ensure minimal loss of time in the later stages

vSphere High Performance
Cookbook

ISBN: 978-1-78217-000-6   Paperback: 240 pages

Over 60 recipes to help you improve vSphere performance and solve problem before they arise

1. Troubleshoot real-world vSphere performance issues and identify their root causes

2. Design and configure CPU, memory, networking, and storage for better and more reliable performance

3. Comprehensive coverage of performance issues and solutions including vCenter Server design and virtual machine and application tuning

Please check **www.PacktPub.com** for information on our titles

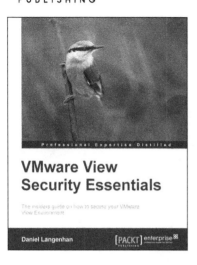

VMware View Security Essentials

ISBN: 978-1-78217-008-2   Paperback: 130 pages

The insiders guide on how to secure your VMware View Environment

1. Discover how to correctly implement View connection, security, and transfer servers

2. Understand all the firewall rules and the basics of multi-layered security

3. Secure all your connections between client and desktop

VMware vSphere 5.1 Cookbook

ISBN: 978-1-84968-402-6   Paperback: 466 pages

Over 130 task-oriented recipes to install configure, and manage various vSphere 5.1 components

1. Install and configure vSphere 5.1 core components

2. Learn important aspects of vSphere such as administration, security, and performance

3. Configure vSphere Management Assistant(VMA) to run commands/scripts without the need to authenticate every attempt

Please check **www.PacktPub.com** for information on our titles

www.ingramcontent.com/pod-product-compliance
Lightning Source LLC
Chambersburg PA
CBHW062052050326
40690CB00016B/3067